ERRATA

A Manual of Comparative R(
Phonology and

by
Henry Mende,

Delete the sub-paragraph letter (d) on page 38 and
change subsequent sub-paragraph letters on pages
38-41 as follows:  (e) to (d),  (f) to (e),  etc.

Delete the sub-paragraph letter  (q) on page 46 and
change subsequent sub-paragraph letters on pages
46-51 as follows:  (r) to (q),  (s) to (r),  etc.

The Catholic University of America Press, Inc.
620 Michigan Avenue, N. E.
Washington, D. C.    20017

# A MANUAL OF COMPARATIVE ROMANCE LINGUISTICS

## PHONOLOGY AND MORPHOLOGY

*by*

HENRY MENDELOFF, Ph.D.
University of Maryland
College Park

The Catholic University of America Press, Inc.
Washington, D. C. 20017

1969

This book is dedicated to my teacher and friend

DR. TATIANA FOTITCH,

in grateful acknowledgment of her constant encouragement, staunch support, and invaluable advice and assistance.

# PREFACE

*A Manual of Comparative Romance Linguistics* has been designed to provide a clear, concise compendium in English of the information concerning the structural evolution of the Romance languages which can be found in the best sources available on the subject. In synthesizing the vast corpus of pertinent data, the author has refined, reordered, and revised whenever necessary, in order that this study and reference manual might best serve the purposes for which it was intended. With these purposes in mind, the author has avoided all linguistic polemics, guiding himself by the consensus of experts in every case; and has omitted all data related only to the external history of the Romance languages, providing instead an ample bibliography for those who seek such information. National languages have been used as criteria throughout, except that Romansch, the fourth national language of Switzerland, is represented by Surselvan, one of the dialects of which it is comprised, and Sardinian, which is an aggregate of dialects, by Logudorese.

The author would like to acknowledge his indebtedness to the Romance scholars whose work constitutes the substance of this *Manual,* and to express his gratitude to Dr. Alessandro S. Crisafulli and Dr. Helmut A. Hatzfeld, both of The Catholic University of America, for their enthusiastic support, and to the staff of The Catholic University of America Press, for preparing the manuscript for publication.

HENRY MENDELOFF, PH.D.

# KEY TO ABBREVIATIONS, DIACRITICS, AND SYMBOLS

Ct. = Catalan
CL = Classical Latin
Eng. = English
Fr. = French
It. = Italian
M = Modern, as in MFr.
O = Old, as in OFr.
Pg. = Portuguese
Pr. = Provençal
Rm. = Rumanian
Sd. = Sardinian
Sp. = Spanish
SS. = Surselvan
VL = Vulgar Latin

N.B. Non-orthographic stress is indicated by boldface letter.

[ ]  Brackets: used for phonetic transcriptions.

ˋ  Signals open *e* [ẹ] and *o* [ọ] of Vulgar Latin, which correspond to Romance [ɛ] and [ɔ], respectively.

•  Signals close(d) *e* [ẹ] and *o* [ọ] of Vulgar Latin, which correspond to Romance [e] and [o], respectively. Also signals the cacuminal *d* [ḍ] of Sardinian.

ˌ  Cedilla: under *c*, (ç), signals the affricate [ts] in Old Spanish orthography, and the [s] sound in French and Portuguese; under *s* (ş) and *t* (ţ), signals the sounds [š] and [ts], respectively, in Rumanian orthography.

ˉ  Macron: used over a vowel in Classical Latin to indicate that it is long.

˘  Breve: used over a vowel in Classical Latin to indicate that it is short; in Rumanian orthography, used over *a* and *i* to indicate that they are partially or totally muted.

>  Used in etymology to mean "becomes, develops into."
<  Used in etymology to mean "came from, developed from."

vii

| | |
|---|---|
| \* | Used in etymology to signal a conjectural form. |
| ~ | Tilde: used in phonetics to signal nasalization; in Spanish orthography (ñ) and, occasionally, in Spanish phonetics [ñ], to signal palatalized *n*. |
| ᷉ | Used in phonetic transcription to signal the semi-consonants and semi-vowels *i* [i̯] and *u* [u̯]. |
| ` | Grave accent: used in orthography to indicate vowel quality and/or stress. |
| ´ | Acute accent: used in orthography to signal stress and/or vowel quality. |
| ^ | Circumflex accent: used in orthography to signal vowel quality and/or length, the loss of an etymological *s*, and one word or form as distinct from another which would otherwise be identical. |
| ' | Apostrophe: used in orthography to signal the elision of a vowel, and in etymology, to signal the loss of a vowel through syncope. |
| ¨ | Dieresis: used in orthography to signal a hiatus between contiguous vowels (Fr. *Noël*), or the articulation of a vowel which would otherwise be mute (Fr. *exangüe*, Sp. *averigü*). |
| [ɐ] | Sound akin to *a* in Eng. *about*: heard in Pg. *pArede, cousA*, Rm. *sĂptĂmânĂ*. |
| [ə] | Mute *e* (*shwa*): heard in Ct. *cAvall*, Fr. *chEval*, Pg. *partE*. |
| [ø] | Palatal *o*: closed, front, rounded vowel heard in Fr. *pEU, affrEUX*. |
| [œ] | Palatal *o*: open, front, rounded vowel heard in Fr. *jEUne*. |
| [y] | Palatal *u*: heard in Fr. *mUr*. |
| [ƀ] | Fricative *b*: heard in Ct. *saBa*, Pg. *aBa*, Sp. *saBe, laVa*. |
| [đ] | Fricative *d*: heard in Ct. *freDa*, Pg. *a Data*, Sp. *praDo*. |
| [dz] | Affricate heard in It. *romanZo*, OSp. *faZer*. |
| [dž] | Affricate heard in It. *Gente*, Rm. *Ger*, SS. *leGer*. |
| [ǥ] | Fricative *g*: heard in Ct. *preGa*, Pg. *o Gato*, Sp. *aGua*. |
| [ł] | Palatal *l*: heard in Ct. *LLum*, It. *foGLia*, OFr. *fueILLe*, OPr. *aureLHa*, Pg. *fiLHo*, Sp. *caLLe*, SS. *feGL*. |
| [š] | English *sh*: heard in Fr. *CHer*, It. *peSCe*, OSp. *diXo*, Pg. *baStar*, Rm. *Şapte*, SS. *laSCHar*. |
| [θ] | Theta: heard in (Castilian) Sp. *Cinco, conoCer, Zorro*. |
| [ts] | Affricate heard in It. *graZie*, OFr. *Cest*, Osp. *lanÇa*, Rm. *fraŢi*. |
| [tš] | Affricate heard in Ct. *desiG, coTXe*, It. *Cena*, OFr. *CHacier*, Rm. *Cer*. Sp. *muCHo*, SS. *laTG*. |
| [ɥ] | Palatal *u*: semi-consonant heard in *jUin, lUi*. |
| [ž] | English *s* in *leisure*: heard in Ct. *Joc, verGe*, Fr. *Jour*, OSp. *fiJa*, Pg. *Gente, deSde*, SS. *Şchurnal*. |
| [χ] | Spanish *jota*: heard in *Gente, diJo*. |

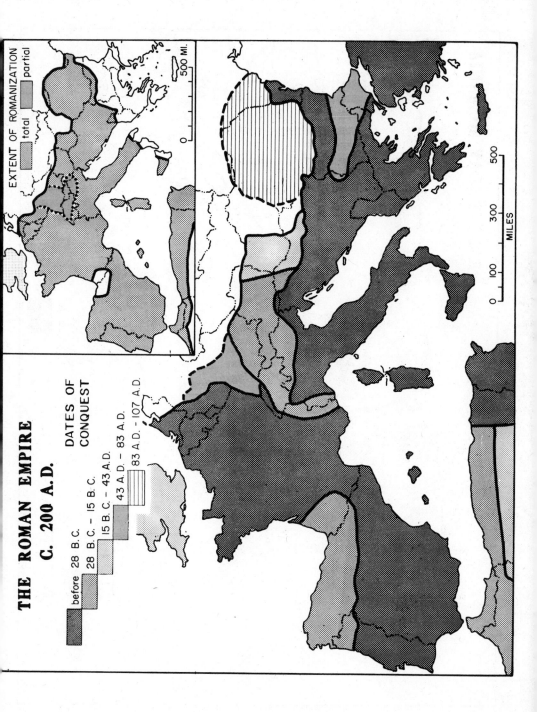

*Figure* 1:    The Roman Empire, *ca.* 200 A.D.

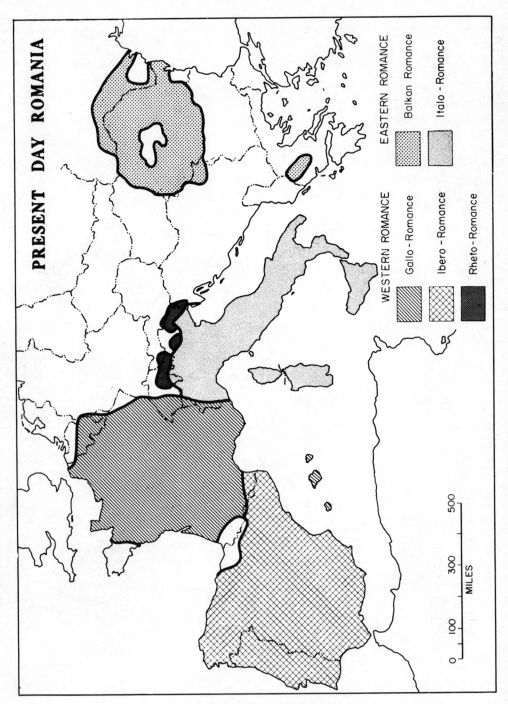

Figure 2: Present-Day Romania

# TABLE OF CONTENTS

# INTRODUCTION

*Origin of Romance Languages*

1. The etymon of all Romance languages is the spoken Latin imported by soldiers, merchants, administrators, and colonizers into the lands of Eastern and Western Europe which, in the wake of military conquest, were destined to become provinces of the Roman Empire. The designation "Romance" was probably derived as a substantivized adverb from the expression *parabolare (fabulare) romanice,* 'to speak in the manner of a citizen of the Roman Empire.' *Romania,* which served to differentiate the Empire from Rome proper, gave rise to *romanicus,* which served, similarly, to differentiate the Roman colonial from the Roman native, the *romanus,* and also from the non-Latin speaking foreigner, the *barbarus.*

*Evolution of Romance Languages*

2. The evolution of the Romance languages was determined, to a greater or lesser extent in each instance, by (1) the languages which were indigenous to the conquered territories (the substratum), (2) the continued exposure of the provinces to the linguistic and cultural influence of Rome, (3) the languages which were superimposed on the same territories by subsequent invasions and conquests (the superstratum), and (4) the unifying influence exerted by Church and State.

*Vulgar vs. Classical Latin*

3. Basic to an understanding of the evolution of any Romance language is a clear distinction between Colloquial or Vulgar Latin and Literary or Classical Latin. Although Vulgar Latin was probably quite heterogeneous in nature, varying, as might be expected, with the social station of the people speaking it, and the regions in which it was spoken, it was unquestionably sufficiently homogeneous to be considered the spoken language of the "people."

*Written Vestiges of Vulgar Latin*

4. The written vestiges of Vulgar Latin are extremely fragmentary, consisting of (1) vernacular passages in classical literature

1

(e.g., the "Cena Trimalchionis" in Petronius' *Satyricon*), (2) technical treatises concerned with agriculture, architecture, veterinary medicine (e.g., Chiron's *Mulomedicina*), and war; (3) inscriptions on gravestones, (4) scribblings on the walls of public buildings, (5) grammatical censures (e.g., the anonymous *Appendix Probi*), (6) writings of Church fathers, and (7) the story of a pilgrimage to the Holy Land supposedly written by a Spanish nun in the fifth century (*Silviae vel potius Aetheriae peregrinatio ad loca sancta*). Most important in the reconstruction of Vulgar Latin has been the comparative study of Romance languages, in which common denominators are tentatively considered to be Vulgar Latin etyma until corroborated or discredited by new written evidence.

## Classification of Romance Languages

5. For purposes of classification, the Romance languages have been divided into Western and Eastern Romance. Western Romance is comprised of Gallo-Romance (French and Provençal, the latter having been reduced to a patois since its "fall from grace" as a flourishing literary language in the thirteenth century), Ibero-Romance (Catalan, Portuguese, and Spanish [Castilian]), and Rheto-Romance (of its three regional dialects, principally Romansch, which, since 1938, has been officially recognized as the fourth national language of Switzerland). Eastern Romance is comprised of Italo-Romance (Italian and Sardinian, the latter consisting of three regional dialects, of which the most prominent is Logudorese), and Balkan Romance (Dalmatian and Rumanian, the former having been extinct since the last decade of the nineteenth century). It must be kept in mind that this schema is far from absolute: both Italian and Sardinian have features in common with Western Romance, and Catalan can as easily be identified with Gallo-Romance (specifically, Provençal) as with Ibero-Romance (specifically, Spanish).

## Western vs. Eastern Romance

6. There are three principal features which distinguish Western from Eastern Romance: (1) in Western Romance, the proparoxytonic stress (' – –) of Vulgar Latin words which had not lost their post-tonic vowel through syncope, became paroxytonic (' –), whereas in Eastern Romance it survived: Compare Sp. *pueblo* with It. *popolo*, Sp. *peine* with It. *pettine* and Rm. *pieptene*; (2) in Western Romance, the unvoiced intervocalic plosives of Vulgar Latin ([k], [p], [t]) were voiced, i.e., pronounced [g], [b], [d], respectively, whereas in Eastern Romance they remained unchanged: compare Sp. *amigo* with It. *amico*, Sp. *lobo* with It. *lupo*, Sp. *marido* with It. *marito*; (3) in Western Romance, the plurals of nouns are marked by final *s*, whereas

in Eastern Romance they are marked by final *e* or *i*: compare Sp. *dueñas* with It. *donne*, Sp. *flores* with It. *fiori*, Sp. *hombres* with It. *uomini* and Rm. *oameni*. It must be remembered that these are generalizations rather than hard and fast rules; for example, with regard to proparoxytonic stress and intervocalic surds, there are many exceptions in Italian. Moreover, the paroxytonic stress of Old French became oxytonic in Modern French, final *e* and all surviving final consonants having become mute.

# Part 1

# PHONOLOGY

*Vocalic System and Accent of Classical Latin*

7. The vocalic system of Classical Latin was characterized by the fact that the phonemic differential between otherwise identical vowels was the duration of articulation. The vocalic system consisted of five long vowels (*ā, ē, ī, ō, ū*), complemented by five correspondingly short vowels (*ă, ĕ, ĭ, ŏ, ŭ*), and three diphthongs (*ae, oe, au*). Accent, which was a variable only in words of three or more syllables, since it was always paroxytonic in words of two syllables, was governed by the length or brevity of the penultimate syllable. The penultimate syllable was considered long, and bore the stress, if it contained a long vowel or a diphthong, or ended in a consonant; if it did not, the antepenultimate syllable was stressed: *amāre, ēventus, perdĕre.*

*Vocalic System of Vulgar Latin*

8. In Vulgar Latin, the distinction between vowels which were otherwise identical was qualitative rather than quantitative, the phonemic differential being the manner, rather than the duration, of articulation, determined by the degree to which the mouth was opened. The long vowels of Classical Latin were the closed vowels of Vulgar Latin, the short vowels were the open vowels, and the three diphthongs were resolved, respectively, as open *e* [ę], closed *e* [ẹ], and closed *o* [ọ], the last with considerable vacillation. At a very remote time, the open and closed *a* of Vulgar Latin merged into a single, medial *a*.

*Vulgar Latin Accent*

9. (a) The accent of Classical Latin was retained in Vulgar Latin, with the following exceptions: (1) stressed *e* or *i* in hiatus became a palatal semi-consonant (yod), the unstressed element of a diphthong: *mu-li-e-rem* and *fi-li-o-lum* were pronounced *mu-lie-re* and *fi-lio-lu*; (2) words of three syllables whose last syllable began with such consonantal groups as *br* and *dr* (the Latin *muta cum liquida*)

4

were stressed on the penultimate, rather than the antepenultimate, syllable: *ca-the-dram* and *te-ne-bras* were pronounced *ca-the-dra* and *te-ne-bras*; (3) prefixed forms were stressed on the stem, rather than the prefix: *re-ci-pit* was pronounced *re-ci-pit*.

(b) The paroxytonic tendency of Vulgar Latin evidenced itself in the loss of unstressed, medial vowels between (1) consonant and l (*oculu*> *oc'lu*), (2) l or r and consonant (*calidu*> *cal'du*, *viride*> *vir'de*), (3) s and t (*positu*> *pos'tu*).

## Variants of the Vulgar Latin Vocalic System: Stressed Vowels

10. In the Vulgar Latin of Italy, and of the West, where the so-called Italic System prevailed, the open *i* merged with the closed *e*, and the open *u* with the closed *o*, thus reducing the total number of Vulgar Latin vowels from nine to seven. In the Vulgar Latin of Sardinia, neither of these vocalic mergers took place; instead, open and closed *e*, *i*, and *u* merged into single phonemes without any qualitative distinctions. In the Vulgar Latin of the Balkans, although open *i* merged with closed *e*, as it did in the Italic System, open and closed *o* and *u* merged, just as they did in the Sardinian System.

| Classical Latin | Vulgar Latin | Italic System | Sardinian System | Balkan System |
|---|---|---|---|---|
| ă, ā | a | a | a | a |
| ĕ, ae | ę | ę | e | ę |
| ē, oe | ẹ | ẹ | e | ẹ |
| ĭ | į | | i | |
| ī | i | | i | |
| ŏ | ǫ | ǫ | o | o |
| ō | ọ | ọ | o | o |
| ŭ | ụ | | u | u |
| ū | u | u | u | u |
| au | au/ǫ | au/ǫ | au | au |

11. The evolution of Vulgar Latin stressed vowels was influenced by one or more of the following factors: (1) a following nasal consonant, (2) a preceding or following palatal element (yod), (3) the checked or unchecked nature of the syllable concerned, (4) the fact that the word ended in one of certain unstressed vowels, (5) dissimilation from a vowel with which the stressed vowel stood in hiatus, (6) the open or closed quality of the vowel, (7) learned influence, which impeded popular development.

### Stressed [a] *in Gallo-Romance*

12. (a) In French, stressed [a] in an unchecked syllable developed as follows: (1) It became *e* [ɛ, e] when not affected by a nasal or palatal (*mare > mer* [ɛ], *amatu > aimé* [e]). (2) It combined with a following yod to form the diphthong [ai̯], which, through assimilation [ei̯], was resolved as [ɛ] or [e] (*ma[g]is > mais* [ɛ], *canta[v]i > chantai* [e]). (3) A following nasal generated a yod with which [a] combined to form the nasalized diphthong [ai̯], later [ei̯], which resolved itself as [ɛ̃] when the nasal was in final position (*pane > pain* [ɛ̃], and as [ɛ] when it was not (*lana > laine* [ɛ]). (4) When preceded by palatalized c [k] (see par. 46, below), [a] became the diphthong [i̯e], which later simplified to [ɛ] or [e] (*capra >* OFr. *chievre>chèvre* [ɛ], *judicare>*OFr. *jugier>juger* [e]). In a checked syllable, stressed [a] remained intact, except that it became nasalized before a nasal consonant in final position (*tantu > tant[ã]*).

(b) The fact that stressed [a], in an unchecked syllable, did not palatalize to *e* in Provençal (*mare > mar, amatu > amat*) is of paramount importance in distinguishing between Northern and Southern Gallo-Romance (medieval *langue d'oïl* vs. *langue d'oc*).

### Stressed [a] *In Ibero-Romance*

13. In Spanish, stressed [a] became *e* [ɛ, e] when followed by (1) the yod which was originated by the vocalization of [k] in *ct* and *x* (*factu > hecho, fraxinu > fresno*), (2) the combination of *p, r,* or *s* plus yod (*sapia > sepa, riparia > ribera, basiu > beso*), (3) the yod originated by the loss of an intervocalic consonant (*canta[v]i > canté*). A similar palatalization took place in Catalan (*factu > fet, basiu > bes, canta[v]i > canté*). The intermediate stage of assimilation [ei̯] through which Spanish and Catalan [ai̯] passed in becoming [ɛ, e] is the norm for Portuguese phonology (*facto > feito, fraxinu > freixo*).

### Stressed [a] *in Rheto-Romance*

14. In Surselvan, stressed [a] followed by *n* diphthongized to *au* in an unchecked syllable, and became *o* in a checked syllable

(*cane> tgaun, annu> onn*) ; followed by *m*, stressed [a] invariably became *o* (*fame > fom, flamma > flomma*).

## Stressed [a] *in Italo-Romance*

15. Stressed [a] remained unchanged in both Italian and Sardinian (*caballu>* It. *cavallo*, Sd. *caḍḍu; cantare>* It., Sd. *cantare*).

## Stressed [a] *in Balkan Romance*

16. In Rumanian, stressed [a], when followed by *n*, or *n* or *m* plus consonant (except *nn* and *mn*), was strongly velarized and pronounced with spread lips. (The resultant sound, which is written â or *î*, is similar to the *y* in Russian *syn*, "son," and to French *un* [œ̃].) Thus, *lana, quando, campu* became *lîna, cînd, cîmp*.

## Stressed [ẹ], [ę] *in Gallo-Romance*

17. In French, stressed [ẹ], in an unchecked syllable, diphthongized to [i̯e] (*pede> pied*). Stressed [ę], in an unchecked syllable, diphthongized to [ei̯] and, through the successive stages [oi̯], [ói̯], ]oɛ], ]u̯ɛ], arrived at Modern French [u̯a], written *oi* (*vēlu > voile, pĭlu > poil*). A following nasal consonant halted the evolution of stressed [ẹ] at [ei̯], which became [ɛ̃] when the nasal was in final position, and [ɛ̃] when it was not (*plenu > plein* [ɛ́], *plena > pleine* [ɛ]). A preceding palatized *c* [k] (see par. 46, below) combined with stressed [ẹ] to form the triphthong [i̯ei̯], which was resolved as [i] (*cera* [tsi̯ei̯ra] *> cire*). In a checked syllable, stressed [ẹ] became [e] and then opened to [ɛ], nasalizing to [ɛ̃], later [ã], before a nasal consonant in syllable or word-final position (*vendiere > vendre* [ã]). In Provençal, stressed [ẹ] and [ę] did noť diphthongize (*pĕde > pe, vēlu > vel*).

## Stressed [ẹ], [ę] in *Ibero-Romance*

18. (a) In Spanish, stressed [ę], if not affected by a yod, diphthongized to [i̯e], regardless of whether the syllable was checked or unchecked (*pĕde > pie, cĕntu > ciento*). The following yods inflected the [ę] to [ẹ], and thus prevented diphthongization: (1) those which inflected stressed [a] (see par. 13, above); (2) those which occurred in the groups *b, d, g, l, m, n* plus yod; and (3) those which originated from the palatalization of *c'l* (>[ɫ]) and *gn* (>[ñ]). Thus, *lĕctu, matĕria, lĕ(g)e* and *spĕc'lu* became *lecho, madera, ley*, and *espejo*. Stressed [ẹ] was similarly inflected to [i] by (1) the groups *b, m, p, r, s* plus yod, (2) the yod originating from the loss of an intervocalic consonant, and (3) to some extent, the groups *d* and *g* plus yod. Thus,

7

*vindēmia, cēreu, lĭmpidu,* and *fastĭdiu* became *vendimia, cirio, limpio,* and *hastío.* A following [ṷ] or a final *ī* had the same effect (*vĭdua > viuda, vēnī > vine*).

(b) In Catalan, stressed [ę], when followed by a palatal, diphthongized to [i̯e]. This diphthong combined with the yod to form the triphthong [i̯ei̯], which was resolved as [i] (*lĕctu > llit, sĕx > sis*). A final *ī* also inflected the [ę] to [i] (*hĕrī > ahir, vĕnī > vine*). Stressed [ę] closed to [i] when affected by one of the following factors: (1) a yod in the final syllable (*sepia > sípia*), (2) final *ī* (*vigintī > vint*), (3) dissimilation from a vowel in hiatus (*vĭa > via*), (4) a following nasal plus consonantal group (*exemplu > eximpli*), and (5) a [ṷ]in the following syllable (*vĭdua > viuda*).

(c) In Portuguese, stressed [ę] did not diphthongize (*pĕde > pe*), but a yod inflected stressed [ę] (*vindēmia > vindima*).

## Stressed [ę], [ẹ] in Rheto-Romance

19. In Surselvan, stressed [ę], in both checked and unchecked syllables, diphthongized to [i̯e] when the Latin etymon ended in *u* (*cĕntu > tschien, caelu > tschiel*). When followed by a nasal consonant, in Latin etyma which did not end in *u*, stressed [ę] closed to [ẹ]. Stressed [ę], when checked, in Latin etyma which did not end in *u*, diphthongized to [i̯a] (*tĕrra > tiara*). Stressed [ẹ], whether etymological (< *ē, ĭ*) or not, diphthongized to [ei̯] in an unchecked syllable (*tēla > teila, bĕne > bein*).

## Stressed [ę], [ẹ] in Italo-Romance

20. In Italian, stressed [ę] diphthongized in an unchecked syllable only (*pede > piede*), and stressed [ẹ] was inflected to [i] by a following palatal (*vĭncere > vincere*).

## Stressed [ę], [ẹ] in Balkan Romance

21. In Rumanian, stressed [ę] diphthongized to [i̯e] in checked and unchecked syllables, when the word ended in *i* or *u* (*hĕrī > ieri, pĕctu > piept*). When the word ended in *ă* or *e*, stressed [ę] diphthongized to [i̯a]. The diphthong [i̯a] which related to final *e* became [i̯e]. Thus, *petră* and its plural *\*petre* (< *petrae*) became *piatra* and *pietre.* Stressed [ẹ], which remained *e* when the word ended in *i* or *u* (*directu > drept, nĭgru > negru*), diphthongized to *ea* [i̯a] when the word ended in *a* or *e*. The diphthong [i̯a] which related to final *e* later monophthongized to *e* [e]. Thus, *directa* and *lege* became *dreapta* and *lege.*

8

*Stressed* [ǫ], [ọ] *in Gallo-Romance*

22. In French, stressed [ǫ] in an unchecked syllable diphthongized to [u̯o] and later, through dissimilation, to [u̯e]. The diphthong [u̯e] finally became the palatal monophthong [ø] or [œ] (*focu > feu* [ø], *novu > neuf* [œ]). In a checked syllable, stressed [ǫ] was retained, except that it nasalized before a nasal consonant in syllable- or word-final position (*ponte > pont* [ɔ̃]). Stressed [ǫ] combined with a following palatal to form the diphthong [u̯i] (*nocte > \*nueit > nuit*). Stressed [ọ] in an unchecked syllable diphthongized to [ou̯], later to [eu̯], and finally monophthongized to [ø] or [œ], thus coinciding with stressed, unchecked [ǫ] (*nepōte > neveu* [ø], *flore > fleur* [œ]). In a checked syllable, stressed [ọ] became [u] (*gutta > goutte, cŭppa > coupe*). Stressed [ọ] combined with a following palatal to form the diphthong [oi̯], which coincided in its development with stressed, unchecked [ẹ] (*voce >* OFr. *voiz > voix), angŭstia > angoisse*). Stressed [ọ] nasalized before a nasal consonant in syllable- or word-final position (*leone > lion* [ɔ̃]). Neither stressed [ǫ] nor stressed [ọ] diphthongized in Provençal (*rŏta > roda, flōre > flor*).

*Stressed* [ǫ], [ọ] *in Ibero-Romance*

23. (a) In Spanish, stressed [ǫ], when not inflected by a yod, diphthongized to [u̯o] and later to [u̯e] (*nŏvu > nuevo*). The yods which inflected stressed [ẹ] (see para. 18(*a*) above), except those of *n* plus yod and *gn*, inflected stressed [ǫ] to [ọ], thus preventing diphthongization (*fŏlia > hoja, pŏdiu > poyo, nŏcte > noche*). Stressed [ọ], when not inflected by a yod, remained intact. In addition to the yods which inflected stressed *a* (see par. 13, above), the combination of *n*·plus yod and *gn* invariably inflected stressed [ọ] to [u], whereas the combination of *b, d, g,* and *m* plus yod did so sporadically (*trŭcta > trucha, pŭgnu > puño, fŭgio > huyo*).

(b) In Catalan, stressed [ǫ] did not diphthongize unless it was followed by a yod, in which case it combined with the yod to form the triphthong [u̯ei̯], later reduced to [u̯i] or [u], the latter before [i] (*cŏmite > comte, cŏctu > cuit, fŏlia > fulla*). Stressed [ọ] remained intact unless it was followed by a yod, in which case it was inflected to [u], combining with the yod of *ct* to form the diphthong [u̯i] (*pugnu > punh, tructa > truita*).

(c) Stressed [ǫ] did not diphthongize in Portuguese, but a following palatal inflected stressed [ọ] to [u] (*nŏvu > novo, pŭgnu > punho*).

9

*Stressed* [ǫ], [o̜] *in Rheto-Romance*

24. In Surselvan, stressed [ǫ], in checked or unchecked syllables, diphthongized to [i̯e] when the Latin etymon ended in *ŭ* (*pŏrcŭ* > *piertg, nŏvŭ* > *niev*). Followed by a nasal consonant, in words whose etyma did not end in *u*, stressed [ǫ] became [o̜]. Stressed [ǫ], whether etymological (< *ō, ŭ*) or not, became [u] (through diphthong [o̜u̯]), which opened to **uo** before *r + cons.* (*scōpa* > *scua, fiōre* > *flur, bŭcca* > *bucca, sŭrdu* > *suord, bŏna* > *buna*).

*Stressed* [ǫ], [o̜] *in Italo-Romance*

25. In Italian, stressed [ǫ], in an unchecked syllable, diphthongized to [u̯o] (*novu* > *nuovo*). After a palatal or an *r*, the first element of the diphthong was often lost (*filiolu* > *figliolo, probat* > *prova*). Stressed [ǫ], when followed by a palatal, was inflected to [u] (*pŭgnu* > *pugno, ŭngula* > *unghia*).

*Stressed* [o] *in Balkan Romance*

26. In Rumanian, stressed [o] (< [ǫ, o̜]), when the etymon ended in *ī* or *ŭ*, became the diphthong [u̯o], which later monophthongized to [o] (*porcŭ* > *porc, porcī* > *porci*). When the etymon ended in *ă* or *e*, stressed [o] diphthongized to [u̯a] written *oa* (*porcă* > *poarca,* \**porce* [< *porcae*] > *poarce*).

*Stressed* [i], [u] *in Romance*

27. Stressed [i] and [u] remained intact in Ibero-, Italo-, and Balkan Romance. In Gallo- and Rheto-Romance, [u] palatalized to [y]. In Surselvan, [y] further palatalized to [i], which remained [i] in an unchecked syllable, and opened to [e] in a checked syllable (*mūru* > *mir, frŭctu* > *fretg*). Similarly, in Surselvan, stressed [i] in a checked syllable opened to [e] (*scriptu* > *scret*).

*Variants of the Vulgar Latin Vocalic System: Unstressed Vowels*

28. In the Italic System, unstressed [ę], [e̜], [i̜] and [ǫ], [o̜], [u̜] merged into the single phonemes [e] and [o], whereas [a], [i], [u] remained intact. In the Sardinian System, open and closed *e, i, o, u* merged into single phonemes, and [a] remained intact. In the Balkan System, unstressed [ę], [e̜], [i̜] and [ǫ], [o̜], [u̜], [u] merged into the single phonemes [e] and [u], whereas [a] and [i̜] remained intact. Thus, the unstressed vowels of Vulgar Latin were reduced to five in the Italic and Sardinian Systems, and to four in the Balkan System.

10

## Unstressed Vowels

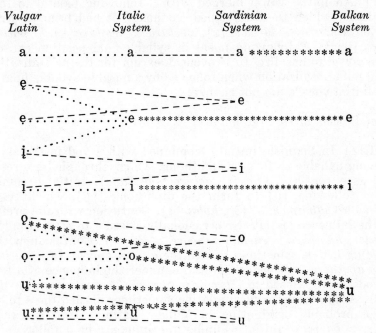

*Evolution of Vulgar Latin Unstressed Vowels*

29. The evolution of the Vulgar Latin unstressed vowels was influenced by one or more of the following factors: (1) the intensity of stress in the language concerned, (2) the perseverance of the vowel, (3) the presence of contiguous consonants, principally nasals and palatals, (4) the fact that the vowel, through the loss of an intervocalic consonant, found itself in hiatus, (5) assimilation to the stressed vowel, (6) dissimilation from the stressed vowel, (7) position within the word, (8) confusion of initial vowels with vowels of articles and prefixes, (9) the fact that the syllable concerned was checked or unchecked.

### Initial Vowels in Gallo-Romance

30. In French, initial *a* after palatalized *c* [k] (see par. 46, below), in an unchecked syllable became *e* and finally [ə] (*caballu > cheval*). In secondary hiatus with a following stressed vowel, it developed similarly, the hiatus eventually resolving itself as a monophthong (*ma[t]uru > OFr. mëur > mûr*). Initial *e* in an unchecked syllable became [ə] (*nepote>neveu*). Initial *o* became [u], written *ou*, except when originating from checked [ǫ] (*mōvere > mouvoir, sŭbinde >*

11

*souvent, dŏrmir > dormir*). Initial *i* remained intact, and *u* palatalized to [y]. An initial vowel merged with a following palatal to form a diphthong, which then developed as though it had been in stressed position (*laxare > laisser* [ɛ], *vectura > voiture* [ũa], *potine > poison* [ųa]). A following nasal in syllable-final position caused an initial vowel to nasalize. In Provençal, except for the palatalization of *u*, and mild nasalization when followed by a nasal in syllable-final position, initial vowels did not change.

## Initial Vowels in Ibero-Romance

31.(a) In Spanish, initial *a* combined with a yod in the same or following syllable to form a diphthong, which, through [eị], resolved itself as *e* (*basiare > besar, lactuca > lechuga*). Initial *a* combined with a following [ų] to form the diphthong [aų], which resolved itself as *o* (*habuimos >* OSp. *hobimos*). Confusion with the prefix *ex*, and the influence of initial *r* occasionally closed *a* to *e* (*abscondere > esconder, anethulu > eneldo, rancore > rencor*). Confusion with the preceding article sometimes caused the *a* to disappear (apheresis), as in *illa apotheca > la bodega*. Initial *e*, under the influence of a following yod or [ų], closed to *i* (*renione > riñón, *equale (< aequale) > igual*). Assimilation or dissimilation sometimes opened the *e* to *a*, the change probably originating in Vulgar Latin (*silvaticu > salvaje, verrere > barrer*). Initial *o*, under the influence of a following yod, closed to *u* (*cognatu > cuñado, dormiamus > durmamos*). Assimilation or dissimilation sometimes caused the *o* to change to *a* or *e* (*colostru > calostro, novacula > navaja, rotundu > redondo*). Initial *i*, through dissimilation, sometimes opened to *e*, the change probably originating in Vulgar Latin (*vicinu > vecino*).

(b) In Catalan, initial *a* and *e* were reduced in pronunciation to mute e [ə], and initial *o* was velarized to [u]. A following yod or nasal, as well as dissimilation from the stressed vowel, closed *a* or *e* to *i* (*lectione > lliçó, singulare > singlar, fenestra > finestra*). A following yod closed *o* to *u* (*muliere > muller*); assimilation to the stressed vowel sometimes opened it to *a* (*novacula > navalla*) ; and dissimilation from the stressed vowel sometimes changed it to *e* (*rotundu > redó*).

(c) In Portuguese, initial *a* and *e* weakened, respectively, to a sound akin to *a* in Eng. *about* [ɐ], and to mute e [ə], with the exception that *e*, when it began the word, closed to [i] (*apertu > aberto* [ɐ], *ferire > ferir* [ə], *evitare > evitar* [i]). Inital *o* velarized to [u] (*nominare > nomear* [u]), unless it began the word, in which case it remained *o* (*operare > operar* [o]). Initial *i*, through dissimilation from stressed *i*, became mute e [*vicinu > vizinho* [ə]).

## Initial Vowels in Rheto-Romance

32. In Surselvan, there was a tendency for initial *o* to become *u* (*dormire, morire* > *durmir, murir*), and for initial *e* to become *a* (*genuculu* > *şchanugl*).

## Initial Vowels in Italo-Romance

33. In Italian, initial *e* normatively closed to *i* (*nepote* > *nipote, fenestra* > *finestra*). A following labial tended to change the *e* to *o* (*debere* > *dovere*).

## Initial Vowels in Balkan Romance

34. In Rumanian, initial *a* weakened to a sound akin to *a* in Eng. *about* [ɐ], unless it began the word (*carbone* > *carbune* [ɐ], *argentu* >argint [a]. Initial *e* weakened similarly after *b, p, r,* or *s* (*peccatu*> *păcat* [ɐ], *septimana* > *săptămână* [ɐ]).

## Pretonic and Post-tonic Vowels in Gallo-Romance

35. (a) In French and Provençal, pretonic *e, i, o,* and *u* were lost through syncope, -*a*- eventually weakening to mute *e* in French, and remaining unchanged in Provençal (*ornamentu* > Fr. *ornement* [ə], Pr. *ornamen*). Other pretonic vowels survived as mute e [ə] to facilitate pronunciation (*\*caprifoliu* > *chèvrefeuille*). The loss of the intervocalic consonant following the pretonic vowel caused the latter to fuse with the stressed vowel (*cantatore* > OFr. *chantëeur* > *chanteur*).

(b) In French, the post-tonic vowels which had survived in Vulgar Latin (see par. 9*b*, above) were lost (*prendere* > *prendre, vendere* > *vendre*). The same occurred in Provençal (*duodecim* > *dotze*), except that it was also possible for the post-tonic to be retained, in which case the final vowel (except *a*) was lost (*vendere* > *vender, persica* > *persega* or *persega*).

## Pretonic and Post-tonic Vowels in Ibero-Romance

36. (a) In Spanish, only pretonic *a* survived (*paradisu* > *paraíso*). If the word had two pretonic vowels, the second was lost (*vicinitate* > *vecindad, recuperare* > *recobrar*). The influence of a root word and the loss of a following intervocalic consonant resulted in the retention of the pretonic vowel (*dolorosu* > *doloroso, cogitare* > *cuidar*). Of the post-tonic vowels which had survived in Vulgar Latin (see par. 9*b*, above), all but *a* were lost (*orphanu* > *huérfano*); however, post-tonic *i* was retained when it preceded an intervocalic consonant which was lost (*tepidu* > *tibio*).

13

(b) In Catalan, only pretonic *a* survived, which weakened to mute *e* [ə] in pronunciation (*paradisu > paradís*). By exception, a pretonic was retained under the following conditions: (1) when its loss would have made pronunciation very difficult (*avellana > avellana*); (2) when it was followed by consonant plus yod (*papilione > papalló*); (3) when it was preceded or followed by *n* (*examinare > eixamenar, lenicare > llenegar*); (4) when it was followed by a suffix (*traditor > traïdor*); (5) when it began the verbal endings -*ĭcare,* -*ĭnare,* and -*ŭlare* (*carricare > carregar, terminare > termenar, tremulare > tremolar*). Of two pretonics, the second was lost (*recuperare > recobrar*).

*Pretonic and Post-tonic Vowels in Rheto-Romance*

37.  In Surselvan, pretonic and post-tonic vowels (except *a*) were lost (*nominatus >numnaus, habitare > avdar, caballariu > cavalier*).

*Pretonic and Post-tonic Vowels in Italo-Romance*

38.  In Italian and Sardinian, there was a strong tendency for pretonics to be retained. In Italian, the pretonic vowel became *e* when followed by *r*, and *i* when followed by any other consonant (\**cantarò* [< *cantare habeo*] *> canterò, septimana > settimana*). The post-tonic vowels were also generally retained (*fraxinu >* It. *frassino, semita >* Sd. *semida*). In Italian, there was some degree of vocalic alteration, the post-tonic vowel becoming *e* before *r*, *o* before *l*, and *a* before a nasal or guttural (*arbore > albero, nubilu > nuvolo, pampinu > pampano*).

*Pretonic and Post-tonic Vowels in Balkan Romance*

39.  In Rumanian, the pretonic and post-tonic vowels generally survived, with some vocalic alteration (*septimana > săptămână, pectine > pieptene*). The loss of final *u* changed proparoxytones to paroxytones (*fraxinu > frasin*).

*Final Vowels in Gallo-Romance*

40.  In French and Provençal, all final vowels were lost except *a*, which became mute *e* [ə] in the former, and *o* in the latter (*bona >* Fr. *bonne, hora >* Pr. *ouro*). In addition to -*a*, final vowels which supported consonantal groups in French and Provençal survived as mute *e* in the former, and as a weakly articulated [e] in the latter (*patre >* Fr. *père*, Pr. *paire*).

*Final Vowels in Ibero-Romance*

41.  (a) In Spanish, final *i* of Vulgar Latin became *e* (*dixī, fecī > dije, hice*). Final *e* became a semi-vocalic yod, written *y*, when it

found itself in hiatus with the stressed vowel through the loss of an intervocalic consonant (*le*[*g*]*e, re*[*g*]*e,* > *ley, rey*). Final *e* was lost after *c, d, l, n, r, s,* and *t,* except in proparoxytones which became paroxytones through syncope (*leone* > *león, sole* > *sol,* but *pectine* > *peine*). Final *u* became *o* (*fructūs* > *frutos*). Final *o* occasionally became *e* (*silvaticŭ* > *salvaje*) or disappeared (*ministeriŭ* > *menester*).

(b) In Catalan, final *a* of Vulgar Latin survived as mute *e* [ə], written *a* when it was the last sound of the word, and *e* when it was followed by a consonant (*porta, portas* > *porta, portes*). All other vowels were lost, except those that survived as supportive mute *e* after consonantal groups of Latin or Romance origin (*fratre* > *frare, comite* > *comte, pauperu* > *pobre*).

(c) In Portuguese, final *a* and *e* of Vulgar Latin weakened, respectively, to a sound akin to *a* in Eng. *about* [ɐ], and to mute *e* (*porta* > *porta* [ɐ], *nocte* > *noite* [ə]). Final *o* became a weakly articulated [u], written *o* (*filu* > *filho* [u]).

## Final Vowels in Rheto-Romance

42. In Surselvan, all final vowels of Vulgar Latin except *a* were lost (*pane* > *paun, caballu* > *cavagl, porta* > *porta*).

## Final Vowels in Italo-Romance

43. (a) In Italian, final *u* of Vulgar Latin became *o* (*lacū* > *lago*), all other final vowels remaining intact (*porta* > *porta, nocte* > *notte, fecī* > *feci, porcŭ* > *porco*).

(b) In Sardinian, the final vowels of Vulgar Latin remained intact (*rota* > *roda, dentes* > *dentes, venī* > *beni, venĭt* > *venit, quando* > *cando, filiu* > *fizzu*).

## Final Vowels in Balkan Romance

44. In Rumanian, final *a* of Vulgar Latin weakened to a sound akin to *a* in Eng. *about* [ɐ], written *ă* (*rota* > *roată*). Final *e* after semi-vowel [u̯] also weakened to [ɐ], written *ă* (*nove* > *nouă*). Final *i* and *u* survived after a consonant plus *l* or *r* (*socri, adflo* > *socri, aflu*); after all other consonants, final *i* weakened or was no longer pronounced, the latter especially when preceded by the affricates [tš], [dž] (*sacĭ, fragĭ* [*satš, fradž*]). When immediately preceded by a vowel, final *i* and *u* were reduced to semi-vowels (*noĭ* [i̯], *vechiŭ* [u̯].

## Diphthong [au̯] in Romance

45. In Gallo-Romance [au̯] monophthongized to [o] in French, but survived in Provençal (*auru* > Fr. *or,* Pr. *aur*). In Ibero-Romance,

15

[au̯] monophthongized to [o] in Spanish and Catalan, with Portuguese arriving at the same solution through the diphthong *ou* [ou̯], whose spelling has been retained (*auru* > Sp. *oro*, Ct. *or*, Pg. *ouro*). In Rheto-Romance (Surselvan), [au̯] survived (*auru* > *aur*). In Italo-Romance [au̯] monophthongized to [o] in Italian, and to [a] in Sardinian (*paucu* > It. *poco*, Sd. *pagu*). In Balkan Romance, [au̯] survived intact (*auru* > *aur*).

## Vulgar Latin Consonantal System

46. The consonantal system of Vulgar Latin differed from that of Classical Latin in the following respects: (1) *H*, which was already weak in Classical Latin, disappeared altogether. (2) Final *m*, except in monosyllables, also disappeared. (3) Final *s* disappeared in the East. (4) Double consonants, except in Italy, were simplified. (5) Intervocalic surds in the West and, to some extent, in Italy, became sonorous. (6) Consonantal groups such as *nf, ns, pt, rs* (*infante, mensa, septe, sursu*) were simplified by the total assimilation of the first phoneme to the second, thus becoming *ff, ss,* and *tt*. (7) $C[k]^{e,i}$ and $g^{e,i}$ (*cera, cilia, gente, gibba*) were palatalized and later assibilated in some regions, thus becoming the affricates [ts] or [tš] and [dž]. (8) Intervocalic *b* and *v* were both pronounced [b̵].

## Evolution of Vulgar Latin Consonants

47. The evolution of Vulgar Latin consonants was conditioned by one or more of the following factors: (1) position within the word, (2) contiguous vowels, (3) a contiguous palatal (yod), (4) contiguous consonants, whose contiguity might have been brought about in Romance through syncope, (5) assimilation to another consonant in the same word, (6) dissimilation from another consonant in the same word.

## Initial Consonants in Gallo-Romance

48. In French and Provençal, initial [ts] ($c^{e,i}$) was eventually simplified to [s], written *c* (*caelu* > Fr. *ciel*, Pr. *cel* [s]). In French, but not in Provençal, initial *c* [k], followed by *a*, palatalized to [tš], which later simplified to [š] (*camera* > *chambre* [š]). In French and Provençal, initial [dž] ($g^{e,i}$) simplified to [ž], written *g* (*generu* > Fr., Pr. *gendre* [ž]). In French, but only sporadically in Provençal, initial *g*, followed by *a*, palatalized to [dž], which later simplified to [ž] (*\*gamba* > *jambe* [ž]). In French and Provençal, initial [i̯] (< CL [i] in hiatus) followed the same pattern as initial [dž], simplifying to [ž] (*iacere* > Fr. *gésir*, Pr. *jazer* [ž]).

16

*Initial Consonants in Ibero-Romance*

49. (a) In Spanish, initial *v* [b̦] merged with initial *b* [b], the etymological spelling being retained in most instances (*ventu* > *viento*, *vota* > *boda* [b]). Within the phrase, except in the environment of a preceding nasal, initial [b] weakened to fricative [b̦] (*te veo* [tebeo], but *en vano* [embano]). Initial *f*, except when followed by *r* or *ue*, and occasionally *ie*, became an aspirated *h*, and then disappeared, the *h* often surviving as an orthographic vestige (*femina, frenu, focu, festa* > *hembra, freno, fuego, fiesta*). Initial *l*, when followed by *ie*, palatalized to [ł], the yod being absorbed in the palatalization (*levat* > \**lieva* > *lleva* [ł]). Initial [ts] (*c^{e,i}*) became [θ], written *c* (*caelu* > *cielo* [θ]). Initial [dž] (*g^{e,i}*) became [i̦], written *y*, when followed by stressed *e* (*generu* > *yerno*), and otherwise disappeared (*germanu* > *hermano*). Initial [i̦] (< CL [i] in hiatus) either survived, written *y* (*iam* > *ya*), or changed to [dž] (> [ž]) and later [χ], written *j* (*iocu* > *juego* [χ]), or disappeared (*iungere* > *uncir*). Initial *r* was strongly trilled.

(b) In Catalan, initial *v* [b̦] merged with *b* [b], as it did in Spanish (*vinu* > *vi* [b]). Initial *l* palatalized to [ł] (*lingua* > *llengua*). Initial [ts] (*c,^{e,i}*) eventually simplified to [s], written *c* (*caelu* > *cel* [s]). Initial [dž] (*g^{e,i}*) and [i̦] ( < CL [i] in hiatus) became [ž] (*gelu* > *gel, iam* > *ja* [ž]). Initial *r* was strongly trilled.

(c) In Portuguese, initial [ts] (*c^{e,i}*) simplified to [s], written *c* (*caelu* > *céu* [s]). Initial [dž] (*g^{e,i}*) and [i̦] (< CL [i] in hiatus) became [ž], written *g* or *j* (*generu* > *genro, iacere* > *jazer* [ž]). Initial *r* was strongly trilled.

*Initial Consonants in Rheto-Romance*

50. In Surselvan, initial [tš] (*c^{s,i}*), written *tsch*, did not change (*caelu* > *tschiel*). Initial *c* [k], followed by *a*, often palatalized to [tš], written *tg* (*cane* > *tgaun*, but *capra* > *caura*). Initial *c* [k], followed by *i* (< [y]) or *ie* (< [ǫ]), also palatalized to [tš] (*cuna* > *tgina, cornu* > *tgiern* [tš]). Initial [dž] (*g^{e,i}*) and [i̦] (< CL [i] in hiatus) became [ž], written *şch* (*gente* > *şchenta, januariu* > *şchaner*).

*Initial Consonants in Italo-Romance*

51. (a) In Italian, initial [tš] (*c^{e'i}*) did not change (*caelu* > *cielo, civitate* > *città* [tš]). Initial [i̦] (< CL [i] in hiatus) merged with [dž] (*g^{e,i}*), both written *g* (*gente* > *gente, iam* > *già* [dž]).

(b) In the Vulgar Latin of Sardinia, initial *c^{s,i}* and *g^{e,i}* did not palatalize. The velar plosives [k] and [g] remained intact, except for the emergence of [b] as a secondary concurrent of [g] (*cena* > *kena, gelare* > *gelare* [g], *belare*). Initial [i̦] (< CL [i] in hiatus) also remained intact (*iuncu* > [iunku]).

*Initial Consonants in Balkan Romance*

52. In Rumanian, initial [tš] ($c^{e,i}$) and [dž] ($g^{e,i}$) did not change (*caelu* > *cer* [tš], *generu* > *ginere* [dž]). Initial *d, l, s, t*, followed by [i̯] or [i̯e] (< VL [ę]) palatalized to [z], [i̯], [š], [tš], respectively, written *z, i, s, t* (*dies* > *zi, lepore* > *iepure, sex* > *şase, terra* > *ţară*).

*Initial Consonantal Groups in Gallo-Romance*

53. In French and Provençal, initial *qu* [ku̯] followed by *a, e,* or *i* was reduced to [k], written *qu* in French, and *c* (before *a*) and *qu* (before *e* or *i*) in Provençal (*quattuor* > Fr. *quatre,* Pr. *catre, quaerere* > Fr. *quérir,* Pr. *querre, qui* > Fr., Pr. *qui*). Initial [di̯] became [dž], which later simplified to [ž], written *j* (*diurnu* > Fr. *jour,* Pr. *jorn*). Initial *s* plus consonant generated a prosthetic [i > e] in Vulgar Latin, which was retained (*sponsu* > Fr. *époux,* Pr. *espos*).

*Initial Consonantal Groups in Ibero-Romance*

54. In Spanish, Catalan, and Portuguese, initial *qu* [ku̯] followed by *e* or *i* was reduced to [k], written *qu*, whereas initial *qu* [ku̯] followed by *a*, written *cua* in Spanish and *qua* in Catalan and Portuguese, was retained (*quaerere* > Sp., Pg. *querer,* Ct. *querre* [k], *quattuor* > Sp. *cuatro,* Ct. *quatre,* Pg. *quatro* [ku̯]). In Spanish, initial *cl, fl, pl* became [ɫ], whereas initial *bl* and *gl* tended to lose their first element (*clave* > *llave, flamma* > *llama, planu* > *llano, \*blastimare* > *lastimare, glattire* > *latir*). In Portuguese, initial *cl, fl, pl* became [š], written *ch* (*clave* > *chave, flamma* > *chama, planu* > *chão*). In Spanish, initial [di̯] became [i̯], or through [dž], became [χ] (*deorsu* > *yuso, diurnale* > *jornal*), whereas, in Catalan and Portuguese, it became [dž], which simplified to [ž] (*diurnu* > Ct. *jorn, diaria* > Pg. *geira*). The prosthetic [i > e] was retained in Spanish, Catalan, and Portuguese (*sponsu* > Sp. *esposo,* Ct. *espos,* Pg. *esposo*).

*Initial Consonantal Groups in Rheto-Romance*

55. In Surselvan, initial *qu* [ku̯] followed by *e* or *i* remained [ku̯], written *qu*, or changed to [tš], written *tg* (*quindecim* > *quendisch, qui* > *tgi*). Initial *qu* [ku̯] followed by *a* did not change (*quattuor* > *quater*). Prosthetic [i > e] was lost (*sponsu* > *spus*).

*Initial Consonantal Groups in Italo-Romance*

56. (a) In Italian, initial *qu* [ku̯] followed by *e* or *i* remained [ku̯], written *qu*, or was reduced to [k], written *ch* (*quindecim* >

18

*quindici, qui > chi*). Initial *qu* [kŭ], followed by *a*, did not change (*quattuor > quattro*). Initial [di̯] became [dž], written *gi* (*diurnu > giorno*). Initial *bl, cl, fl, gl, pl* became [bi̯], [ki̯], [fi̯], [gi̯], [pi̯], written *bi, chi, fi, ghi, pi* (*\*blastimare > biasimare, clave > chiave, flamma > fiamma, glande > ghianda, planu > piano*). Prosthetic [i] was lost (*sponsu > sposo*).

(b) In Sardinian, initial *qu* [kŭ], followed by *a, e,* or *i*, became [b] or [k] (*quindecim > bindighi, quid >* [ki], *quattuor > battoro*). Initial *pl* became *pr* (*plenu > prenu*). Prosthetic [i] was retained (*scala > iskala*).

## Initial Consonantal Groups in Balkan Romance

57. In Rumanian, initial *qu* [kŭ], followed by *e* or *i*, became [tš], written *c* (*quaerere > cere*). Initial *qu* [kŭ], followed by *a*, became [p] or [k], the latter written *c* (*quattuor > patru, quando > când*). Initial *cl, gl* became [ki̯], [gi̯], written *chi, ghi* (*clave > \*[ki̯ei̯e] > cheie* [kei̯e, by dissimilation], *glacia > ghiață*). Prosthetic [i > e] was lost (*scala > scară*).

## Intervocalic Consonants in Gallo-Romance

58. (a) In French: (1) *-p-* became *-b-* and then *-v-* (*ripa > rive*); (2) *-[b]-* (*< -b-, -v-*) became *-v-* before *a, e, i* (*faba > fève, bovariu > bouvier*), and disappeared before *o, u* (*pavone > paon, avunculu > oncle*); (3) *-t-* and *-d-* became *-[đ]-* and then disappeared (*maturu > mûr, nudare > nouer*); (4) *-s-* voiced to [z], written *s* (*causa* [s] *> chose* [z]); (5) *-[ts]-* (*-cᵉ,ⁱ*) became [dz] and then [i̯z], written *is*, [i̯] forming a diphthong with the preceding vowel (*vicinu > voisin* [oi̯ > u̯ɛ > u̯al]); (6) *-[dž]-* (*-gᵉ,ⁱ*) became [i̯], forming a diphthong with the preceding vowel (*rege > roi* [oi̯ > u̯ɛ > u̯a]); (7) *-c* [k]-, followed by *a*, and preceded by *o* or *u*, became *-[g]-* and then disappeared (*locare > louer*); preceded by *a, e,* or *i*, it became [i̯], which formed a diphthong with the preceding vowel (*necare > noyer* [oi̯ > u̯ɛ > u̯a]); (8) *-g-*, followed by *a*, and preceded by *o* or *u*, disappeared (*ruga > rue*); preceded by *a, e,* or *i*, it became [i̯], which formed a diphthong with the preceding vowel (*legale > loyal, plaga > plaie*).

(b) In Provençal; (1) *-p-* became *-b-* (*sapere > saber*); (2) *-t-* became *-d-* (*rota > roda*); (3) *-d-* became *-[đ]-* and then *-[z]-*, written *z* (*videre > vezer*); (4) *-s-* became *-[z]-*, written *s* (*causa* [s] *> causa* [z]); (5) *-[ts]-* (*cᵉ,ⁱ*) became *-[dz]-, -[i̯z]-*, and finally *-[z]-*, written *z* (*placere > plazer*); (6) *-[dž]-* (*-gᵉ,ⁱ*) became [ž], written *g* (*sagitta > sageta* [ž]).

## Intervocalic Consonants in Ibero-Romance

59. (a) In Spanish: (1) *-p-* became *-b-* and then *-[b]-* (*lupu > lobo* [b]); (2) *-t-* became *-d-* and then *-[đ]-* (*maturu > maduro* [đ]),

which was lost in some instances (*cantatis* > *cantades* > *cantáis*) and weakened in others (*cantatu* > *canta[d]o*); (3) -*d*- became -[đ]-, which was retained (*nudu* > *nudo*) or lost (*tepidu* > *tibio*); (4) -*g*-, followed by *a, o,* or *u,* which was probably already [g̶] in Vulgar Latin, survived in some instances (*legumen* > *legumbre*), and was lost in others (*legale* > *leal*); (5) -*c*[k]- followed by *a, o,* or *u* became -[g]- and then -[g̶]- (*lactuca* > *lechuga*); (6) -*f*- became -[b̶]-, written *v* (*profectu* > *provecho*), unless it was felt to be initial (following a prefix), in which case, when not followed by *r* or *ue*, it was aspirated and then lost (*defensa* > *dehesa*); (7) -[ts]- (-*c*$^{e,i}$) became -[dz]-, [z]-, -[đ]-, and finally -[θ]- written *c* (*facere* > *hacer*); (8) -[dž]- (-*g*$^{e,i}$) became [i̯] and then disappeared (*frigidu* > *frío, lege* > *ley*); (9) -[b̶]- (< -*b*-, -*v*-) survived, most often with the etymological spelling (*caballu* > *caballo, vivere* > *vivir*); (10) -*s*- became -[z]-, and then reverted to [s] (*casa* [z] > *casa* [s]).

(b) In Catalan: (1) -*p*- became -*b*-, pronounced [b] or [b̶] (*ripa* > *riba*); (2) -*f*- merged with -[b̶]- (< -*b*-, -*v*-), written *v* (*defensa* > *devesa, probare* > *provar, cavare* > *cavar*), which disappeared before *o* or *u* (*sabucu* > *saüc*); (3) -*t*- became -*d*-, pronounced [d] or [đ] (*rotundu* > *rodó*); (4) -*d*- was lost when preceded and followed by an unstressed vowel (*tepida* > *tèbea*); when it followed the stressed vowel, it became -[z]-, spelled *s* (*lampreda* > *llampresa* [z]); when it preceded the stressed vowel, it was lost (*sudare* > *suar*); (5) -*s*- survived as [z], written *s*, when it followed the stressed vowel; when it preceded the stressed vowel, it disappeared (*rasore* > *raor*); (6) -*c*[k]-, followed by *a, o,* or *u,* became *g* (*formica* > *formiga*); (7) -[ts]- (< -*c*$^{e,i}$) became -[z]- and then disappeared (*placere* > *plaer*); (8) -*g*-, followed by *a,* survived when it was in post-tonic position (*negat* > *nega*), but disappeared in pretonic position (*regale* > *real*); followed by *o* or *u,* the reverse was true (*jugu* > *jou, legumen* > *llegum*); (9) -[dž]- (-*g*$^{e,i}$) became [i̯], which survived (*brugitu* > *bruit*) or disappeared (*magistru* > *maestre, mestre*); (10) -[i̯]- survived as -[ž]-, written *j* (*maiore* > *major* [ž]).

(c) In Portuguese: (1) -*p*- became -*b*- (*sapere* > *saber*); (2) -*f*- and -[b̶]- (< -*b*-, -*v*-) became -[v]- (*profectu* > *proveito, caballu* > *cavalo, clave* > *chave*); (3) -*t*- became -*d*- (*rota* > *roda*); (4) -*d*- was lost (*pede* > *pé*); (5) -*s*- became -[z]-, written *s* (*casa* [s] > *casa* [z]); (6) -*l*- was lost (*caelu* > *céu*); (7) -[ts]- (< *c*$^{e,i}$) became -[dz]- and then -[z]-, written *z* (*vicinu* > *vizinho*); (8) -[dž]- (-*g*$^{e,i}$) simplified to -[ž]-, written *g* (*\*fugire* > *fugir* [ž]), or disappeared (*grege* > *grei*); (9) -*c*[k]-, followed by *a, o* or *u,* became -*g*- (*pacare, dico, securu* > *pagare, digo, seguro*); (10) -*n*- was lost, having first nasalized the preceding vowel; the resulting vocalic combinations resolved themselves as *ã* < -[ãn]*a* (*lana* > *lã*); *o* < -*ã*[*n*]*u*, -*ã*[*n*] *e*, -*ō*[*n*]e (*sānu* > *são, cāne* > *cão, sapōne* > *sabão*); *ãos* < -*ã*[*n*]*os*, (*germānos* > *irmãos*); *āes* < -*ā*[*n*]*es* (*cānes* > *cães*); *ões* < *ō*[*n*]*es* (*lectiōnes* > *licões*); *eia* < -*ē*[*n*]*a* (*vēna* > *veia*) ; *eio* < -*ē*[*n*]*u* (*plēnu* > *cheio*); *im* [*ī*] < -*ī*[*n*]*e* (*fīne* > *fim*); *om* [*ō*] < -*o*[*n*]*u* (*bonu* > *bom*) ; -*inha*, -*inho* < -*ī*[*n*]*a*, -*ī*[*n*]*u* (*farina* > *farinha*, *vinu* > *vinho*).

## Intervocalic Consonants in Rheto-Romance

60. In Surselvan: (1) -*p*- became -*v*- (*ripa* > *riva*); (2) -[ƀ]- (< -*b*-, -*v*-) became -[v]-, written *v* (*caballu* > *cavagl*, *nova* > *nova*); (3) -*t*- became -*d*- (*rota* > *roda*); (4) -*d*- was lost (*pede* > *pei*); (5) -*s*- became -[z]-, written *s* (*casa* [s] > *casa* [z]); (6) -[tš]- (-*c*$^{e,i}$) became -[dž]-, and finally -[ž]-, written *şch* (*vicinu* > *vişchin*); (7) -[dž]- (-*g*$^{e,i}$) was retained (*fugere* > *fugir*); (8) -[g]- (-*g*$^{a,o,u}$) was lost (*augustu* > *uost*).

## Intervocalic Consonants in Italo-Romance

61. (a) In Italian: (1) -*p*- survived (*sapere* > *sapere*); (2) -[ƀ]- (< -*b*-, -*v*-) became -[v]-, written *v* (*caballu* > *cavallo*, *clave* > *chiave*); (3) -*t*- survived (*rota* > *ruota*); (4) -*d*- survived (*pede* > *piede*); (5) -*s*- became -[z]-, written *s*, and, in some cases, reverted to -[s]- (*nasu* > *naso* [s], *casu* > *caso* [z]); (6) -[tš]- (-*c*$^{e,i}$) survived, written *c* (*vicinu* > *vicino* [tš]); (7) -[dž]- (-*g*$^{e,i}$) was reinforced [d·dž] or became [i], the latter absorbed by a following stressed *e* or *i* (*exagiu* > *saggio*, *magistru* > *maestro*); (8) -*c*[k]-, followed by *a*, *o*, or *u*, was retained or became -*g*-, some words showing both developments (*amica* > *amica*, *fricare* > *fregare*, *amicu* > *amico*, *acutu* > *acuto*, *aguto*).

(b) In Sardinian: (1) -*p*-, -*t*-, -[*k*]- became [ƀ], [đ], [g] (*nepote* > *ne*[ƀ]*o*[đ]*e*); (2) -[ƀ]- (< -*b*-, -*v*-), -*d*-, -[g]- (< -*g*$^{a,o,u}$) were lost (*caballu* > *kaḍḍu*, *coda* > *koa*, *iugu* > *yu*); (3) -*c*$^{e,i}$, -*g*$^{e,i}$ became [g], which, in the latter case, disappeared (*acetu* > *aghedu* [g], *legere* > *leere*).

## Intervocalic Consonants in Balkan Romance

62. In Rumanian: (1) -*p*- survived unchanged (*ripa* > *rîpa*); (2) -*t*-, -*d*-, -*s*-, which otherwise survived unchanged (*muta* > *mută*, *cruda* > *crudă*, *formosa* > *frumoasă*), palatalized before *i* to [ts] (written *ţ*), [z] (written *z*), [š] (written *ş*) : *lati* > *laţi*, *cades* > *\*cadi* > *cazi*, *formosi* > *frumoşi*; (3) -[ƀ]- (< -*b*-, -*v*-) was lost (*caballu* > *cal*, *novu* > *nou*); (4) -[tš]- (-*c*$^{e,i}$) survived, written *c* (*vicinu* > *vecin* [tš]) ; (5) -[dž]- (-*g*$^{e,i}$) survived, written *g* (*\*fugire* > *fugi*) ; (6) -*l*- became -*r*- (*sole* > *soare*).

## Vulgar Latin Double Consonants in Romance

63. (a) The double consonants of Classical Latin, other than *cc* *ll*, *nn*, and *rr*, survived only in the Vulgar Latin of Italy and Sardinia,

simplifying in all other Romance areas. The simple consonants thus derived did not undergo the changes which affected the original intervocalic consonants; for example, the surds did not become sonorous in Western Romance (*cuppa* > Fr. *coupe*, Sp. *copa*).

(b) In French, Portuguese, Provençal, Rumanian, and Surselvan, *-ll-* became *-l-*, but this derived *-l-* remained intact, whereas the original intervocalic *-l-* regularly changed to *-r-* or disappeared (*caelu, caballu* > Pg. *céu, cavalo*, Rm. *cer, cal*). In Spanish and Catalan, *-ll-* palatalized to [ï], written *ll* (*caballu* > Sp. *caballo*, Ct. *cavall*). In Sardinian, *-ll-* became cacuminal [ḍ·ḍ] (*caballu* > *kaḍḍu*). In Rumanian, derived *-l-* followed by *i* became *-i-* and disappeared (*gallina* > *găină*); before *-a-*, it became [ṷ], which survived after stressed *-i-* and *-a-* (*stella illa* > *steaua*), and otherwise disappeared (*stella* > *stea*). In Italian, *-ll-* was distinguished by its doubly lengthened articulation.

(c) In Spanish and Catalan, *-nn-* palatalized to [ñ], written *ñ* and *ny*, respectively (*annu* > Sp. *año*, Ct. *any*). In French, Portuguese, Provençal, Rumanian, and Surselvan, *-nn-* simplified to *-n-*, which remained where intervocalic *n* normally disappeared (*annu, sanu* > Pg. *ano, são*). In Italo-Romance, *-nn-* survived intact (*annu* > It. *anno*, Sd. *annu*).

(d) The fate of *-cc-* was determined by (1) the following vowel, (2) the fact that the second *c* was in syllable-initial position, and (3) assimilation in Italian of the first *c* to palatalized $c^{e,i}$: *vacca* > Fr. *vache* [tš > š], It. *vacca* [k.k], Sp. *vaca* [k]; *accessu* > Fr. *accès* [ks], It. *accesso* [t.tš], Sp. *acceso* [kθ].

(e) In Ibero-Romance, *-rr-*, like *r-*, is strongly trilled. In Modern French, originally trilled *-rr-* was reduced to a single velar or uvular *-r-* through the influence of Parisian pronunciation. In Rheto- and Balkan Romance, *-rr-* was simplified, whereas in Italo-Romance, it was retained intact.

*Medial Consonantal Groups in Gallo-Romance*

64. (a) In French: (1) *-pl-, -p'l-* became *-bl-* (*duplu* > *double*, *cap[u]lu* > *cable*); (2) *-pr-, -p'r-, -br-, -b'r-* became *-vr-* (*aprile* > *avril*, *paup(e)re* > *pauvre*, *libra* > *livre*, *lib(e)rare* > *livrer*); (3) *-tr-, -dr-, -d'r-* became *-[đr]-* and then *-r-* or *-rr-* (*patre* > *pedre* > *père*, *quadratu* > *carré*, *cred(e)re* > *croire*); (4) *-t'l-* became *-tr-* (*epist(u)la* > *épître*); (5) in *-x*[ks]*-, -c'r- -ct-, -gr-, -g't-, -g'd-*, the first element became a semi-vocalic yod [i̯] (*coxa* > *cuisse*, *fac(e)re* > *faire*, *factu* > *fait*, *fragrare* > *flairer*, *dig(i)tu* > *doigt*, *frig(i)du* > *froid*); (6) *-l* + yod-, *-c'l-, -g'l-*, with exceptions, became [ï], written *il* in final, and *ill* in non-final position (*folia* > *feuille*, *vermic(u)lu* > *vermeil*, *vig(i)lare* > *veiller*); (7) *-lv'r-* became *-oudr-* (*absolv(e)re* > *absoudre*); (8) *-mn-, -m'n-* became *-mm-* through assimilation (*somnu*

22

> *somme, fem(i)na* > *femme*) ; (9) -*n'm*- became -*m*- (*an(i)ma* > *âme*); (10) -*m'l*- -*m'r*- became more pronounceable through the intrusion of an unetymological *b* (*cum(u)lare* > *combler, num(e)ru* > *nombre*) ; (11) -*n'r*- became -*ndr*- (*ten*(e)*ru* > *tendre*) ; (12) -*n* + *yod*-, -*gn*-, -*ng*-, with exceptions, became [ñ], written *gn*, occasionally *ign* (*Spania* > *Espagne, agnellu* > *agneau, plangente* > *plaignant*); (13) in -*s* + cons.-, *s* disappeared, lengthening the vowel which preceded it (*costa* > *côte, as(i)nu* > *âne* ); (14) -*p* + yod became [tš > š], written *ch* (*sapia* > *sache*); (15) -*b* or *v* + yod became [dž > ž], written *g* or *j* (*rubeu* > *rouge, diluviu* > *déluge*); (16) -*t* + yod became [i̯z], written *is* (*potione* > *poison*); (17) -cons. + *t* + *yod* became -*ss*-, also written *c* or *z* (*\*captiare* > *chasser*); (18) -*st* + yod became -*iss*- (*angustia* > *angoisse*) ; (19) -*d* + yod was reduced to [i̯] (*\*gaudia* > *joie*); (20) -*s* + yod became [i̯z], written *is* (*mansione* > *maison*); (21) -[ts] (-*c*^{e,i}) + yod was reduced to [s], written *c* or *ss* (*\*facia* > *face, facia* > *fasse*); (22) -*nd* + yod became [ñ], written *gn* (*ver[e]cundia* > *vergogne*) ; (23) -*m* or *mn* + yod became [nž], written *ng* or *nj* (*simia* > *singe*); (24) in -*l* + cons.-, *l* became [u̯] after *a, e, i, o*, and disappeared after *u* (*alta* > *haute, caballos* > *chevaux, pul[i]ce* > *puce*).

(b) In Provençal: (1) -*br*-, through [br̥], became [u̯r] (*fabru* > *faure*) ; (2) -*tr*-, -*dr*-, through [dr̥], became [i̯r] (*petra* > *peira, quadru* > *caire*); (3) in -*b* or *m* + yod, the yod might be retained (*cavea* > *gabia, vindemia* > *vendemia*); (4) in -*l* + cons.-, the *l* might be retained (*alba* > *alba*); (5) in -*s* + cons.-, the *s* survived during the Middle Ages, and is still perceptible in some regions (*castellu* > *castel, \*blastimare* > *blasmar*); (6) -*ct*- generally became [tš], written *ch* (*factu* > *fach, nocte* > *nuech*); (7) -*mn*-, -*m'n* survived in the literary language (*\*damnaticu, fem[i]na* > *damnatge, femna*); (8) -*n'r*-, -*l'r*-, -*s'r*- survived without the instrusion of *d* (*cinere* > *cenre, molere* > *molre*) ; (9) in -*pt*-, -*bt*-, the first element survived (*cap[i]tale, dub[i]tare* > *capdal, doptar*); (10) in -*v't*-, the *v* became [u̯] (*civ[i]tate* > *ciutat*).

*Medial Consonantal Groups in Ibero-Romance*

65. (a) In Spanish: (1) the combination of -*l, m, n, r*, or *s* + cons.- remained intact (*saltu* > *salto, \*tempu* > *tiempo, porta* > *porta, musca* > *mosca*) except for Vulgar Latin assimilations (see par. 46, above, and the developments described in (2)-(8) following); (2) -*mb*-, through assimilation, became -*m*- (*lumbu* > *lomo*); (3) -*mn*-, through assimilation and palatalization, became -*ñ*- (*damnu* > *daño*); (4) -*sc*^{e,i} [sts]- became [θ], written *c* or *z* (*miscere* > *mecer*); (5) -*rg*^{e,i} [rdž]- became [rdz], [rd̦], and finally [rθ], written *rc* or *rz* (*spargere* > *esparcir*); (6) -*ng*^{e,i} [ndž]- became [ndz], [nd̦], and finally [nθ], written *nc* or *nz* (*singellu* > *sencillo*), -*ñ*- (*\*ringere*

> *reñir*), or -n- (*quingenti* > *quinientos*); (7) in -cons. + $c^{e,i}$ [ts]-, [ts] became [θ], written *c* or *z* (*vincere* > *vencer*); (8) in -*lc*-, -*lp*-, -*lt*-, *l* became [u̯] if preceded by *a* (*alteru* > *\*autro* > *otro*), and [i̯] if preceded by *u*, the [i̯] being retained if the group was in final position (*multu* > *muy*) or if pronunciation made further development impossible (*vulture* > *buitre*), and otherwise disappearing (*multu* > *mucho*); (9) *in* -[u̯k]-, -[u̯p]-, -[u̯t], the [u̯] prevented the voicing of the consonant (*paucu* > *poco*, *autumnu* > *otoño*); (10) in -cons. + *r* or *l*, the first element developed as though it had been intervocalic (*duplare* > *doblar*, *aprile* > *abril*, *patre* > *padre*, *socru* > *suegro*), voiced consonants surviving (*quadru* > *cuadro*) or disappearing (*quadraginta* > *cuarenta*); (11) -*d* or *g* + yod became [i̯], written *y* (*podiu* > *poyo*, *exagiu* > *ensayo*); (12) -*t* or *c* + yod became [z], [d̦], and finally [θ], written *c* or *z* (*ratione* > *razón*, *minacia* > *amenaza* [θ]); (13) -cons. + *t* or *c* + yod became -cons. [ts]- and finally -cons. [θ]-, written *c* or *z* (*martiu* > *marzo*, *lancea* > *lanza*); (14) -*n* + yod became -*ñ*- (*vinea* > *viña*); (15) -*l* + yod became [ž] and finally [χ], written *j* (*folia* > *hoja*); (16) -*n'c*- became -*ng*- (*domin*[*i*]*cu* > *domingo*); (17) -*al'c^{e,i}* became [au̯θ] (*sal*[*i*]*ce* > *sauce*), and -*ul'c* became -*ulg*- (*\*pulica* > *pulga*); (18) -*p't*-, -*p'd*-, -*b't*-, -*v't*- became -*bd*- and finally -[u̯d] or -*d*- (*cap*[*i*]*tale* > *caudal*, *rap*[*i*]*du* > *raudo*, *cub*[*i*]*tu* > *codo*, *civ*[*i*]*tate* > *ciudad*); (19) -*c'l*-, -*g'l*-, -*t'l*- (> -*c'l*-) became [ł], [ž], and finally [χ], written *j* (*\*vet*[*u*]*lu* > *\*vec*[*u*]*lu* > *viejo*, *oc*[*u*]*lu* > *ojo*, *teg*[*u*]*la* > *teja*); (20) -*m'n*-, -*m'r*- became -*mbr*-, -*m'l*- became -*mbl*-, and -*n'r*- became -*ndr*- (*hom*[*i*]*ne*, *hum*[*e*]*ru* > *hombre*, *hombro*; *trem*[*u*]*lare* > *temblar*, *ingen*[*e*]*rare* > *engendrar*); (21) -*c^{e,i}t*- became -[dzd]-, -[dz]-, -[z]-, -[d̦]-, and finally [θ], written *c* or *z* (*plac*[*i*]*tu* > *plazo*); (22) -*g^{e,i}t*- became -*t*-, then -*d*- [d], and finally -*d*- [d̦] (*dig*[*i*]*tu* > *dedo*); (23) -*t'c*-, -*d'c*- became [dg], and then [d̦g], written *zg* (*portat*[*i*]*cu* > *portazgo*, *iud*[*i*]*care* > *juzgar*); (24) -*d'c*- became [dz], [z], [d̦], and finally [θ], written *c* or *z* (*tred*[*e*]*cim* > *trece*); (25) -cons. + *c'l*- became -cons. *ch*- or -*ch*- (*\*manc*[*u*]*la* > *mancha*, *masc*[*u*]*lu* > *macho*); (26) -*ng'l*- became -*ñ*- (*ung*[*u*]*la* > *uña*).

(b) In Catalan, (1) -*pt*-, -*bt*- became -*tt*- and then -*t*- (*captivu* > *catiu*, *subtile* > *sotil*); (2) -*p't*- became -*bd*- (*cap*[*i*]*tale* > *cabdal*); (3) -*b't*- became [u̯t] (*deb*[*i*]*tu* > *deute*); (4) -*br*-, -*b'r*- became [u̯r] (*libra* > *lliura*, *bib*[*e*]*re* > *beure*); (5) -*v'cons*.- became -[u̯] cons.- (*civ*[*i*]*tate* > *ciutat*); (6) -*t'd*-, through -*tt*-, became -*t*- (*nit*[*i*]*da* > *neta*); (7) -*t'n*- became -*nn*-, also written *tn* and *gn* (*pat*[*i*]*na* > *panna*, *cut*[*i*]*na* > *cotna*, *ret*[*i*]*nas* > *regnes*); (8) -*tr*- became -*dr*- or -*r*- (*petra* > *pedra*, *fratre* > *frare*); (9) -*dr*- became -*r*- (*cathedra* > *cadira*), passing through [ir], still evidenced in *caire* < *quadru*; (10) -*d'c^{e,i}*- became [dz], written *tz* (*duod*[*e*]*cim* > *dotze*); (11) -*sm*-, -*s'n*- became [im], [in] (*aes*[*ti*]*mare* > *aimar*, *mans*[*io*]*nata* > *mainada*); (12) -*sc^{e,i}*- became [š], written *x* or *ix*

24

(*crescere* > *créixer*) ; (13) -*ct*-- became [it], which (a) combined with diphthongized [ę] to form the triphthong [iei], later reduced to [i] (*lectu* > *llieit* > *llit*), or (b) was absorbed by preceding stressed *i* (*\*ficta* > *fita*), or (c) combined with stressed [a] or [ę] to form the diphthong [ei], later reduced to *e* (*facta* > *feita* > *feta*), or (d) combined with stressed [ǫ], [ọ] (< ŭ) to form the diphthong [ui] (*cocta* > *cuita, tructa* > *truita*); (14) -*c't*- became -*st*- (*amic*[*i*]*tate* > *amistat*), or [ud] (*lic*[*i*]*ta* > *lleuda*), or [id] (*voc*[*i*]*tare* > *buidar*); (15) -*c'r*- became [ur] (*plac*[*e*]*re* > *plaure*); (16) -*gr*- became -*r*- (*pigritia* > *peresa*) ; (17) -*x*- [ks] became [š], written *ix* (*coxa* > *cuixa*) ; (18) -*c'm*-, -*gm*- became [um] (*dec*[*i*]*mu, phlegma* > *deume, fleuma*); (19) -*gn*- became [ñ], written *ny* (*agnellu* > *anyell*); (20) -*g'd*- became -*d*-, and -*g'c*- became -*c*- (*frig*[*i*]*da* > *freda, fig*[*i*]*care* > *ficar*); (21) -*mn*- through dissimilation became -*mr*- and, by intrusion, -*mbr*- (*fem*[*i*]*na* >*fembra*); (22) -*mt*- remained intact (*com*[*i*]*te* > *comte*); (23) -*nd*- became -*n*- (*demandare* > *demanar*); (24) -*ns*- became [z], written *s* (*defensa* > *devesa* [z]); (25] -*ng*ᵃ,ᵒ,ᵘ- was retained (*onganicia* > *llonganissa*), but -*ng*ᵉ,ⁱ- became [ñ], written *ny* (*plangere* > *plànyer*); (26) -*nc*ᵃ,ᵒ,ᵘ- was retained (*anchora* > *àncora*), but -*nc*ᵉ,ⁱ- became [s], written *c*, in pretonic position (*\*mancipa* > *macip*), and [ns], written *nc* in post-tonic position (*vincere* > *vèncer*); (27) -*pl*- became -*bl*- (*duplicare* > *doblegar*), but -*p'l*- became [ł] (*pop*[*u*]*lu* > *poll*); (28) -*b'l*- became [u] (*fabula* > *faula*); (29) -*c'l*-, *g'l*- became [ł], written *ll* (*acuc*[*u*]*la* > *agulla, reg*[*u*]*la* > *rella*); (30) -*s'l*- became[ł], written *ll* (*ins*[*u*]*la* > *illa*) ; (31) -*t'l*-, -*d'l*, -*i'l*, -*g'l*- became [łł], written *tll* (*quat*[*i*]*la* > *guatlla, \*amid*[*du*]*la* > *ametlla, bai*[*u*]*lu* > *batlle, vig*[*i*]*lat* > *vetlla*).

   (c)   In Portuguese: (1) *c, t, d, p,* and *b* in the groups -*cr*-, -*tl*-, -*tr*-, -*dl*-, -*dr*-, -*pl*-, -*pr*-, -*br*- developed as though they were intervocalic, *l* becoming *r: lacrima* > *lágrima, petra* > *pedra, duplare* > *dobrar, laborare* > *lavrar;* (2) -*b'l*- became -*l*-, the *b* assimilating itself completely to the *l* (*fabulare* > *falar*) ; (3) -*gr*- became [i] (*integru* > *inteiro*) ; (4) -*gn*-, -*ng'l*- became [ñ], written *nh* (*cognatu* > *cunhado, ungula* > *unha*) ; (5) -*ct*- became [it] (*factu* > *feito*); (6) -*c'l*-, -*g'l*- became [ł], written *lh* (*oculu* > *ôlho, tegula* > *telha*); (7) -*x*- [ks] became [s], written *ss* (*dixit* > *disse*), or [š] written *x* (*coxa* > *coxa*); (8) preceded by a vowel, -*qu*ᵃ- became [gu], and -*qu*ᵉ,ⁱ,ᵒ,ᵘ became [g], written *g* or *gu* (*aqua* > *água, antiquu* > *antigo, aquila* > *águila*); (9) preceded by a consonant, -*gu*ᵃ- became [gu] (*lingua* > *lingua*), and -*gu*ᵉ,ᵒ- became [g], written *g* or *gu* (*distinguo* > *distingo, sangue* > *sangue*); (10) -[lu]-, [du]-, -[nuᵃ]-, -[nuᵉ]- became -*lv*- (*valuisset* > *valvesse*), -*v*- (*\*creduit* > *creve*), -[ngᵘ]- (*manuale* > *mangual*), -*n*- (*januelle* > *janela*) ; (11) -*v'g*- became [gu], through vocalization of the *v* and metathesis of the [u] and *g* (*fabrica* > *frágua*) ; (12) preceded by a consonant, *c*ᵉ,ⁱ (ts) became [s], written *c* (*mercede* >

*mercê*); (13) *-sc^{e,i}-* became [i̯s], written *ix* (*pisce* > *peixe*); (14) preceded by a consonant, *-g^{e,i}-* became [ž], written *g* or *j* (*argilla* > *argila, angelu* > *anjo*); (15) *-c* [ts] + yod became [s], written *ç* or *c* (*bracchiu* > *braço, facie* > *face*); (16) preceded by a consonant, *-t* + yod became [s], written *ç* or *c* (*lenteu* > *lenço*); preceded by a vowel, *-t* + yod became *z* (*ratione* > *razão*); (17) preceded by a vowel, *-d* + yod became [ž], written *j* (*video* > *vejo*); preceded by a consonant or diphthong, *-d* + yod became [s], written *ç* (*audio* > *ouço*); (18) *-g* + yod became [ž], written *j* (*fugio* > *fujo*); (19) preceded by a vowel, *-l* or *-ll* + yod became [i̯], written *lh* (*filiu* > *filho, alliu* > *alho*); (20) preceded by a vowel, *-n* + yod became [ñ], written *nh* (*vinea* > *vinha*); (21) preceded by a vowel, *-s* + yod became [ž] (*basiu* > *beijo*); (22) *-ss* and *-sc* + yod became [i̯s], written *ix* (*passione* > *paixão, fascia* > *faixa*); (23) in *-^{a}lp,t,s-*, *l* vocalized to [u̯] (*alteru* > *outro*); (24) the *l* in *-^{u}lt-* vocalized to [i̯] (*multu* > *muito*), which, in most cases, disappeared (*cultellu* > *cuitello* > *cutelo*); (25) *-mn-* assimilated to *-n-* (*damnu* > *dano*); (26) *m'd* assimilated to *-nd-* (*comite* > *conde*); (27) *-mpt-* lost *p*, and *-mt-* assimilated to *-nt-* (*computare* > *contar*); (28) *-mpl-, -nfl-* became *-nch-* [nš] (*amplu* > *ancho, inflare* > *inchar*), and *-mpl-* also became *-mpr-* (*implicare* > *empregar*); (29) *-mbl-* became *-mbr-* (*similare* > *sembrar*).

## Medial Consonantal Groups in Rheto-Romance

66. In Surselvan: (1) *-c'l-, -g'l-* became [i̯], written *gl* (*oc[u]lu, coag[u]lu* > *egl, cuagl*); (2) *-c^{e,i}, d, l, n, p, t* + yod became, respectively, [tš], written *tsch* (*glacia* > *glatscha*); [z], written *z* (*hodie* > *oz*); [i̯], written *gl* (*filia* > *feglia*); [ñ], written *gn* (*vinea* > *vegna*); [ppi] (*sapiam* > *sappi*); [ts], written *zz* (*platea* > *plazza*); (3) *-x-* [ks] became [i̯s], written *iss* (*fraxinu* > *fraissen*) (4) *-ct-* became [tš], written *tg* (*lacte* > *latg*); (5) *-s* + cons.- became *-[š]* + cons.- (*festa* > *fiasta* [š]); (6) *-mn-* became *-nn-* or *-n-* (*somnu* > *sien*); (7) *-gn-* became *-nn-* (*lignu* > *lenn*) or *-[ñ]* (*pugnu* > *pugn*); (8) *-n'gl-* remained *-ngl-* (*ung[u]la* > *ungla*); (9) *-sc^{e,i}* became [š], written *sch* (*pisce* > *pèsch*).

## Medial Consonantal Groups in Italo-Romance

67. (a) In Italian: (1) when preceded by a vowel, *-pl- (-p'l), -bl-, (-b'l), -fl- (-f'l-), -cl- (-c'l-), -gl (-g'l-), -t'l- (> c'l)* became, respectively, [ppi̯] (*cop[u]la* > *coppia*), [bbi̯] (*fib[u]la* > *fibbia*), [ffi̯], [k.ki̯], written *cchi* (*oc[u]lu* > *occhio*), [g.gi̯], written *gghi* (*teg[u]la* > *tegghia*), [k.ki̯] (*vet[u]lu* > *vecchio*); (2) when preceded by a consonant, the groups in (1), above, became, respectively, [pi̯] (*templu*

26

> *tempio*), [bi̯], [fi̯] (*conflat* > *gonfia*), [ki̯], written *chi* (*sarc*[*u*]*lu* > *sarchio*), [gi̯], written *ghi* (*cing*[*u*]*la* > *cinghia*), [ki̯] written *chi* (*fist*[*u*]*la* > *fischio*) ; (3) -*dl*- (-*d'l*-), -*nl*- (-*n'l*-), -*tl*- (-*t'l*), the last when it was formed too late to become -*c'l*-, assimilated to -*ll*- (*ad lo* > *allo*, *spin*[*u*]*la* > *spilla*, *spath*[*u*]*la* > *spalla*) ; (4) -*cr*- (-*c'r*-), -*pr*- (-*p'r*-), -*tr*- (-*t'r*-) developed into the geminates -*cr*-, -*gr*- (*lacrima* > *lacrima*, *lagrima*), -*pr*-, -*vr*- (*supra* > *sopra*, *sovra*), and the concurrent -*tr*-, -*dr*- (*petra*, *matre* > *pietra*, *madre*) ; (5) -*dr*- was retained (*quadru* > *quadro*); (6) -*gr*- was either retained (*pigru* > *pigro*) or reduced to -*r*- (*nigru* > *nero*); (7) -*lr*-, -*llr*-, -*nr*- assimilated to -*rr*- (*tollere* > *torre*, *ponere* > *porre*); (8) -*br*-, -*fr*- became -*bbr*-, -*ffr*- (*fabru* > *fabbro*, *Africa* > *Affrica*); (9) -*m'r*-, -*s'r*- became -*mbr*-, -*sdr*- (*memorare*, \**exradiare* > *membrare*, *sdraiare*); (10) -*p*[u̯]-, -[bu̯]-, -*t*[u̯]-, -*d*[u̯]-, -*l*[u̯]-, -*r*[u̯]- assimilated to -*pp*-, -*bb*-, -*tt*-, -*dd*-, -*ll*-, -*rr*-, the last two sometimes becoming -*lv*-, -*rv*- (*sapui* > *seppi*, *habuit* > *ebbe*, *potuit* > *potte*, \**caduit* > *cadde*, *voluit* > *volle*, *paruit* > *parve*); (11) -*d*[i̯]- became [d.dž], written -*gg*- (*radiu* > *raggio*), less commonly [d.dz], written -*zz*- (*razzo*); (12) -*b*[i̯]-, -*m*[i̯]-, -*p*[i̯]- became -*bbi*-, -*mmi*-, -*ppi*-, when preceded by a vowel (*habeamus* > *abbiamo*, *simia* > *scimmia*, *sapiamus* > *sappiamo*), and -*bi*-, -*mi*-, -*pi*-, when preceded by a consonant; (13) -[ki̯]- and -[ti̯]- became [t.tš], written *cci*, and [t.ts], written *zz*, when preceded by a vowel (*placeo* > *piaccio*, *puteu* > *pozzo*) ; and [tš], written *ci*, and [ts], written *z*, when preceded by a consonant (*urceu* > *orcio*, *martiu* > *marzo*); (14) -[li]-, -[lli]- became [ɫ], written *gl* (*filiu* > *figlio*, \**tolliamus* > *togliamo*) ; (15) -[ni̯]-, -[lni̯]-, -[mni̯]-, [ndži̯]-, (*nge,i*), -[nni̯]- became [ñ], written *gn* (*vinea* > *vigna*, *balneu* > *bagno*, *somniu* > *sogno*, *spongia* > *spugna*, \**pinnione* > *pignone*); (16) -[si̯]- became [ž], written *gi* (*occasione* > *cagione*); (17) -[ssi̯]-, -[stši̯]- (*sce,i*), -[sti̯]- became [š], written *sci* (\**revessiu* > *rovescio*, *fascia* > *fascia*, *angustia* > *angoscia*) ; (18) -[ri̯]- became [i̯] (*area* > *aia*) ; (19) -*m't*-became -*nt*- (*com*[*i*]*te* > *conte*) ; (20) -[ndž]- normally survived, (*piangere* > *piangere* [dž]); (21) -*sce,i*- became [š], written *sc* (*pisce* > *pesce*); (22) -*gna,o,u*- became [ñ], written *gn* (*dignu* > *degno*); (23) -*x*- [ks] became [š], written *sc* (*exit* > *esce*), or [s], written *ss* (*dixit* > *disse*).

(b)  In Sardinian: (1) -*cr*-, -*pr*-, -*tr*- remained unchanged (*socru*, *capra*, *petra* > *sokru*, *kapra*, *petra*); (2) -cons. + *l*- became -cons. + *r*- (*oc*[*u*]*lu* > *okru*); (3) -*sce,i*- became -*sk*- (*pisce* > *piske*); (4) -*gn*- and -*mn*- became -*nn*- (*ligna* > *linna*, *somnu* > *sonnu*); (5) -*ct*- became -*tt*- (*nocte* > *notte*), and -*x*- [ks] became -*ss*- (*fraxinu* > *frassu*); (6) -*gua*- became -*mb*- (*lingua* > *limba*), and -*qua*- became -*bb*- (*aqua* > *abba*); (7) -[bi̯]-, -[li̯]-, -[ni̯]-, -[ri̯]-, -[si̯]-, [ti̯]- became, respectively, [i̯], (*rubeu* > *ruiu*), [dz] (*folia* > *fodza*), [ndz] (*vinea* > *bindza*), [rdz] (*coriu* > *kordzu*), [z] (*caseu* > *kasu*), [t.t] (*puteu* > *puttu*).

## Medial Consonantal Groups in Balkan Romance

68. In Rumanian: (1) -bl- (-b'l-) became -ul- (stab[u]lu > staul) ; (2) -c'l- became [ki̯], written chi (oc[u]lu > ochiu); (3) -scl- (-sc'l), -ngl- (-ng'l-) became [sk] (written sch) and [ngi̯] (written nghi), respectively (discludit > deschide, ung[u]la > unghie); (4) -br- (-b'r-) became [ur̯] (fabru > faur) ; (5) -mn- (-m'n-) became [un̯] when preceded by a (scamnu > scaun); (6) -gn- became mn (pugnu > pumn) ; (7) -cs$^{e,i}$- became [št], written st (pisce > peste) ; (8) -ct- became -pt- (nocte > noapte); (9) -pt- remained unchanged (septe > șapte); (10) -nct- became -nt- (sanctu > sînt); (11) -x- [ks] became -ps- (coxa > coapsa); (12) -[ti̯]- and -[ki̯]- became [ts] written ț (puteu > puț, bracchiu > braț), except when followed by stressed o or u, in which case they became [tš], written ci (titione > taciune, urceolu > ulcior) ; (13) -[bi̯]-, -[di̯]-, -[li̯]-, -[ni̯]-, -[si̯]- became, respectively, [i̯b] (rubeu > roib), [z] (*radia > raza), [i̯] (folia > foaie, vinea > vie), [š] (*ceresia > cireașa); (14) -[rdi̯]- became -rz (hordeu > orz); (15) -qu$^a$ preceded by a vowel became -p- (aqua > apa); -qu$^{e,i}$ preceded by a consonant became [tš], written c (quinque > cinci) ; (16) -gu$^{e,i}$ preceded by a consonant became [dž], written g (sangue > sînge); -gu$^a$ preceded by a consonant became -b- (lingua > limba).

## Final Consonants in Gallo-Romance

69. (a) In French: (1) -m disappeared, except in monosyllables, in which it survived as -n (rem > rien); (2) -n disappeared (nomen > nom [nõ]); (3) -s survived, but became mute very soon, reserving a latent [z] for liaison (nos > nous [nu], nous avons [nuzavõ]); (4) -x [ks] survived as -[s], written x, its first component having become yod (sex > *[si̯ei̯s] > six); (5) post-vocalic -t survived only when the loss of the final vowel made it post-consonantal (videt > voit), being pronounced only in liaison (dort-il); (6) post-consonantal -t survived in such forms as chantent < cantant, but was soon muted, except in liaison (chantent-ils [til]); (7) -d, -c disappeared; (8) -r became internal (quattor > quatre); (9) -l survived (mel > miel); (10) -p (< -p-) became -f, through -v (capu > chef); (11) -[ƀ] (< -b-, -v-) became -f (novu > neuf); (12) -t (< -t-) survived briefly in participial forms such as chantet < cantatu, but soon disappeared (natu > né); -d (-d-) never materialized (nudu > nu); (13) -[ts]- (< -c$^{e,i}$) became [i̯ts] in final position, written iz (voce > voiz), the affricate disappearing in Modern French, and the diphthong [oi̯] becoming [ u̯a] (voix [vu̯a]); (14) -[dž]- (< g$^{e,i}$) became [i̯] in final position (lege > loi [oi̯ > u̯a]) ; (15) -c (< -c$^{o,u}$) did not materialize (focu > feu); (16) -r, -s (< -r-, -s-) survived in Old French but then became mute (cantare, nasu > chanter [e], nez [e]);

(17) -l ($<$ -l-), -m ($<$ -m-), -n ($<$-n-) survived, the latter two soon serving only to nasalize the preceding vowel (sale, vinu $>$ sel, vin [vɛ̃]).

(b) In Provençal: (1) -s survived and, unlike French, was never muted (feminas $>$ femnas); (2) -t did not survive (cantat $>$ canta, cantant $>$ cantan); (3) -p ($<$ -p-) remained intact (capu $>$ cap); (4) -[ƀ] ($<$ -b-, -v-) became -[u̯] (nive $>$ neu); (5) -t ($<$ -t-), -d ($<$ -d-) both became -t (natu, nudu $>$ nat, nut), but -d occasionally disappeared (pede $>$ pé); (6) -c ($<$ -c$^{o,u}$) was retained (focu $>$ foc); (7) -[ts] ($<$ -c$^{e,i}$) was retained, written tz (voce $>$ votz); (8) -[dž] ($<$ -g$^{e,i}$) became [i̯] (lege $>$ lei); (9) -s ($<$ -s-) was retained and, unlike French, was never muted (nasu $>$ nas); (10) -r ($<$ -r-) was retained and, unlike French, was never muted (cantare $>$ cantar); (11) -m, -n ($<$ -m-, -n-) were retained, except that -n might also disappear (homo, vinu $>$ om, vin, vi).

*Final Consonants in Ibero-Romance*

70. (a) In Spanish: (1) -m survived in monosyllables only, as -n (quem $>$ quien); (2) -n survived in en, disappeared in no ($<$ non), and became internal r by dissimilation in nombre ($<$ nomen); (3) -r became internal (sartor $>$ sastre); (4) -l survived in monosyllables (fel $>$ hiel); (5) -s survived without exception (homines $>$ hombres); (6) -t ($<$ -t-) became -d (caritate $>$ caridad); (7) -d ($<$ -d-) survived in polysyllables (mercede $>$ merced), and disappeared in monosyllables (pede $>$ pie); (8) -n ($<$ -n-) survived without exception (pane $>$ pan); (9) -l ($<$ -l-) survived without exception (sale $>$ sal); (10) -r ($<$ -r-) survived, sometimes dissimilating to -l (amare $>$ amar, arbore $>$ árbol); (11) -s ($<$ -s-) survived without exception (tra[n]sve[r]se $>$ través); (12) -[ts] ($<$ -c$^{e,i}$), [ki̯], [ti̯]) survived as -[ts], written z, and then became [θ] (cruce, solaciu, pretiu $>$ cruz, solaz, prez).

(b) In Catalan: (1) -s survived without exception (homines $>$ homes); (2) -m survived as -n in some monosyllables (tam $>$ tan); (3) -n, -l, -r survived in monosyllables (in, mel, cor $>$ en, mel, cor), -r becoming internal in polysyllables (semper $>$ sempre); (4) -n ($<$ -n-) generally disappeared (planu $>$ pla), but reappeared in plurals (hòmens), certain proclitic monosyllables (ben, bon), and in compound indefinite pronouns used adjectivally (algun, ningun); (5) -r ($<$ -r-) survived only orthographically (cantare $>$ cantar [kantá]), except that it was pronounced in certain monosyllables (mar, car), before enclitic personal pronouns (sentir-vos), and in the first person singular of the present tense of verbs whose stem ended in r (sospir); (6) -[ƀ] ($<$ -b-), -[đ] ($<$ -d-), [dz] ($<$ -c$^{e,i}$) became [u̯] (debet $>$ deu, leve $>$ lleu, pede $>$ peu, voce $>$ vou $>$ veu); (7) -[b], -[d], -[g], -[z] ($<$ -p-, $<$ -t-, $<$ -c$^{o,u}$, $<$ -s-), and -[dž] ($<$ -j-,

-$g^{e,i}$) became -p, -t, -c, -s (*capu, pratu, locu, herbosu* > *cap, prat, lloc, herbós*), and -[tš], written *ig* (*maju* > *maig, fageu* ⪈ *faig*) ; (8) -nt, -st became -n, -s (*cantant* > *canten, est* > *es*); (9) -x (ks) was reduced to -s, the first element having become yod (*sex* > *sis*); (10) -l's, -n's, -p's remained intact (*vol[e]s* > *vols, pan[e]s* >*pans, op[u]s* > *ops*); (11) -d's (< -*tis*) became -ts and then -[u̯] (*cantatis* > *cantats* > *cantau*) ; (12) -st, -sc^u, -mf, -rm, -rn, -rt, -rc^u, -rp, having become final, remained unchanged (*repostu* > *rebost, friscu* > *fresc, triumphu* > *triomf, firmu* > *ferm, cornu* > *corn, cohorte* > *cort, porcu* > *porc, serpe* > *serp*) ; (13) -gn-, -ng^{e,i}, -nn-, -mn-, having become final, became [ñ], written *ny* (*stagnu* > *estany, longe* > *lluny, annu* > *any, damnu* > *dany*) ; (14) -ll-, having become final, remained unchanged (*caballu* > *cavall*); (15) -cl-, having become final, became -[ɨ], written *ll* (*vec[u]lu* > *vell*) ; (16) -ct- > -yt-, -t-, having become final, remained unchanged (*factu* > *feyt* > *fet, fructu* > *fruit*) ; (17) -mb-, having become final, became -m (*columbu* > *colom*) ; (18) -nd-, having become final, became -n (*grande* > *gran*).

(c) In Portuguese: (1) -m survived in monosyllables, but only as a nasal resonance (*quem* > *quem* [kẽ]); (2) -s survived as [š] or [ž], depending upon sentence phonetics (*coronas* > *coroas*) ; (3) -r became internal (*inter* > *entre*); (4) -l-, -r-, -n-, -s-, having become final, survived, except that -n served only as a nasal resonance, indicated by -m or tilde (*aprile* > *abril, mare* > *mar, latrone* > *ladrom* > *ladrão*).

## Final Consonants in Rheto-Romance

71. In Surselvan: (1) -m, -n disappeared (*iam, nomen* > *gia, num*); (2) -s survived (*feminas* > *femnas*), except in *plus, magis, est* (> *pli, mai, ei*), and in such forms as *cantamus* (> *cantein*); (3) -x [ks] survived as -s (*sex* > *sis*); (4) -t survived in monosyllabic verbal forms such as *dat, stat* (< *dat, stat*); (5) -r survived (*cor, semper* > *cor, semper*); (6) -l survived (*mel* > *mel*); (7) -p-, -b-, -[b]- (< -b-, -v-), having become final, became [v] and then [f], written *f* or *v* (*lupu, nive* > *luf, neiv* [f]); (8) -t (< -t-) survived (*site* > *seit*); (9) -d (< -d-) disappeared (*pede* > *pei*); (10) -c^{e,i}, having become final, became [š], written *sch* (*nuce* > *nusch*) ; (11) -g^{e,i}, -j-, having become final, were pronounced [tš], and written *tg* (*maju* > *matg*); (12) -r (< -r-) survived (*colore* > *colur*), but was not pronounced in infinitive endings such as -ar, -er, -ir (*cantar* [kantà], *temer* [temé], *finir* [finí]), nor in the masculine noun ending -er (*nurser* [nursè]).

## Final Consonants in Italo-Romance

72. (a) Final consonants did not survive in Italian. Latent -d (< -d, -t) materialized in *ad* (< *ad*) and *ed* (< *et*) when followed

by a word beginning with a vowel. Final *-s* became -[i̯], which (1) survived after the stressed vowel in monosyllables (*nos > noi*), or (2) in polysyllables, formed a transitional diphthong with the preceding unstressed vowel (*vides > *vedei > vedi*), or (3) disappeared (*plus > più*).

(b) In Sardinian: (1) *-m* disappeared (*iam > ya*); (2) *-n* survived (*nomen > nomen*) or became intervocalic through the accretion of a paragogic *-e* (*nomene*); (3) *-s* survived (*feminas > feminas*), but, in sentence phonetics, a following consonant other than *p-, t-, k-* caused it to become *-r* (*ipsas dentes > sar dentes*) or to assimilate itself to the consonant concerned (*ipsas manos > sa mmanos*); (4) *-t* survived (*cantat > cantat*) or became intervocalic through the accretion of a paragogic *-a* (*cantata*); (5) *-r* survived (*cor > kor, semper > semper*) or became intervocalic through the accretion of a paragogic vowel (*quattuor > battoro*); (6) *-l* survived as an intervocalic through the accretion of a paragogic *-e* (*mel > mele*).

*Final Consonants in Balkan Romance*

73. In Rumanian: (1) *-m* survived as intervocalic *-n-* through the accretion of a paragogic *-e* (*quem > cine*), or disappeared (*cum > cu*); (2) *-n* disappeared (*nomen > nume*); (3) *-s* developed in the same way as in Italian (see par. 72(a), above) (*nos > noi, vides > vezi*); (4) *-r* became internal (*quattuor > patru*); (5) *-l* became intervocalic through the accretion of a paragogic *-e* (*mel > *mele > miere*).

31

# Part 2

# MORPHOLOGY

## Vulgar Latin Nominal System

74. The three genders of Classical Latin nouns were reduced in Vulgar Latin to two, most neuter nouns becoming masculine, and some collective neuter plurals (*folia, opera,* etc.) becoming feminine singular. The five Classical Latin declensions (*rosa, -ae; lupus, -ī; canis, -is; fructŭs, -ūs; spēs, -ĕī*) were reduced to three, the fifth merging principally with the first (*materiēs > materia*), and the fourth with the second (*fructŭs, -ūs > frŭctus, -i*). The six Classical Latin cases (vocative, nominative, genitive, dative, accusative, and ablative) were reduced to two, the nominative and the accusative. The vocative merged with the nominative, and the accusative, with the aid of prepositions, assumed the functions of the genitive, dative, and ablative. There was a tendency to equalize the nominatives and accusatives of third declension imparisyllabics (other than those naming people) by adding a syllable to the nominatives (*leo, leone > leonis, leone; bonitas, bonitate > bonitatis, bonitate*).

## The Noun in Gallo-Romance

75. (a) The two-case declensional system of Vulgar Latin survived in Old French and Old Provençal. The declension of masculine nouns whose nominative ended in *-s* (*murs, mur, mur, murs*) served eventually as the prototype of all other masculines, e.g., *fredre(s), fredre, fredre, fredres.* Similarly, the declension of feminine nouns whose nominative ended in *a* (OFr. *porte, porte,* analogical *portes* [CL *portae*], *portes;* OPr. *porta, porta,* analogical *portas, portas*) served as the prototype for all other feminines. Imparisyllabics which designated people, and whose accent shifted from the nominative to the accusative were declined as follows: OFr. *sire, seignor, seignor, seignors;* OPr. *senher, senhor, senhor, senhors.* Proper nouns and a few common nouns (*pute, nonne*) were declined according to the pattern of *Hugo, Hugone >* OFr. *Hüe, Hüon;* OPr. *Uc, Ugo.* Imparisyllabics with fixed accent were declined like OFr. *om, ome,* analogical *ome* (CL *homines*), *omes* or *cuens, conte,* analogical *conte* (CL *comites*), *contes.* Phonetic consequences of the clustering of consonants before

32

final -*s* resulted in such disparities as *cers, cerf* < *cervus, cervu,* and *chevaus, cheval* < *caballus, caballu.*

(b) The two-case declensional system of Old French and Old Provençal had collapsed by the XIVth and XIIIth centuries, respectively, the nominative case having virtually disappeared. Vestiges of the nominative case in Modern French include (1) proper names such as *Louis* and *Charles,* (2) the personal imparisyllabics such as *ancêtre, prêtre, soeur,* and (3) such exceptions as *fils.* Some nominative-accusative doublets have survived, but with distinct meanings, e.g., *sire-seigneur, gars-garçon.*

(c) The final -*s* which marked the accusative plural survived only orthographically in French, and not at all in Provençal. Normatively, the definite article is the only structural marker of plurality in spoken French and in both spoken and written Provençal: Fr. *les* [le(z)], Pr. *li.* In some instances, Old French plurals survived which, for phonological reasons, had developed differently from their respective singulars (*chevaux* = OFr. *chevaus* vs. *cheval; cieux* = OFr. *cieus* vs. *ciel,* etc.), or new unetymological plurals were formed on the pattern of their respective accusative singulars (*hôtels* vs. OFr. *osteus; conseils* vs. OFr. *conseus,* etc.).

(d) Gender, in many instances, was a variable until it was fixed by the grammarians of the XVIIth century. The structural marker of gender in French is the definite article (*le, la*), unless the noun begins with a vowel or mute *h,* in which case *le* or *la* is elided (*l'*), and gender is no longer marked. In Provençal, besides the definite articles (*lou, la*), final -*o* also serves as a structural marker of feminine gender (*la montagno*).

## The Noun in Ibero-Romance

76. (a) In pre-literary times, the two cases of the Vulgar Latin nominal system in the Iberian Peninsula were reduced to one, the accusative. There are sporadic vestiges of the Vulgar Latin nominative in Spanish, Catalan, and Portuguese, but these are only of archeological interest (e.g., Sp. *Carlos, juez;* Ct. *lladre, hom;* Pg. *Deus, bufo*).

(b) In Spanish, nouns developed roughly along the lines of the three declensions which had survived in Vulgar Latin: (I) feminine nouns ending in *a,* (II) masculine nouns ending in *o,* and (III) feminine and masculine nouns ending in *e* or a consonant. The rigor of the generic aspect of the nominal system was modified by the incorporation of masculines (e.g., *cura, día, tema*) into the vestigial first declension, and of a few feminines (e.g., *mano, nao*) into the second. Many nouns of the Latin third declension changed gender in Spanish (e.g., *grege,* m. > *grey,* f.; *arbore,* f. > *árbol,* m.). Third-declension nouns of ambiguous gender have either remained ambiguous (e.g., *fronte, ordine*, m., f. > *frente, orden*, m., f., with distinct meaning in each case), or assumed specific gender (e.g., *cutis*, m., f. > *cutis*, m.). The *-s* of the Latin accusative remained the structural marker of plurality (*casas, hombres, muros*), except that it became *-es* when the word ended in a consonant (*pared, paredes*), a diphthong (*rey, reyes* [OSp., also *reys*], *pie, pies* [OSp., also *piees*]), or a stressed vowel (*rubí, rubíes*), further exception being made for paroxytones ending in *s*, which remained invariable (*crisis, crisis*), and for the possible use of *-s* after stressed vowels in certain instances (*mamá, mamás; bajá, bajás*).

(c) In Catalan, Latin *-s* remained the structural marker of the plural regardless of whether the singular noun ended in a vowel or a consonant (*arbre, arbres; llum, llums*). Nouns whose singular ended in unstressed *-a* changed this *a* to *e* before adding plural *-s* (*casa, cases*), orthographic changes being made to preserve the original pronunciation of the consonants (*soca, soques; paga, pagues; puça, puces*). Monosyllabic words which ended in a vowel, and polysyllabics which ended in a stressed vowel, whose Latin etyma had a post-tonic *-n-*, recovered this *n* in the plural (*pa < pane, pans; dofí < delphinu, dofins*). Words whose singular forms ended in [s], written *-s* or *-ç*, or [š], written *-ix*, were expressed in the plural by *-es*, later *-os* (*cos, cosses > cossos; peix, peixes > peixos*). Latin gender was usually preserved in Catalan, except that (1) some feminines became masculine (*arbor*, and the names of all trees not ending in *-a*); (2) some masculines became feminine (all abstracts in *-ore*, [*amore, dolore > amor, dolor*], and such words as *dente, flore > dent, flor*); (3) some nouns vacillated between genders (*somnu*, m. > *son*, m., f.; *fronte*, f. > *front*, m., f.).

(d) In Portuguese, nouns of the three Vulgar Latin declensions normally developed as follows: (I) f., *-a, -as* > f., *-a, -as*; (II) m., *-u, -os* > m., *-o, -os*; (III) m., f., *-e, -es* > m., f., *-e* or *-*; *-es, -s, -is*. Preceding vowels came into hiatus with the initial vowels of endings because of the fall of intervocalic consonants, with the following consequences: (1) a preceding tonic *o* fused with *-a, -as*, resulting in *-ó, -ós* (*mola, molas > mó, mós*); (2) a preceding tonic *ã* fused with *-a, -as*, resulting in *-ã, -ãs* (*germana, germanas > irmã, irmãs*): (3) a preceding tonic *a* or *e* caused *-o, -os* to close to *-u, -us* (*caelu, caelos > céu, céus*); (4) a preceding tonic *u* caused *-o, -os* to close to *-u, -us*, and then to contract with the tonic *u* (*mūlu > mu*); (5) a preceding tonic *ã* fused with *-o, -os* to form *-ão, -ãos* (*granu, granos > grão, grãos*); (6) a preceding tonic *õ* fused with *-o, -os* to form *-om, -ons* (*sonu, sonos > som, sons*); (7) a preceding tonic *ũ* fused with *-o, -os* to form *-um, -uns* (*unu, unos > um, uns*). Final *-o* closed tonic [ɔ] to [ǫ], but final *-os* did not (*populu > p[o]vo, populos > p[ɔ]vos*). Final *-o* and *-os* closed stressed [ɛ] to [e]: *catĕllu, catêllos > cad[e]lo, cad[e]los*. Preceding consonants had the following effects upon the endings of

34

the third declension: (1) -*e* fell when it followed *c, l, n, r, s,* or [tị], but -*es* either remained intact or became -*is* in hiatus (*vice* >*vez, sole* > *sol, mare* > *mar, duritie* > *durez, canes* > *cães, soles* > *sóis*); (2) in the plurals of nouns with -*n* in stem-final position, the nasalization of the vowel preceding -*n* affected the *e* of -*es*, and the two vowels either formed a nasal diphthong or contracted (*fines* > *fĩis* > *fins, homines* > *omẽes* > *homens*).

## The Noun in Rheto-Romance

77. Of the three declensions which had survived in Vulgar Latin, only the first (feminine nouns in -*a*) remained discernible in Surselvan, the others having become indistinguishable because of the loss of final -*o* and -*e*. Final -*a* became the structural marker of feminine gender for first declension nouns, the definite article serving to mark the gender of feminine nouns of the third declension, and of masculine nouns of the second and third declensions: *la vacca, la fin, l'alva, il paun, igl amitg*. Final -*s* is the invariable sign of the plural (*sora, soras; frar, frars*).

## The Nouns in Italo-Romance

78. (a) Italian nouns correspond to the three declensions of Vulgar Latin, deriving their respective singulars from the accusative case, and their plurals from the nominative case, except that the plurals of third-declension nouns are analogical to those of the second declension: *casa, -e; lupo, -i; chiave, -i*. Plurals of feminines whose stems end in *c* [k] or *g* [g] preserve the hard pronunciation of these consonants, which are then written *ch* or *gh* (*amica, amiche; lega, leghe*). Plurals of masculines whose stems end in *c* [tš] vacillate between an etymological development (*amico, amici* [tš]) and one which is analogical to the singular (*fuoco, fuochi* [k]). Plurals of masculines whose stems end in *g* [dž] tend to develop analogically (*lago, laghi* [g] vs. *astrologo, astrologi* [dž]).

(b) The noun in Sardinian developed along the lines of Western Romance, its plural being derived from the accusative, rather than the nominative (*filiu, filios* > *fizzu, fizzos; rota, rotas* > *roda, rodas; homine, homines* > *omine, omines*). Latin neuters survived in Sardinian in their nominative-accusative form (*tempus, cor, lumen* > *tempus, kóro* [paragogic -*o*], *lumene* [paragogic -*e*]), with analogical plurals in -*s*, -*os* (*tempos, koros, lumenes*).

## The Noun in Balkan Romance

79. (a) Rumanian nouns fall into the following three classes: (I) feminine nouns in -*ă*, -*e* (*cară, care*); (II) masculine nouns in

*-cons.*, *-i* (*lup, lupĭ*), and in *-u, -i* (*socru, socri*); (III) feminine and masculine nouns in *-e, -ĭ* (f., *muiere, muierĭ*; m., *iepure, iepurĭ*).

(b)  In Class I, certain nouns, particularly those ending in *-ca*, *-ga, -ra, -ta*, form their plurals with *-ĭ*, rather than *-e* (*vaca, vacĭ*; *sluga, slugĭ, țara, țarĭ; porta, porțĭ*). Other nouns have plurals with analogical *-ur-*, having distinct *meaning* (*ierbĭ*, "grasses", vs. *ierburĭ*, "herbs").

(c)  In Class II, final *-u* was lost except in *-clu, -cru, -dru, -gru*, *-tru* (*lup* vs. *socru*). Certain nouns have evolved with etymological *-ur-* (*tempora* > *timpurĭ*).

(d)  In Class III, the feminines include the substantivized infinitives (*atingere, batere*, etc.), and nouns whose atonic *a*, after a palatal, became *e* (*area* > *arie*). Some feminines have elongated plurals, with analogical *-ur-* (*carne, carnurĭ*).

(e)  It should be noted, with regard to plurals, that final *-ĭ*, now written *i*, is either pronounced [ə], or, more often, not pronounced at all.

(f)  The case system of Classical Latin developed uniquely in the Vulgar Latin of the Balkans, in that there survived an identical nominative-accusative, an identical genitive-dative, and a vocative with Slavic overtones. Properly speaking, it is not the Rumanian noun that is inflected, but rather the definite article which is appended to it, and the indefinite article which precedes it (see par. 97, below).

*Vulgar Latin Verbal System*

80.  The four Classical Latin conjugations (*-āre, -ēre, -ere, -īre*) were retained in Vulgar Latin, but there was considerable shifting from one to the other, especially between the second and the third. Of the simple indicative tenses of Classical Latin, the future was replaced by a periphrastic combination of the infinitive plus the present tense of *habēre* (originally indicating obligation or necessity); and the conditional, which was expressed by the subjunctive mood in Classical Latin, was expressed analogically by the infinitive plus the imperfect tense of *habēre* (*amabo* = *amare habeo, amavissem* = *amare habeba*[m]). Of the perfect indicative tenses, the pluperfect (*amaveram* > *amara*) functioned also as an imperfect subjunctive. In the subjunctive mood, the pluperfect (*amavissem* > *amasse*) replaced the imperfect (*amarem*), the latter having become indistinguishable from the perfect (*amaverim*), which had lost its distinctive phonemes through syncope and the neutralization of final *i*. A system of compound perfects in the active voice, unknown to Classical Latin, evolved on the pattern of the passive participle (used as a past active participle) plus the appropriate tense of *habēre* (*amatu habeo, amatu habea*). Similarly, the passive voice was expressed periphrastically

36

by the passive participle plus the appropriate tense of the verb
*essere (amor = amatu sum).

## The Verb in Gallo-Romance

81. (a) The four conjugations of Vulgar Latin survived in French,
the infinitives evolving as follows: -āre > -er, -ier (the latter after
palatals, in Old French only [see par. 12, above]), -ēre > -oir, '-ere
> -re, -īre > -ir (cantare > chanter, iudicare > jugier > juger, debere
> devoir, rendere > rendre, partire > partir). The gerunds of the sec-
ond, third, and fourth conjugations (-endu, -iendu) were patterned
after that of the first conjugation (-andu), and all four gerunds
remained invariable (chantant, devant, rendant, partant). The present participles of the second, third, and fourth conjugations (-ente,
-iente) were patterned after that of the first conjugation (-ante), lost
their verbal function, and became declinable adjectives (chantant,
chantante, chantants, chantantes). The passive participles, having
become active past participles, evolved etymologically: the weak forms
developed as -é, -ée (< atu, -ata), -u, -ue (< -utu, uta), -i, -ie (< -itu,
-ita), and the strong forms as -t, -te (< -tu, -ta), Old French forms
in -s (ars, ris, etc.) having disappeared. The Modern French participles mis, pris are analogical to the corresponding strong preterites.

(b) The four conjugations of Vulgar Latin survived in Provençal,
the infinitives evolving as follows: -are > -ar, -ere > -er, '-ere > re,
('-er), -ire > -ir (cantare > cantar, debere > dever, rendere > rendre,
vincere > venser, partire > partir). The third conjugation infinitive
developed as '-re when the loss of the post-tonic vowel of the Vulgar
Latin infinitive resulted in a pronounceable consonantal cluster, and
as '-er, when it did not. Anomalous third conjugation infinitives for
second conjugation verbs (deure < debere, moure < movere) developed sporadically. The gerunds of third and fourth conjugation verbs
were patterned on that of the second conjugation verbs, all four
gerunds remaining invariable (cantan, vezen, venden, dormen). The
passive participles, having become active past participles, evolved
etymologically: the weak forms developed as -at, -ada (< -atu, -ata),
-ut, -uda (< -utu, -uta), -it, -ida (< -itu, -ita), and the strong forms
as -s (< -su) and -t/-ch (cf. par. 64 (b, 6), above) (< -tu). The weak
forms in -ut were often built on the corresponding preterite stems
(vengut, degut, conogut, etc.).

(c) The present indicative, through Old French (indicated parenthetically), evolved as follows in Modern French: chante (chant),
chantes, chante (chante[t]), chantons, chantez, chantent; vois (voi),
vois, voit, voyons (veons), voyez (veez), voient; vends (vent), vends
(venz), vend (vent), vendons, vendez, vendent; dors (dorm), dors,
dort, dormons, dormez, dorment; finis (fenis), finis (fenis), finit
(fenist), finissons (fenissons), finissez (fenissez), finissent (fenis-

*sent*). The -*e* of (*je*) *chante* (L. *canto*) is analogical to the supportive -*e* of *tremble, entre,* etc.; the -*ons* of *chantons, voyons,* etc., is derived from *sumus* > \**sons* > *ons*; the -*ez* of *voyez, vendez,* etc., is analogical to the -*ez* of *chantez* (< *cantatis*); the -*s* of *vois, vends, dors,* became a structural marker of the first person singular early in the history of the language; the *d* of *vends, vend* is a mere orthographic restitution; the stress of *vendons, vendez* (L. *vendimus, venditis*) is analogical to that of the corresponding forms of the other three conjugations (*chantons, chantez, voyons, voyez,* etc.)

(d) The pattern of stress in the present indicative, which fell (1) upon the stem in the first, second, and third persons singular, and in the third person plural, and (2) upon the ending in the first and second persons plural, had phonological effects which resulted in dichotomous conjugations (*trouver: je truef, nous trouvons; laver: il lève*[*t*], *nous lavons; amer: tu aimes, vous amez,* etc.). In most instances, one of the two forms predominated (*je trouve, il lave, vous aimez,* etc.); in some instances, two distinct conjugations developed (*plier, ployer*); and many conjugations remained dichotomous (*tenir: je tiens, nous tenons; venir: je viens, nous venons,* etc.).

(e) In Provençal, the present indicative developed as follows: *cant, cantas, canta, cantam, cantatz, cantan/canton; vei ,ves, ve, vezem, vezetz, vezon; ven, vens, ven, vendem, vendetz, vendon; dorm, dorms, dorm, dormem, dormetz, dormon; finisc/finis, finis/finisses, finis, finem, finetz, finiscon/finisson.* Final -*am* in *cantam* reveals an anomalous loss of final -*s* (L. *cantamus*); final -*on* in *canton, vezon,* is analogical to the -*on* of the third and fourth conjugations (L. -*unt,* -(*i*)*unt*); final -*em,* -*etz* of *dormem, dormetz, finem, finetz* are analogical to the corresponding forms of the second conjugation; the stress of *vendem, vendetz* is analogical to that of the corresponding forms of the other three conjugations.

(f) In Modern French, the imperfect indicative endings, which had developed from those of the Old French second conjugation (indicated parenthetically), became generalized for all four conjugations: -*ais* (-*oie* < -*eie*), -*ais* (-*oies* < -*eies*), -*ait* (-*oit* < -*eit*), -*ions* (-*iiens*), -*iez* (-*iiez*), -*aient* (-*oient* < -*eient*). First conjugation endings in Old French (-*oe,* -*oes,* etc.) were soon replaced by those of the second conjugation. Modern French -*ais* in (*je*) *chantais* and -*ions* in *chantions* are strictly unetymological, the latter being attributable to the influence of present tense -*ons*.

(g) In Provençal, the imperfect indicative of the first conjugation developed regularly from the Latin (*cantava, cantavas, cantava, cantavam, cantavatz, cantavan*), the variant *cantavon* for the third person plural being attributable to an anomalous intrusion of the -*unt* ending. The second conjugation provided the pattern for the third and fourth (*vezia, vendia, dormia,* -*ias,* -*ia,* -*iam,* -*iatz,* -*ian* (< -*e*[*b*]*a,* -*e*[*b*]*as,* -*e*[*b*]*at,* etc.).

(h) In Modern French, the weak preterite of the first conjugation evolved through Old French (indicated parenthetically) as follows: *chantai, chantas, chanta, chantâmes (chantasmes), chantâtes (chantastes), chantèrent*. The *-âmes* ending is analogical to *-âtes*.

(i) In Provençal, the weak preterite of the first conjugation was patterned after the strong preterite of *dedi* (*diei, dest, det, dem, detz, deron*) and evolved as follows: *cantei, cantest, cantet, cantem, cantetz, canteron*.

(j) In Modern French, the weak preterites of the third and fourth conjugations evolved through Old French (indicated parenthetically) as follows: *vendis (vendi), vendis, vendit (vendiet), vendîmes, (vendismes), vendîtes (vendistes), vendirent (vendierent); dormis (dormi), dormis, dormit, dormîmes, dormîtes, dormirent*. In the *vendre* paradigm, the key vowel, *i*, is etymological only in (*je*) *vendis* (< *\*vendiei* < *\*vende[d]i*) and (*tu*) *vendis* (< *\*vendesti*), and analogical in all other forms, whereas it is etymological in all forms of the *dormir* paradigm. The *-s* of (*je*) *vendis, dormis* is strictly unetymological; the *-îmes* of *vendîmes, dormîmes* is an analogue of *-îtes*.

(k) The strong preterites in *-ī, -sī*, and *-uī* of the second, third, and fourth conjugations evolved in Modern French through Old French (indicated parenthetically) as follows: [*vidi*] *vis (vi), vis, (veïs), vit, vîmes (veïmes), vîtes (veïstes), virent;* [*dixi*] *dis, dis (desis), dit (dist), dîmes (desimes), dîtes, (desistes), dirent (distrent);* [*habui*] *eus (oi), eus (ous), eut (out), eûmes (oumes), eûtes (oustes), eurent (ourent)*.

(l) In Provençal, the strong perfects in *-ī, -sī, -uī* of the second, third, and fourth conjugations evolved as follows: [*vidi*] *vi, vist, vi, vim, vitz, viron;* [*dixi*] *dis, dissist, dis, dissem, dissetz, diron/disseron;* [*habui*] *aic, aguist, ac, aguem, aguetz, agron*. Like Catalan (see par. 82(*n*), below), Old Provençal could also express the perfect by a periphrasis consisting of the present indicative of *anar* and the infinitive (e.g., *va dir, van partir*).

(m) The French and Provençal future and conditional evolved from the Vulgar Latin etyma as follows: *\*cantarayo (cantare habeo), \*cantarea (cantare habeba)*: (French) *chanterai, -as, -a, -ons, -ez, -ont; chanterais* (OFr. *-oie* < *-eie* [see par. 81 (*f*), above]); *-ais, -ait, -ions, -iez, -aient;* (Provençal) *cantarai, -as, -a, -em, -etz, -an; cantaria, -ias, -ia, -iam, -iatz, -ian*. The second, third, and fourth conjugations conformed to the following patterns: (French) *verrai, verrais; vendrai, vendrais; dormirai, dormirais;* (Provençal) *veirai, veiria; vendrai, vendria; dormirai, dormiria*.

(n) The perfect indicative tenses in French and Provençal were derived from the Vulgar Latin periphrasis *\*habere cantatu* for transitive verbs, *\*essere venutu* for intransitive verbs, and *\*se essere levatu* for reflexive verbs: thus, *j'ai chanté*, (*ieu*) *ai cantat*; *je suis venu*, (*ieu*) *soi vengutz*; *je me suis levé*, (*ieu*) *me soi levatz*.

(o) The present subjunctive of Modern French evolved through Old French (indicated parenthetically) as follows: *chante* (*chant*), *chantes* (*chanz*), *chante* (*chant*), *chantions* (*chantons*), *chantiez* (*chantez*), *chantent*; *voie*, *voies*, *voie*, *voyions* (*voiions*), *voyiez*, *voient*; *vende*, *vendes*, *vende*, *vendions* (*vendons*), *vendiez* (*vendez*), *vendent*; *dorme*, *dormes*, *dorme*, *dormions* (*dormons*), *dormiez* (*dormez*) *dorment*; *finisse*, *finisses*, *finissions* (*fenissons*), *finissiez* (*fenissez*), *fenissent*. Unetymological forms include the first and second persons plural of all conjugations, the three singular forms of the first conjugation (which appear to be analogical to those of the third), and all of the forms of the inchoative fourth conjugation.

(p) The present subjunctive of Provençal evolved etymologically, as follows: *cant, cantz, cant, cantem, cantetz, canten; veia, veias, veia, veiam, veiatz, veian; venda, vendas, venda, vendam, vendatz, vendan; dorma, dormas, dorma, dormam, dormatz, dorman; finisca, finiscas, finisca, finiscam, finiscatz, finiscan*.

(q) The imperfect subjunctive (CL pluperfect subjunctive) of Modern French evolved through Old French (indicated parenthetically) as follows: *chantasse, chantasses, chantât* (*chantast*), *chantassions* (*chantissons*), *chantassiez* (*chantissez*), *chantassent*; *visse* (*veïsse*), *visses* (*veïsses*), *vît* (*veïst*), *vissions* (*veïssons*), *vissiez* (*veïssez*), *vissent* (*veïssent*); *vendisse, vendisses, vendît* (*vendist*), *vendissions* (*vendissons*), *vendissiez* (*vendissez*), *vendissent*; *dormisse, dormisses, dormît* (*dormist*), *dormissions* (*dormissons*), *dormissiez* (*dormissez*), *dormissent*; *finisse* (*fe-*), *finisses, finît* (*fenist*), *finissions* (*finissons*), *finissiez* (*finissez*), *finissent*. The *-ons* and *-ez* endings in Old French, and the *-ions*, *-iez* endings in Modern French, are analogical to present subjunctive endings.

(r) In Provençal, the imperfect subjunctive developed as follows: *cantes, cantesses, cantes, cantessem, cantessetz, cantessen* (*cantesson*); *vendes, vendesses, vendes, vendessem, vendessetz, vendessen* (*vendesson*); *partis, partisses, partis, partissem, partissetz, partissen* (*partisson*). The stressed *e* of the first conjugation, instead of etymological *a* (**amasse*), is an analogue of the stressed vowel of the preterite (see par. 81 (*i*), above).

(s) The perfect subjunctives in French and Provençal developed from the Vulgar Latin periphrases consisting of the present and imperfect subjunctive of *habere* or **essere* and the past participle of (1) transitive and (2) intransitive or reflexive verbs, respectively: thus, (1) Fr. *j'aie, j'eusse chanté; je sois, je fusse venu, -e; je me sois, je me fusse levé, -ée*, and (2) Pr. *ieu aia, agues cantat; ieu sia, fos vengutz, -uda; ieu me sia, fos levatz, -ada*.

(t) The passive voice in French and Provençal developed along the lines of the Vulgar Latin periphrasis of the Classical Latin form

(VL *sum amatu* vs. CL *amor*), the periphrasis being modeled on the Classical Latin perfect passive: Fr. *je suis aimé(e)*, Pr. *ieu soi amat, amada*. The auxiliary serves to express the passive in all persons, tenses, and moods.

(u) The affirmative imperative evolved in Modern French through Old French (indicated parenthetically) as follows: *chante, chantez; vois (voi), voyez (veez); vends (vent), vendez; dors (dorm), dormez; finis, finissez*. The singular forms were derived from the Latin imperative (*canta, vide, vende*, etc.), the final *-s* of the second, third, and fourth conjugation forms being analogical to the second person singular in all tenses and moods; the plural forms were borrowed from the second person plural of the present indicative. In Old French, the imperative was negated in the singular by negating the infinitive (or, possibly, a vestige of the Latin subjunctive perfect [*cantaveris*], which became identical to the infinitive). In Modern French, the negative singular and plural are mere negations of the corresponding affirmative forms.

(v) The imperative evolved in Provençal as follows: *canta, cantatz; ve, veez; ven, vendetz; dorm, dormetz; finis, finissetz*. The singular forms were derived from the Latin imperative, and the plurals from the present indicative. Negation followed the same pattern as Old French in the singular, but the negative plurals were derived from subjunctive forms.

## The Verb in Ibero-Romance

82. (a) The four conjugations of Vulgar Latin were reduced to three in Spanish, the third Latin conjugation fusing largely with the second and, to some extent, with the fourth (*vendere > vender, ridere > reír*). The infinitives evolved as *-ar, -er, -ir (cantar, tener, partir)*. The gerunds of the first and second conjugations developed etymologically (*-ando < -andu, -iendo < -endu*), whereas the gerund of the third (Latin fourth) developed by analogy to the second, the *i* of CL *-iendu* having been lost in Vulgar Latin. The present participles developed similarly (*-ante < -ante, -iente < -ente*), but lost their verbal function completely and survived as nouns and/or adjectives (**currente* > corriente, ridente > riente, ponente > poniente*, etc.). The weak passive participles, having become active past participles, evolved etymologically in the first and third conjugations (*-ado < -atu, -ido < -itu*), and analogically in the second conjugation (*tener, tenido*). The weak participles in *-udo* (*< -utu*), such as *metudo, vençudo*, etc., which may have been Gallicisms, did not survive beyond the fourteenth century. The strong participles include *abierto, cubierto, dicho, escrito, hecho, muerto, puesto, roto, visto, vuelto*.

(b) The four conjugations of Vulgar Latin survived in Catalan, the second only minimally, and the third under the guise of two different infinitives, as in Provençal (see par. 81(b), above). For purposes of conjugation, the second is grouped with the third, the total conjugational scheme being resolved as follows: (I) -ar (< -āre), e.g., cantar; (II) -er (< ēre), e.g., valer; '-er (< '-ere), e.g., créixer; -re (< '-ere), e.g., caure, metre; (III) -ir (< -īre), e.g., dormir. The Vulgar Latin gerunds -andu, -endu, *-indu became -ant, -ent, -int in Catalan (cantant, havent, partint). The present participles developed as they did in Spanish (see par. 82(a), above): ant < ante, ent < ente (cantant, corrent, vivent, etc.). The weak passive participles, having become active past participles, developed as follows: -at, -ada (< -atu, -ata), -ut, -uda, (< -utu, -uta), -it, -ida (< -itu, -ita), as in cantat-cantada, perdut-perduda, sentit-sentida. The strong participles became -s, -sa (< -su, -sa), -t, -ta (< -tu, -ta), as in mes-mesa, dit-dita. Strong participles in -ert (obert, sofert, etc.) gave rise to analogical weak participles such as omplert, establert.

(c) The four conjugations of Vulgar Latin evolved as three in Portuguese, exactly as they did in Spanish (see par. 82(a), above), except that the Portuguese infinitives developed an anomalous conjugation of their own. The forms of the so-called "personal infinitive" were derived from the Latin perfect subjunctive or future perfect, which are largely identical, the latter being the more likely etymon. The endings which serve as structural markers for the second person singular and the first, second, and third persons plural are as follows: -es, -mos, -des, -en. The first and third persons singular are expressed by an uninflected form which is identical to the infinitive, although it is a derivative of the corresponding forms of the perfect subjunctive (canta[ve]rim, canta[ve]rit) or the future perfect (canta[ve]ro, canta[ve]rit). The present participles (-ante, -ente, more rarely -inte, an analogical form) developed as nouns and/or adjectives (cantante, poente, ouvinte, etc.). The weak past participles developed as in Spanish (see par. 82(a), above). The strong participles include aberto, coberto, dito, escrito, feito, morto (besides morrido), posto, roto (besides rompido), vindo, visto.

(d) In Spanish, first and second conjugation verbs developed etymologically in the present indicative: canto, cantas, canta, cantamos, cantáis (< OSp. cantades < cantatis), cantan; temo (< VL *temo < CL timēo), temes, teme, tememos, teméis (< OSp. temedes < timētis), temen. Verbs of the Latin third conjugation which had been incorporated into the Spanish second conjugation developed a paradigm which was identical to that of the latter: vendo, vendes, vende, vendemos (CL vendimus), vendéis (CL venditis, but OSp. vendedes [by analogy]), venden (CL vendunt). The third (Latin fourth) conjugation was etymological except for the third person plural, which was analogical to the second conjugation: parto (<VL

*parto < CL partio), partes, parte, partimos, partís (< OSp. partides < partītis), parten (CL partiunt). Paradigmatic deviations are due to the phonological consequences of (1) stress on VL [ę] and [ǫ] (pienso vs. pensamos, cuento vs. contamos), (2) a yod which inflects the stressed vowel (vestio > visto), (3) analogy to other forms in the same conjugational framework (vistes, viste, visten).

(e) In Catalan, the conjugations developed in the present indicative as follows: (I) canto, cantes, canta, cantem, canteu, canten; (II) temo, tems, tem, temem, temeu, temen; (III) sento, sents, sent, sentim, sentiu, senten; pateixo, pateixes, pateix, patim, patiu, pateixen. The -o [u] ending is a later development of supportive -e [ə] (see par. 41(b), above), which had become generalized; this development may have been prompted by the need to distinguish between the first and third persons singular. Cantem, canteu are analogical to the corresponding forms of the present subjunctive. Latin verbs of the third conjugation which had been incorporated into the second conjugation of Catalan developed an anomalous first person ending (-c) by analogy to corresponding etymological forms (dic, estrenc, planc < dico, stringo, plango): bec (beure), escric (escriure), entenc (entendre), venc (vendre), etc.

(f) In Portuguese, the conjugations developed in the present indicative as follows: (I) canto, cantas, canta, cantamos, cantais (< OPg. cantades < cantātis), cantam; (II) devo, deves, deve, devemos, deveis (< OPg. devedes < debētis), devem; (III) parto, partes, parte, partimos, partis (< OPg. partides < partītis), partem. As in Spanish (see par. 82(d), above), Latin third conjugation verbs which had been incorporated into the second conjugation developed identically, with shift of accent in the first and second persons plural (vendemos, vendeis), and an analogical third person plural (vendem). The pronunciation of -am [ɐu̯] is analogical to that of vão (< vadunt). The third person plural of the third (Latin fourth) conjugation is analogical to the corresponding form of the second conjugation.

(g) In Spanish, the imperfect indicative developed along the lines of -aba, -eba, -iba, the last being a form which originated in Vulgar Latin by analogy to forms with stressed i in the fourth conjugation. There was a shift of stress in the first and second persons plural from the penult to the antepenult, by analogy to the etymological stress of the other forms. The -b- of the -eba endings disappeared by analogy to the -b- of debe(b)a, habe(b)a, which had done so through dissimilation; and the -b- of the -iba forms, by analogy to the -eba forms. Thus, the Spanish imperfect conjugations evolved as follows: (I) cantaba, cantabas, cantaba, cantábamos (CL cantabāmus), cantabais (CL cantabātis), cantaban; (II, III) temía, sentía, -ías, -ía, -íamos (CL -ebāmos), -íais (CL -ebātis), -ían. Old Spanish had -ie, -ie endings alongside the ía endings, final -a having assimilated itself to stressed i, with the stress shifting more often than not

43

to the more open element of the new ending, thus creating a diph-thong.

(h) The imperfect indicative developed in Catalan just as it did in Spanish (see par. 82(*g*), above), except that it had a strong, as well as a weak, second conjugation: (I) *cantava, cantaves, cantava, cantàvem, cantàveu, cantaven;* (II) *temia, temies, temia, temíem, temíeu, temien; creia, creies, creia, crèiem, crèeu, creien;* (III) *sentia, senties, sentia, sentíem, sentíeu, sentien.*

(i) The imperfect indicative developed in Portuguese just at it did in Spanish (see par. 82(*g*), above): (I) *amava, amavas, amava, amávamos, amáveis* (< OPg. *amávades*), *amavam* [ɐu̯]; (II, III) *devia, partia, -ias, -ia, -íamos, -íeis* (< OPg. *-íades*), *-iam* [-iɐu̯].

(j) Of the weak perfects of the Latin first, second, and fourth conjugations, only those of the first and fourth survived as preterites in Spanish. The paradigms of the first and fourth conjugation pret-erites developed from the contracted forms of Vulgar Latin, in which the stress of the second person singular and plural, and of the third person plural, shifted from the penultimate to the antepenultimate vowel (*a* and *i*, respectively), thus making the stress pattern uni-form for all persons: *canté* (< *cantai* < *cantavi*), *cantaste* (< *cantasti* < *cantavistī*), *cantó* (< *cantaut* < *cantavit*), *cantamos* (< *cantamus* < *cantavimus*), *cantasteis* (< *cantastis* < *cantavistis*), *cantaron* (< *cantarunt* < *cantavērunt*); *partí* (< *partii* < *partivi*), *partiste* (< *partisti* < *partivisti*), *partió* (< *partiut* < *partivit*), *partimos* (< *partimus* < *partivimus*), *partisteis* (< *partistis* < *partivistis*), *partieron* (< *partierunt* < *partiverunt*). The endings *-asteis* and *-isteis* are analogical to the corresponding endings of the present in-dicative. The Latin second and third conjugations, which fused into the Spanish second conjugation, developed a weak perfect on the basis of *dedi* and by analogy to the *i*-stressed third (Latin fourth) conjugation; *vendí, vendiste, vendió, vendimos, vendisteis, vendieron.*

(k) The only strong perfect of the Latin first conjugation which survived in Spanish was that of *dare* (*dedi, dedisti, dedit, dedimus, dedistis, dederunt* > *di, diste, dio, dimos, disteis, dieron* [haplological dissimilation throughout, shift of stress for the sake of uniformity, and analogy to the weak fourth conjugation]). The strong perfects of the second conjugation (Latin second and third conjugations) developed as follows: (*-i: vidi, vidisti,* etc.) *vi, viste, vio, vimos, visteis, vieron;* (*-si: dixi, dixisti,* etc.) *dije, dijiste, dijo, dijimos, dijisteis, dijeron;* (*-ui: habui, habuisti,* etc.; *potui, potuisti,* etc.) *hube, hubiste, hubo, hubimos, hubisteis, hubieron* (< OSp. [h]*oue*, [h]*ouiste,* etc.); *pude, pudiste, pudo, pudimos, pudisteis, pudieron.* Of the strong perfects of the third (Latin fourth) conjugation, only those in *-i* (*veni, venisti,* etc.) survived: *vine, viniste, vino, vinimos, vinisteis, vinieron.* The etymologically correct *-i-* of *vine* became analogically uniform for the whole conjugation; final *-o*, *-isteis*, *-ieron* are strictly analogical, just as they are in *hubo*, *pudo*, etc.

(l) The weak perfect of the Latin first and fourth conjugations developed in Catalan as follows (Old Catalan forms indicated parenthetically) : *cantí, (canté), cantares (cantast, cantàs, cantist), cantà, cantàrem* (cantam), *cantàreu (cantast, cantats), cantaren; partí, partires (partist), partí, partírem (partim), partíreu (partist, partits), partiren.* The Latin second and third conjugations developed a weak perfect on the pattern of *dedi* (Old Catalan forms indicated parenthetically) : *venguí (vené), vengueres (venist), vengué (vené), venguérem (venem), venguéreu (venest), vengueren (veneren).* The *-i* of *cantí* and *venguí* is analogical to the etymological *-i* of *partí*; the Modern Catalan second person singular, and first and second persons plural, are analogical to the third person plural; the velarization of the stem consonant in the *vendre* forms ($d > g$) is analogical to similar velarizations in the strong perfects.

(m) Of the Latin and Old Catalan strong perfects, only three in *-i* survived, those of *ésser (ser), fer*, and *veure; fui, fores (fost), fou, fórem (fom), fóreu (fórets), foren; fiu, feres, féu, férem, féreu, feren; viu, veres (veieres), véu (veié), vérem (veiérem), véreu (veiéreu), veren (veieren).* Originally strong perfects in *-ui* and *-si* developed as follows in Modern Catalan (Old Catalan forms indicated parenthetically) : (*-ui: debui, debuisti*, etc.) *deguí (dec), degueres (deguist), degué (dec), deguérem (deguem), deguéreu (deguets), deueren (degren)* ; (*-si: dixi, dixisti*, etc.) *diguí (dix), digueres (dixist), digué (dix), diguérem (dixem), diguéreu (dixets), digueren (diren, dixeren).* The velarization of the final stem consonant of a strong perfect was generally carried over into the corresponding weak perfect.

(n) In Modern Catalan, the perfects of Latin origin have largely been replaced in use by a periphrasis consisting of the present tense of *anar* and the infinitive of the verb concerned; thus, *vaig cantar = cantí, vas cantar = cantares*, etc.

(o) In Portuguese, the weak preterites developed as they did in Spanish (see par. 82(*j*), above) : *cantei, cantaste, cantou, cantamos, cantastes, cantaram* (OPg. *-arom*) ; *vendideste* (OPg. *-iste*), *vendeu* (OPg. *-e*), *vendemos, vendestes, venderam* (OPg. *-erom*); *parti, partiste, partiu, partimos, partistes, partiram* (OPg. *-irom*). The stressed *-a-* of *cantamos* is pronounced [a] by analogy to the other stressed *a*'s of the conjugation; the stressed *-e-* of *vendeste* is analogical to the other stressed *e*'s of the conjugation; the *-u* of *vendeu* is analogical to the *-u* of *cantou, partiu*. Medieval *-om*, the orthographic equivalent of unstressed *-ão*, was replaced by *-am*, which originally represented stressed *-ão* only.

(p) As in Spanish (see par. 82(*k*), above), the only strong perfect of the Latin first conjugation to survive in Portuguese was that of

45

*dar*: *dei, deste, deu, demos, destes, deram* (OPg. *derom*). Strong perfects in *-ui* and *-si*, of the Latin second and third conjugations developed as follows: (*-ui*: *habui, habuisti*, etc.; *potui, potuisti*, etc.) *ouve, ouveste, ouve, ouvemos, ouvestes, ouveram* (OPg. *ouverom*) ; *pude, pudeste, pôde, pudemos, pudestes, puderam* (OPg. *poderom*) ; (*-si*: *dixi, dixisti*, etc.) *disse, dissesté, disse, dissemos, dissestes, disseram* (OPg. *disserom*). In all instances, the stressed e [ɛ] of the second person singular, and the first and second persons plural, is analogical to that of the third person plural, and to all forms of the pluperfect indicative and future subjunctive (see 82(*w*),(*ee*), below). The initial *u* of the second singular and all plural forms of *poder* is orthographically analogical to the etymological *u* of *pude*, since its pronunciation would have been identical to the latter's even as etymological initial *o* [u].

(q) The strong preterites of *ler, rir*, and *ver* resemble weak preterites because (1) their third persons plural became paroxytonic through syncope, rather than shift of stress (*lēgĕrunt* > *\*legron* > *leram*), and (2) their stem vowels fused with the initial vowels of their endings, often as a result of the loss of intervocalic *d* or *g* (*lēgĭstis* > *leestes* > *lêstes*) : thus, *li, lêste, leu, lêmos, lêstes, leram*; *ri, vi, -iste, -iu, -imos, -istes, -iram* (OPg. *-iron*). The forms *leu, riu, viu* are strictly analogical. The strong preterites of *fazer, querer*, and *vir* form a miscellaneous group of their own: *fiz, fizeste, fêz, fizemos, fizestes, fizeram* (OPg. *fizerom*); *quis, quiseste, quis, quisemos, quisestes, quiseram* (OPg. *quiserom*); *vim, vieste, veio (veiu), viemos, viestes, vieram* (OPg. *vierom*).

(r) In Spanish, the future and conditional followed the patterns of the corresponding Vulgar Latin periphrases (inf. + *habeo*, inf. + *habeba*), with the stress shifting in the future from the infinitive-stem to the auxiliary-ending in the second and third persons singular, and the third person plural, by analogy to the fixed etymological stress of the conditional: *cantaré, temeré, partiré, -ás, -á, -emos, -éis, -án*; *cantaría, temería, partiría, -ías, -ía, -íamos, -íais, -ían*. Since the infinitive was unstressed, the vowel of the infinitive ending came into pretonic position, with the corresponding phonological consequences (see par. 36(*a*), above). Until Modern Spanish, there were many instances of (1) the loss of pretonic *e* or *i* (*perdrás, recibrían*), (2) metathesis of the final consonant of the infinitive stem and the *-r* of the infinitive ending (*verná*), (3) intrusion of a consonant between the consonants involved in (2), above (*combré, doldrá*), (4) assimilation of the consonants involved in (2) and (3), above (*verrá, terría*), (5) the interpolation of one or more pronouns between the infinitive and the auxiliary (*dar le has, dezir vos lo he*); and a few instances of the loss of a stem-final fricative (*di*(*z*)*ré* > *diré*). In Modern Spanish, the infinitive and the auxiliary were no longer separable, and the full infinitive survived or was restored, with the following exceptions: *caber* (*cabré, cabría*),

46

*decir* (*diré, diría*), *poder* (*podré, podría*), *poner* (*pondré, pondría*), *querer* (*querré, querría*), *saber* (*sabré, sabría*), salir (*saldré, saldría*), *tener* (*tendré, tendría*), *valer* (*valdré, valdría*), *venir* (*vendré, vendría*). The future and conditional forms of *hacer* (*haré, haría*) were derived from the contracted infinitive *far*. Conditional endings developed in the same way as those of the imperfect second and third conjugations (see par. 78 (*g*), above).

(s) In Catalan, the future and conditional originated as they did in Spanish (see par. 82 (*r*), above), but developed somewhat differently: (1) the *e* of the infinitive endings -*er* and -*re* was lost through syncope; (2) when the loss of *e* in the -*er* infinitive resulted in the consonantal group *l'r*, an intrusive *d* served to bridge the two consonants; (3) an intrusion identical to that of (2), above, took place in the *n'r* of *tenir* and *venir*, which had lost the vowel of the infinitive ending, by exception to all other -*ir* verbs; (4) the stem vowel of *tenir* and *venir* closed anomalously to *i*. The modern future and conditional conjugations are as follows: *cantaré, temeré, podré, correré, veuré, sentiré, tindré, vindré, -às, -à, -em, -eu* (OCt. -*ets*), -*an; cantaria, temeria, podria,* etc., -*ies, -ia, -iem, -ieu* (OCt. -*iets*), -*ien*. In Old Catalan, infinitives in -*ir* whose stems ended in -*r*, regularly lost the *i* of the infinitive ending through syncope (*ferré, ferria*); in these cases, the complete infinitive was restored in Modern Catalan.

(t) In Portuguese, the future and conditional originated as they did in Spanish and Catalan (see par. 82 (*r*),(*s*), above), but developed differently, in that the infinitive and auxiliary have always been separable, and continue to separate, to permit the interpolation of one or more pronouns: *cantarei* (*cantar ... hei*), *deverei* (*dever ... hei*), *partirei* (*partir ... hei*), -*ás* ( ... *hás*), -*á* ( ... *há*), -*emos* ( ... *hemos*), -*eis* ( ... *heis*), -*ão* ( ... *hão*); *cantaria* (*cantar ... ia*), *deveria* (*dever ... ia*), *partiria* (*partir ... ia*), -*ias, -ia, íamos, -íeis, -iam*. The periphrases *hei* (*havia*) + *de* + *inf.* developed alongside the corresponding forms of the future and conditional (*hei de cantar = cantarei, havia de cantar = cantaria,* etc.). Of the syncopated forms in Old Portuguese (*terrei, porrei, verrei,* etc.), only *trarei* has survived. The forms *direi, farei* are believed to have originated in Vulgar Latin.

(u) In Spanish, the perfect indicative forms developed as periphrases consisting of the respective tenses of *haber* and the active past (Latin passive) participle. The simple pluperfect was derived etymologically in the Spanish first conjugation; by analogy to the pluperfect of *dare* (*de*[d]*era* > *\*deera* > *diera, de*[d]*eras* > *dieras,* etc.) in the Spanish second conjugation (Latin second and third) ; and by analogy to the Spanish second conjugation in the Spanish third (Latin fourth) conjugation: *cantara, cantaras, cantara, cantáramos, cantarais* (< *cantárades*), *cantaran; temiera, vendiera, partiera, -ieras, -iera, -iéramos, -ierais* (< -*iérades*), -*ieran*. In all conjugations, the stress

47

shifted in the first and second persons plural from the Latin penult to the Spanish antepenult (*canta*[ve]*rāmus* > *cantáramos, canta*[ve] *rātis* > *cantárades* > *cantarais*). Until Modern Spanish, the simple pluperfect served to express not only the pluperfect indicative but also the imperfect and pluperfect subjunctive, and the conditional and conditional perfect. In Modern Spanish, it serves as a concurrent to the *-se* form of the imperfect subjunctive (see par. 82(*aa*), below); as a literary concurrent to the *-ía* form of the simple conditional (see par. 82 (*r*), above); and as a literary concurrent to the periphrastic pluperfect.

(v) In Catalan, the periphrastic indicative perfects developed as they did in Spanish (see par. 82(*u*), above). The simple pluperfect was derived etymologically in the Old Catalan first and third (Latin fourth) conjugations, and analogically in the Old Catalan second conjugation (Latin second and third conjugations), with the same shift of stress in the first and second persons plural as in Spanish (see par. 78(*u*), above): *cantara, cantares, cantara, cantàrem, cantàreu (cantarets), cantaren; batera, bateres, batera, batérem, batéreu (baterets), bateren; partira, partires, partira, partírem, partíreu (partirets), partiren*. The simple pluperfect, having performed the same functions as in pre-Modern Spanish (see par. 83 (*u*), above), disappeared in Modern Catalan, except in the auxiliaries, as a concurrent to the conditional.

(w) In Portuguese, the periphrastic indicative perfects developed as combinations of the respective tenses of *ter* and the active past (Latin passive) participle. The simple pluperfect was derived etymologically from the Latin first and fourth (Portuguese third) conjugations, and by analogy to the pluperfect of *dare* for the Latin second and third conjugations (Portuguese second conjugation), with the same shift of stress in the first and second persons plural as in Spanish and Catalan (see par. 82(*u*),(*v*), above) : *cantara, cantaras, cantara, cantáramos, cantáreis (<cantárades), cantaram* [ɐᴜ]; *devera, deveras, devera, devéramos, devéreis (< devérades), deveram* [ɐᴜ] ; *partira, partiras, partira, partíramos, partíries (< partírades), partiram* [ɐᴜ]. In Modern Portuguese, the simple pluperfect serves as a strong concurrent to the periphrastic pluperfect in the written language, and as a much weaker concurrent in the spoken language.

(x) In Spanish, the present subjunctive developed etymologically, as follows, with the yod of the Vulgar Latin second conjugation (first person only), irregular third conjugation, and fourth conjugation, disappearing, occasionally after having inflected the initial vowel (*dormiamus* > *durmamos*): *cante, cantes, cante, cantemos, cantéis (< cantedes), canten; tema, parta, -as, -a, -amos, -áis (< -ades), -an*.

(y) In Catalan, the present subjunctive forms, with very few exceptions, developed unetymologically, as follows: (I) *canti, -is, -i, -em, -eu (< -ets), -in*; (II) *temi, -is, -i, -em, -eu, -in*; (III) *senti, -is,*

48

*-i, -im, -iu, -in.* The singular forms of the first conjugation developed a supportive *e* by analogy to those verbs whose final consonantal group (consonant + liquid) required one (*entre, omple*). The endings *-es, -e* closed to *-is, -i,* in order to differentiate themselves from the *-es, -a* of the present indicative, with which they coincided in pronunciation; the first person singular and the third person plural assumed their endings by analogy. The singular forms and the third person plural of the second and third conjugations appear to be altogether analogical to the corresponding forms of the first conjugation. The first and second persons plural of the second and third conjugations became identical to the corresponding forms of the present indicative. By analogy to the etymological *-g-* in such subjunctive forms as *digui, dugui* (*dir, dur*), a stem-final *g* became the rule for all *-re* verbs (*aprengui, begui, caigui,* etc.). *Cabre* and *sabre* developed somewhat anomalous subjunctive forms: *càpiga, sàpiga, -gues, -ga,* etc.

(z) In Portuguese, the present subjunctive developed etymologically in the first and third (Latin fourth) conjugations, the yod of the Latin fourth conjugation falling in Vulgar Latin for analogical or phonological reasons, in some cases after inflecting the stem vowel (*sĕrvĭo* > OPg. *s[e]rvo*): *cante, -es, -e, -emos, -eis* (< *edes*), *-em; parta, -as, -a, -amos, -ais* (< *-ades*), *-am* (ɐ̨). The present subjunctive of the Latin second and third conjugations fused in Portuguese, the yod of the second conjugation disappearing completely, and that of the irregular third conjugation being attracted to the stressed syllable: *deva* (< *debea*), *venda* (< *venda*), *saiba* (< *sapia*), *-as, -a, -amos, -ais* (< *ades*), *-am* [ɐ̨].

(aa) The Spanish imperfect (Latin pluperfect) subjunctive developed etymologically in the first conjugation, from the contracted Vulgar Latin forms (< *-asse, -asses,* etc.), the stress shifting in the first and second persons plural from the penult to the antepenult: *cantase, -ases, -ase, -ásemos* (< *assemus*), *-aseis* (< *ássedes* < *-assetis*), *-asen.* The Spanish second conjugation (Latin second and third) developed by analogy to *dare* (*-dedisse, -dedisses,* etc.), with the same shift of stress as in the first conjugation: *temiese, vendiese, -ieses, -iese, -iésemos* (< *-[d]essemus*), *-ieseis* (< *-iéssedes* < *-[d]essetis*), *-iesen.* The Spanish third (Latin fourth) conjugation is analogical to the second (*partiese, -ieses,* etc.). The concurrence of the *-se* forms and the *-ra* forms (the latter derived from the Latin pluperfect indicative) has already been indicated (see 82(*u*), above).

(bb) The Catalan imperfect (Latin pluperfect) subjunctive developed etymologically in the first and third (Latin fourth) conjugations, from the contracted Vulgar Latin forms (*-asse, -isse*), with the same shift of stress as in Spanish (see par. 82(*aa*), above). The stressed *a* of the first conjugation (*cantàs, cantasses,* etc.) closed to *e* by analogy to the second conjugation (Latin second and third); and the final (unstressed) *e* of the second person singular, and of all the plural persons, closed to *i* by analogy to the present subjunctive (see par. 82(*y*), above): *cantés, -essis, -és, -éssim, éssiu* (OCt. *-ássats*), *-essin*. The second conjugation (Latin second and third) was derived, as in Spanish (see par. 82(*aa*), above), by analogy to *dare*, with the same shift of stress, and the same closing of final *e* to *i*, as in the first and third conjugations: *temés, -essis, -és, -éssim, -éssiu* (OCt. *-éssets*), *-essin*. The third (Latin fourth) conjugation experienced the same analogical change with regard to final *e* as the other two conjugations: *sentis, -issis, -is, -ĭssim, -ĭssiu* (OCt. *-ĭssets*), *-issin*.

(cc) The Portuguese imperfect (Latin pluperfect) subjunctive developed etymologically in the first and third (Latin fourth) conjugations, from the contracted Vulgar Latin forms, with the same shift of stress as in Spanish and Catalan (see pars. 82(*aa*),(*bb*), above): *cantasse, -asses, -asse, -ássemos, -ásseis* (< *ássedes*), *-assem; partisse, -isses, -isse, -íssemos, ísseis* (< *íssedes*), *-issem*. The second conjugation (Latin second and third) was derived, as in Spanish and Catalan, by analogy to *dare*, with the same shift of stress as in the other conjugations: *vendesse, -esses, -esse, -éssemos, -ésseis* (< *éssedes*), *-essem*.

(dd) In Spanish, the future subjunctive, which has been largely replaced in usage by the present indicative and the present subjunctive, was derived from the Vulgar Latin fusion of the future perfect indicative and the perfect subjunctive. The etymological -*o* of the first person singular survived until the end of the fourteenth century, when it was superseded by an -*e* which was analogical to the third person singular. The first conjugation developed etymologically; the second (Latin second and third), by analogy to *dare* (-*de*[*d*]*ero* > *\*deero* > -*diero* > -*diere*); the third (Latin fourth), by analogy to the second: *cantare, -ares, -are, -áremos, -areis,* (OSp. *-áredes*), *-aren; temiere, vendiere, partiere, -ieres, -iere, -iéremos, -iereis* (OSp. *-iéredes*), *-ieren*.

(ee) In Portuguese, the future subjunctive was derived as it was in Spanish (see par. 82(*dd*), above), The etymological -*o* of the first person singular became -*e* by analogy, as in Spanish, and then fell. The first and third (Latin fourth) conjugations developed etymologically; the second (Latin second and third), as in Spanish, by analogy to *dare: cantar, -ares, -ar, -armos, -ardes, -arem; dever, vender, -eres, -er, -ermos, -erdes, -erem; partir, -ires, -ir, -irmos, -irdes, -irem*.

(ff) The perfect subjunctives evolved in Spanish as periphrases of the present, imperfect, and future subjunctive of *haber* and the past participle; in Catalan, as periphrases of the present and imperfect subjunctive of *haver* and the past participle; in Portuguese, as periphrases of the present, imperfect, and future subjunctive of *ter* and past participle.

(gg) The passive voice in Spanish and Portuguese, which was originally expressed in terms of the Vulgar Latin periphrasis *essere amatu, -a* (CL passive perfect) only, eventually differentiated, for transitive verbs of perfective action, between the passive of action (*ser* + past part.) and the passive of state (*estar* + past part.). No such differentiation materialized in Catalan, which continued to express passive of action and passive of state by the periphrasis *ésser* plus the past participle. The tenses and moods of the passive voice in all three languages are expressed by the auxiliary.

(hh) The affirmative imperative developed etymologically in Spanish and Portuguese, the Classical Latin third conjugation forms having fused, in Vulgar Latin, with those of the second conjugation: *canta, cantate* > Sp. *canta, cantad*; Pg. *canta, cantade* > *cantai*; *tĭmē, tĭmēte* > Sp. *teme, temed*, Pg. *teme, temede* > *temei*; *vende, \*vendete* > Sp. *vende, vended*; Pg. *vende, vendede* > *vendei*; *partī, partīte* > Sp. *parte, partid;* Pg. *parti* > *parte, partide* > *parti*. Catalan, which followed the same pattern as Spanish and Portuguese in the singular (*canta, tem, ven, part*), derived its plural from the corresponding form of the present indicative (*canteu, temeu, veneu, partiu*). In Spanish, Catalan, and Portuguese, affirmative imperatives are negated in the present subjunctive: Sp. *no cantes, no cantéis*, etc.; Ct. *no cantis, no canteu*, etc.; Pg. *no cantes, no canteis*, etc.

### The Verb in Rheto-Romance

83. (a) The four conjugations of Vulgar Latin survived in Surselvan, the infinitives developing regularly as *-ar, -er, '-er, -ir* (*levar, temer, vènder, sentir*). The gerund of the first conjugation was derived from *-andu* (*levond*), whereas the gerunds of the other three conjugations were derived from *-endu* (*temend, vendend, sentend*). Similarly, the present participle of the first conjugation was derived from *-ante* (*levont*), whereas the present participles of the other three conjugations were derived from *-ente* (*tement, vendent, sentent*). The weak forms of the active past participles were derived from the weak passive participles, with anomalous nominative forms for the masculine singular and plural. Thus, the active past participles for transitive verbs are *-au* (< *-atu*) for the first conjugation, and *-iu* (< *-utu, -itu* [which coincide phonologically]) for all other conjugations. For intransitive and reflexive verbs, and as predicate nominatives, the active past participles are *-aus* (< *atus*), *-ada* (< *ata*), *-ai* (< *-ati*), *-adas* (< *-atas*) for the first conjugation, and *-ius* (< *-utus, -itus*), *-ida* (< *uta, -ita*), *-i* (< *-uti, -iti*), *-idas* (< *-utas, -itas*) for all other conjugations; e.g., *cumprau, temiu, vendiu, sentiu; levaus, levada, levai, levadas; fugius, fugida, fugi, fugidas*. Strong past participles include the following: *ars* (*arder*), *buiu* (*beiber*), *cotg* (*cuer*), *dau* (*dar*), *detg* (*dir*), *fatg*

*(far)*, *mess* *(metter)*, *morts, morta (murir)*, *ris (rir)*, *scret (scriver)*, *spons (sponder)*, *tratg (trer)*, *viu (ver)*, *viult (volver)*.

(b) The present indicative evolved with a single set of endings for the first three conjugations: *-el, -as, -a, -ein, -eis, -an*. The fourth conjugation, which otherwise coincided with the rest, developed etymologically in the first and second persons plural (*-in, -is*). The anomalous ending *-el* has been explained as enclitic *-illu* or as an analogue of etymological *affel* (< *afflo*) ; the ending *-as, -a, -an* are etymological for the first conjugation, and analogical to the first for the other three conjugations; unetymological *-ein, -eis*, in the first conjugation, were derived from archaic present subjunctive forms; e.g., *level, temel, vendel, sentel; levein, temein, vendein*, but *sentin, sentis*.

(c) The imperfect indicative, except for the first person singular, *-avel, -evel* (see par. 83 (*b*), above), developed etymologically in the first and second conjugations, with a shift of accent in the first and second persons plural: *-abas, -abat, -abamus, -abatis, -abant* > *-avas, -avat, -avan, -avas, -avan; -ebas, -ebat, -ebamus, -ebatis, -ebant* > *-evas, -eva, -evan, evas, -evan*. The third and fourth conjugations are analogical to the second: *vendevas, vendeva; sentevas, senteva*, etc.

(d) The Latin perfect indicative did not survive. The simple past and the present perfect were both expressed by the periphrasis *habere* (for transitive verbs) or *\*essere* (for intransitive and reflexive verbs) + past part.; thus, *jeu hai cumprau*, but *jeu sun levaus (levada)* and *jeu sun selegraus (selegrada)*.

(e) The future was derived from the periphrasis *venire a(d)* + infinitive, *ad* being used before infinitives beginning with a vowel: *jeu vegnel a clamar (ad esser), ti vegns . . ., el vegn . . ., nus vegnin . . ., vus vegnis, . . .els vegnan . . .*

(f) The conditional was derived from the imperfect (CL pluperfect) subjunctive, with change of stress in the first and second persons plural. The first and second conjugations developed etymologically, the third and fourth by analogy to the second: *purtass, -asses, -ass, -assen* (< VL *\*portassemu* < CL *portavissēmus*), *-asses* (< VL *\*portassetis* < CL *portavissētis*), *-assen; savess, vendess, vegness, -esses, -ess, -essen, -esses, -essen*.

(g) The pluperfect, future perfect, and conditional perfect developed in conformance to the following patterns; *jeu erel levaus (levada), jeu (ha) vevel cumprau; jeu vegnel ad esser levaus (levada), jeu vegnel ad haver cumprau; jeu vegness ad esser levaus (levada), jeu vegness ad haver cumprau.*

(h) The present subjunctive developed largely unetymological paradigms, which were identical in the first three conjugations, the fourth conjugation maintaining its distinctive forms for the first and second persons plural: *levi, temi, vendi, -ies, -i, -eien, -eies, -ien; fineschi, senti, -ies, -i, ien, -ies, -ien.*

52

(i) The imperfect (CL pluperfect) subjunctive, in order to distinguish itself from the conditional (see par. 83 (*f*), above), developed endings which were analogical to those of the present subjunctive (see par. 83 (*h*), above): *levassi, temessi, vendessi, sentessi, -ies, -i, -ien, -ies, -ien.*

(j) The perfect subjunctives developed as periphrases consisting of the present or imperfect subjunctive of *esser* or *haver* and the past participle.

(k) The passive voice developed as a periphrasis consisting of *vegnir* and the past participle (*jeu vegnel clamaus, -ada*), the preposition *da* (*dad* before a vowel) serving to introduce the agent of passive action.

(l) The affirmative imperative, which was originally etymological in the singular (*porta, vende, dormi*), remained etymological in the first conjugation only, the other conjugations developing forms analogical to those of the first: *leva, tema, venda, finescha, senta.* The plural forms are identical in the first three conjugations: *levei, temei, vendei,* but *fini, senti.* The imperatives are negated by *buc* (*buca* before a consonant), which may precede or follow the verb (*buca leva, leva buc*).

## The Verb in Italo-Romance

84. (a) In Italian, the four Vulgar Latin infinitives survived, but the second and third conjugations became one: thus, (I) *-are*, (II) *-ere, '-ere*, (III) *-ire* (*cantare, vedere, vendere, partire* [*finire*]). The gerund developed etymologically, the *i* component of the Classical Latin endings for the irregular third and the fourth conjugations having been lost in Vulgar Latin (*cantando, vedendo, vendendo, partendo*). The present participle, functioning only as a noun or adjective, developed similarly (*cantante, tenente, corrente, partente*). The weak forms of the active past (Latin perfect passive) participle developed etymologically in the first and fourth conjugations (*-atu* > *-ato, -itu* > *-ito*), and by analogy to the *-uto* participles of verbs with strong perfects in *-ui*, in the second and third conjugations (*tenuto, venduto*). The strong participles include (1) etymological forms in *t* (*detto, fatto, giunto, morto, pianto, scritto, visto* [cf. *veduto*]), (2) etymological forms in *s* (*chiuso, corso, riso, raso, sparso*), and (3) unetymological forms in *st*, analogical to *posto, visto*, etc. (*risposto, rimasto*).

(b) In Sardinian, the four Vulgar Latin conjugations originally survived, but the second soon merged with the third (*cantare, bíere* [L. *vidēre*], *vendere, dormire*). The Old Sardinian gerunds in *-ande, -ende, -inde* have survived alongside subsequent levelings, such as analogical *-ende* for the first and third (Latin fourth) conjugations. The unetymological *-e* of the gerund has been explained (1) as a mistaken restitution of etymological -o, which had been lost through elision, and (2) as an analogue of the final e of the infinitive. The -nde of the gerund has been explained as a vestige of (i)nde, which was often appended to gerunds as a pleonastic enclitic, e.g., kurrendinde (cf. It. correndosene), and was mistakenly appended to verb stems, to form the gerund. The weak forms of the active past (Latin perfect passive) participle developed etymologically in the first and third (Latin fourth) conjugations (-atu, -itu > -a[đ]o, -i[đ]o). Strong forms developed anomalously in the second (Latin second and third) conjugation, by the generalization of the '-itu forms of the Latin third conjugation (venditu > bendi[đ]u). Other strong forms include (1) those in t([ar]ruttu, cottu, fattu, iskrittu, kurtu [cf. kúrri(đ)u], tentu [cf. ténni(đ)u]), (2) those in st (postu), and (3) those in s (tusu, frissu [cf. fritto]).

(c) In Italian, the present indicative developed as follows, with Old Italian forms indicated parenthetically: (I) amo, ami (ama, [very rare], ame), ama, amiamo (amamo), amate, amano (aman); (II) vedo, vedi (vede [very rare]), vede, vediamo (vedemo), vedete, vedono (vedon); credo, credi (crede), crede, crediamo (credemo), credete, credono (credon); (III) sento, senti, sente, sentiamo (sentimo), sentite, sentono (senton). The -i of the second person singular of the first three conjugations has been explained phonologically (see par. 72(a) above) and morphologically, the latter in terms of borrowing the etymological -i of the fourth conjugation in order to differentiate the second from the third person singular after the loss of final s. The morphological explanation also maintains that, in Old Italian, the second person singular of the first conjugation borrowed the final e of the second conjugation (vede < vides) before final i became generalized for all four conjugations; thus, cantas > canta > cante > canti. The intrusion of the present subjunctive form (see par. 84(o), below) in the first person plural has been explained as a carry-over of the corresponding hortatory form. The unetymological -o of the third person plural has been explained (1) as being analogical to the -o of such forms as diedero, fecero, videro, derived from Latin proparoxytones ending in unt, and (2) as being paragogic in nature, relieving etymologically final n from its untenable nonconformity with the sound system of the language; -ono has been explained as an analogue of sono, whose final o has itself been explained (1) as an analogue of the etymological -o of the corresponding person of regular verbs, and (2) as an echo of stressed o. In most instances, the yod of such forms as video and sentio was lost in Vulgar Latin; thus, vedo and sento.

(d) In Sardinian, the present indicative developed as follows, with Old Sardinian forms indicated parenthetically: (I) kanto; kanta[š], kanta[š]a (kantas); kantat, kanta[đ]a (kantat); kantamus, kantamos (kantamus); kanta[đ]es (kantates); kantana (kantan, kan-

*tant*); (II) *respundo; respunde[š], respunde[š]e; respundet, re-spunde[đ]e (respundet, respundit); respundimus, respundimos (respundemus, respundimus), respundi[đ]es (respundites), respun-dene (respunden); bendo, bende[š], bende[š]e,* etc.; (III) *dormo, dormi[š], dormi[š]i (dormis), dormit, dormi[đ]i (dormit); dormi-mus, dormimos (dormimus); dormi[đ]es (dormites); dormini (dormin).* The *o*, instead of etymological *u*, of the first person plural ending, has been explained as an analogue of the first person singular. The *e*, instead of the etymological *i*, of the second person plural ending has been explained as an analogue of the substantival ending in *-e(s)*.

(e) In Italian, the imperfect tense of the indicative developed as follows, with Old Italian forms indicated parenthetically: (I) *cantavo (cantava), cantavi (cantave), cantava, cantavamo, cantavate, can-tavano (cantavan);* (II) *vedevo (vedeva, vedea), vedevi (vedea), vedeva (vedea), vedevamo (vedeamo), vedevate (vedeate), vedevano (vedevan, vedean); vendevo (vendeva, vendea), vendevi (vendea),* etc.; (III) *finivo (finiva, finia), finivi (finia), finiva (finia), finivamo (finiamo), finivate (finiate), finivano (finivan, finian).* The *-o* of the first person singular is an analogue of the corresponding form of the present indicative, and serves to differentiate the first from the third person singular. The *-i* of the second person singular has been ex-plained phonologically (see par. 72(a) above) and morphologically, the latter on the analogy of the corresponding form of the present and preterite tenses (see 84(c), above, and pars. 84(g) and (i), below). Phonologically, Old Italian *-ea*, which had developed on the analogy of *avea, devea* (< *habe[b]a, debe[b]a*) should have become *-ia*; it undoubtedly remained unchanged so that it might serve to differen-tiate the second conjugation from the third. For final *o* of the third person plural, see par. 84(c), above. OIt. *cantave* is an analogue of the corresponding form of the present indicative (see par. 84(c), above).

(f) In Sardinian, the imperfect tense of the indicative developed as follows, with Old Sardinian forms indicated parenthetically: (I) *kantao, kantaia (kantava); kanta[š]a, kantai[š]a; kanta[đ]a, kantaia[đ]a (kantavat); kantaiamus; kantaia[ž]is; kantana, kan-taiana (kantavan);* (II, III) *biia, (biea, biia), biias, biiat, biiamus, biia[ž]is, biiana (biean, biian); bendia (bendea, bendia), bendias,* etc.; *dormia (dormia), dormias, dormiat (dormiat),* etc. The first conjugation endings in *-ao, -a[š]a,* etc., correspond to etymological *-a[ƀ]a, -a[ƀ]as,* etc.; those in *-aia, -aí[š]a,* etc. are analogues of the second-third conjugation endings, except that the *o* of *-ao* is an ana-logue of the corresponding form of the present tense (see par. 84(d), above).

(g) In Italian, the weak preterites of the first and third (Latin fourth) conjugations developed as follows from the corresponding Vulgar Latin perfects, with Old Italian forms indicated partheti-cally: (I) *cantai, cantasti, cantò (cantào), cantammo, cantaste, can-*

*tarono (cantaro, cantor[o]no; cantoro, cantonno)*; (III) *partii (partì)*, *partisti, partì (partío), partimmo, partiste, partirono (partiro, partinno)*. The weak preterites of the Italian second (Latin second and third) conjugation developed on the analogy of the strong *dedi* and *detti* preterites (see par. 84(*i*), below: (II) *vendei* and *vendetti*, *vendesti, vendè (vendèo)* and *vendette, vendemmo, vendeste, venderono (vendero, vendenno)* and *vendettero*. The etymon of *cantò* is *\*cantaut < cantav(i)t*. The -*mm*- of the first person plural was the result of the gemination which took place when -v- was lost, and *m* found itself in the phonetic context -*aimo*, -*eimo*, -*iimo*. Tonic *e* of *vendemmo* is an analogue of the tonic vowel of *vendeste*. The ending of the Modern Italian third person plural is analogical to the corresponding ending of the present and imperfect tenses (see pars. 84(*c*) and (*e*), above). OIt. *cantor[o]no* is an analogue of the third person singular.

(h) In Old Sardinian, the weak preterite is attested for the first and third conjugations only: (I) *kantavi, kantai; kantasti; kantait, kantat; kantaimus; kantaistis; kantarun, kantaint*; (III) *dormivi, ...*, *dormivit, dormivimus; ...; dormirun*. During the sixteenth and seventeenth centuries, there was a concurrence of these weak preterites and new forms in -*e[š]i*, -*ei*, which consisted of endings derived from strong -*s*- *preterites* (see par. 84(*j*) below) appended to present or preterite stems: *prende[š]i, fe[dž]i[š]i, appe[š]i*, etc. The Old Sardinian weak preterites disappeared altogether in the eighteenth century. In Modern Sardinian, virtually all weak preterites have been replaced by present perfect forms (see par. 84(*p*) below).

(i) In Italian, the strong preterite of *dare* developed from Latin *dedi, dedisti*, etc., with haplological dissimilation of the unstressed stem syllable; geminated -*m*- in the first person plural; and tonic *e* in the first person plural, on the analogy of the second person plural: *diedi < dedi, desti < (de)disti, diede < dedit, demmo < de(di)mus, deste < (de)distis, diedero < dederunt*. On the analogy of the corresponding preterite forms of Latin *stare*, the following forms emerged as concurrents of *dedi, diede*, and *diedero*, respectively: *detti, dette, dettero*. The strong preterites of the second (Latin second and third) conjugation are as follows: (1) (-*i*: *vidi, vidit, viderunt; feci, fecit, fecerunt*) *vidi, vide, videro; feci, fece, fecero*; (2) (-*si*: *misi, misit, miserunt; dixi, divit, dixerunt*) *misi, mise, misero; dissi, disse, dissero*; (3) (-ui: *habui, habuit, habuerunt; naqui, naquit, naquerunt; parui, paruit, paruerunt*) *ebbi, ebbe, ebbero; nacqui, nacque, nacquero; parvi, parve, parvero*. The weak forms of the remaining persons are analogical to *(de)disti, de(di)mus*, and *(de)distis*: thus, *vedesti, vedemmo, vedeste; mettesti, mettemmo, metteste; avesti, avemmo, aveste*. The strong preterite in -*i* of the third (Latin fourth) conjugation developed on the analogy of *tenni < tenui: venni, venne, vennero*.

(j) The Old Sardinian strong preterites, which had the same development as their weak counterparts (see par. 84(*h*), above), included the following: (1) (-i) bendi, bidi, binki, feki; (2) (-si) dissi, iskripsi, lesi, posi, remasi; (3) (-ui) appi, benni, petti, potti, tenni.

(k) In Italian, the future indicative developed from the Vulgar Latin periphrasis consisting of the infinitive and the present tense of habere: (I) canterò (OIt., also canteraggio, canterabbo), canterai, canterà, canteremo (OIt., also cantereno), canterete, canteranno. The unstressed a of the infinitive ending, since it was followed by r, became e, which is the normal phonological development; (II) venderò, venderai, etc.; (III) partirò, partirai, etc. OIt. -eno is a reconstruction on the analogy of the apocopated form of -emo (-en-) before an enclitic, e.g., farenvi (= vi faremo). The conditional developed as an analogue of the future, consisting of the infinitive and the imperfect or perfect of habere, only the latter surviving in this context in Modern Italian: (I) canterei (OIt., also canteria), canteresti, canterebbe, canteremmo, cantereste, canterebbero; (II) venderei (OIt., also venderia), venderesti, venderebbe, etc.; (III) partirei (OIt., also partiria), partiresti, partirebbe, etc. The loss of the unstressed infinitive vowel through syncope is sporadic in all three conjugations: andrò, andrei (andare); dovrò, dovrei (dovere); morrò, morrei (morire); potrò, potrei (potere); vedrò, vedrei (vedere), etc. This syncope is occasionally accompanied by the assimilation of the stem consonant to the r of the infinitive: terrò, terrei (tenere), verrò, verrei (venire), vorrò, vorrèi (volere).

(l) In Sardinian, the future developed from the Vulgar Latin equivalents of the periphrases habeo ad cantare, debeo cantare, becoming, respectively, appo a kkantare and deppo kantare. The conditional developed as an analogue of habeo ad cantare, imperfect habebam replacing habeo.

(m) In Italian, the perfect indicatives are derived from Vulgar Latin periphrases consisting of the various tenses of the auxiliaries habere and *essere, and of the past participles of (1) transitive, and (2) intransitive and reflexive verbs, respectively: thus, ho cantato; sono partito, -a; mi sono divertito, -a. In Modern Italian, the past participle with avere generally agrees only with a preceding direct object pronoun; with essere, it always agrees with the subject.

(n) In Sardinian, the perfect indicatives were derived from Vulgar Latin periphrases consisting of the past participles of (1) transitive, and (2) intransitive and reflexive verbs, and the various tenses of the auxiliaries habere and *essere, respectively: thus, kantatu appo; benni[đ]u so.

(o) In Italian, the present subjunctive developed as follows, with Old Italian forms indicated parenthetically: (I) ˙canti (cante), canti (cante), canti (cante), cantiamo, cantiate, cantino; (II, III) venda (vendi), venda (vende, vendi), venda (vendi), vendiamo, vendiate, vendano (vendino); parta (parti), parta (parte, parti), etc. The -i of the second person singular of the first conjugation developed either

57

phonologically (see par. 72(a), above), or morphologically, the latter on the analogy of the corresponding form of the present indicative or to differentiate the second person from the first and third. This -i became generalized for the endings of all the stem-stressed forms of the first conjugation, and appeared sporadically in the corresponding forms of the second and third conjugations. The endings of the first and second persons plural are analogues of *abbiamo, abbiate* (< *habeamus, habeatis*), *siamo, siate* (< *\*siamus, \*siatis*).

(p) In Sardinian, the present subjunctive developed as follows, with attested forms in Old Sardinian indicated parenthetically: (I) *kante* (*kante*), *kantes*, *kantet* (*kantet*), *kantemus* (*kantemus*) *kante[d]es*, (*kantetes*), *kantene* (*kanten*); (II, III) *benda* (*benda*), *bendes* (*bendas*), *bendat* (*bendat*), *bendamus* (*bendamus*), *benda[d]-das, bendana* (*bendant*) ; *dorma* (*dorma*), *dormes* (*dormas*), etc. (N.B. There is no standard conjugation of the present subjunctive in Logudorese. The preceding forms are those of the Orani sub-dialect, which is considered to adhere most closely to the historical development of Logudorese.) The final *e* of *-e[d]es* (L. *-etis*) and the final *a* of *-a[d]as* (L. *-atis*), instead of etymological *i*, are explained as analogues of the respective third person endings *-ene, -ana*.

(q) In Italian, the imperfect subjunctive developed from the Vulgar Latin contracted forms of the Classical Latin pluperfect subjunctive, with displacement of accent in the first and second persons plural: *cantasse, vendesse, partisse; -asses, -esses, -isses; -asset, -esset, -isset; -assemus, -essemus, -issemus, -assetis, -essetis, -issetis; -assen, -essen, -issen*; thus, *cantassi, vendessi, partissi* (OIt., also *-asse, -esse, -isse*) ; *cantassi, vendessi, partissi; cantasse, vendesse, partisse* (OIt., also *-assi, -essi, -issi*) ; *cantassimo, vendessimo, partissimo; cantaste, vendeste, partiste* (OIt., also *-assi, -essi, -issi*) ; *cantassero, vendessero, partissero* (OIt., also *-asseno, -esseno, -isseno; -asserono, -esserono, -isserono*). The *-i* of the first person singular is an analogue of the corresponding form of the strong preterites (see 84(i), above). The *-i* of the second person singular is either phonological (see par. 72(a), above) or analogical to the corresponding form of other tenses. The *-i* of the Old Italian third person singular is an analogue of the first person singular. The *-assi, -essi, -issi* of the Old Italian second person plural have been attributed to an effort to avoid using *-aste, -este, -iste*, which clash morphologically with the endings of the weak preterites. The *-assero, -essero, -issero* of the third person plural are analogical to the corresponding forms of the strong preterites. The *-asserono, -esserono, -isserono* of the Old Italian third person plural are combinations of the *-assero* and *-asseno* endings.

(r) In Old Sardinian, the etymological imperfect subjunctive developed as follows: (I) *kantare, -ares, -aret, -aremus, [-aretis], -aren[t]*; (II) *bendere, -eres, -eret*, etc.; (III) *dormire, -ires, -iret*, etc. In the eighteenth century, these forms were replaced by a single paradigm

58

for all conjugations, on the analogy of the weak preterite forms in *-esi* (see par. 84(*h*), above) for stress and thematic vowel: *-ere, -eres, -eret, -eremus, -ere[đ]es, -erent*.

(s) In Italian, the perfect subjunctives developed from Vulgar Latin periphrases consisting of the present and imperfect subjunctive of *habere* or *\*essere* and the past participle of (1) transitive and (2) intransitive and reflexive verbs, respectively; thus, *abbia (avessi) cantato; sia (fossi) partito, -a; mi sia (fossi) divertito, -a.*

(t) In Sardinian, the perfect subjunctives developed from Vulgar Latin periphrases consisting of the past participle of (1) transitive and (2) intransitive or reflexive verbs, and the present and imperfect subjunctive of *habere* or *\*essere*, respectively; thus, *kantatu appa (aere), partitu, -a sia (sie), essere.*

(u) The passive voice in Italian and Sardinian is expressed by the periphrases *essere amato, -a,* and *amatu, -a essere,* respectively, no structural differentiation being made between passive of action and passive of state. The various tenses and moods of the passive voice are indicated in both languages by the auxiliary.

(v) In Italian, the singular imperative developed etymologically in the first and third (Latin fourth) conjugations, and analogically in the second (Latin second and third) conjugation: *canta < canta; vedi, vendi* (L. *vede, vende*); *parti < parti.* The plural imperative either developed etymologically in the first and third conjugations (*cantate, partite*), and analogically in the second, *vendite* becoming *vendete* on the analogy of *vedete,* or simply adopted the corresponding forms of the present indicative. The singular imperative is negated by *non* and the infinitive (or possibly a vestige of the Latin perfect subjunctive [*cantaveris*], which became identical to the infinitive): *non cantare, vedere,* etc. The plural imperative is negated by *non,* with no morphological change.

(w) In Sardinian, the singular imperative developed etymologically in all three conjugations: *kanta, bende, dormi.* The plural imperative developed etymologically in the first and third (Latin fourth) conjugations (*kanta[đ]e, kantae; dormi[đ]e, dormie*), and analogically in the second, *videte* becoming *bii[đ]e, biie,* on the analogy of *bendi[đ]e, bendie.*

## The Verb in Balkan Romance

85. (a) In Rumanian, the four Vulgar Latin conjugations survived. The etymological infinitives (*-are, -eare -ere, '-ere, -ire*) assumed an exclusively substantival function (see par. 79(*d*), above), relinquishing their verbal function to apocopated derivatives (*-a, -ea, -e, -i*), usually introduced by *a*: thus, *cîntare* vs. *a cînta, tacere* vs. *a tacea, facere* vs. *a face, simţire* vs. *a simţi.* The gerunds of the second and third conjugations conformed analogically to the etymological ger-

59

und of the first conjugation, whereas the gerund of the fourth conjugation maintained itself distinctively: thus, *cîntând, tăcând, făcând, simţind*. The Latin present participles did not survive in Rumanian, their Romance function as verbal adjectives being assumed by (1) declinable gerunds, and (2) derivatives of Latin adjectives in *-torius*, with final stem-vowels to correspond to the respective gerunds (*cîntător, tăcător, făcător, silitor*). The weak forms of the active past (Latin perfect passive) participles developed etymologically in the first and fourth conjugations (*-atu > -at, -itu > -it*); in the second and third conjugations, the analogical pattern was established by etymological *-ut* (*< -utu*) of verbs whose perfects ended in *-ui*: thus, *cîntat, tăcut, făcut, simţit*. Strong participles in *t* include *copt, fript, rupt, supt*; strong participles in *s* include *ars, mers, ris*, and analogical forms, such as *pus, scris, tras, zis*.

(b) The present tense of the indicative evolved etymologically, but with variant, infixed paradigms in the first and fourth conjugations: (I) *cînt, cînţi, cîntă, cîntam, cîntaţi, cîntă; lucrez, lucrezĭ, lucreză, lucrăm, lucraţi, lucrează*; (II) *tac, tacĭ, tace, tacem, taceţi, tac*; (III) *vind, vinzĭ, vinde, vindem, vindeţi, vînd*; (IV) *dorm, dormĭ, doarme, dormim, dormiţi, dorm; vorbesc, vorbeşti, vorbeşte, vorbim, vorbiţi, vorbesc; hotărăsc, hotărăşti, hotărăşte, hotărîm, hotărîţi, hotărăsc*. First person *-u* survived after cons. + *l* or *r* (see par. 44, above): thus, *aflu, suflu*. Second person *-i* has been explained in the same way as the corresponding form in Italian (see pars. 72(*a*), 84(*c*), above). First person *-ăm*, instead of phonologically correct *-am*, is attributed to the analogical influence of *dăm, stăm*. Third person *-unt* must have prevailed in the second, as well as the third and fourth, conjugation in Vulgar Latin, to judge from the modern forms which evolved in that person. Especially noteworthy is the retention of Latin stress in the first and second persons plural of the third conjugation.

(c) The imperfect indicative developed as follows, with Old Rumanian forms indicated parenthetically: *cîntam (cînta), cîntaĭ, cînta, cîntam, cîntaţi, cintaŭ (cînta); taceam, vindeam, (-ea), -eaĭ, ea, -eam, -eaţi, -eaŭ (-ea); dormeam (dormia), dormeai (dormiaĭ), dormea (dormia), dormeam (dormiam), dormeaţi (dormiaţi), dormeaŭ (dormia)*. First person *-am* and third person *-au* are thought to be analogical to the corresponding forms of the present indicative of *habere (a avea)*. Modern fourth conjugation endings are analogical to those of the second and third conjugations.

(d) The weak preterites of the Vulgar Latin first and fourth conjugations developed as follows, with Old Rumanian forms indicated parenthetically: (I) *cîntai (cîntaiŭ), cîntaşi, cînta, cîntarăm (cîntamu), cîntarăţi (cîntatu), cîntară*; (IV) *dormii (dormiiŭ), dormişi, dormi, dormirăm (dormimu), dormirăţi (dormitu), dormiră*. The modern first and second persons plural are analogical to the third persons plural of their respective paradigms.

(e) The weak preterites of the Rumanian second and third conjugations have their roots in the strong Vulgar Latin preterites in *-ui*, which became weak by shifting the stress to *u* in the first and third persons singular by analogy to the preterite of *essere (*fui, *fusti, *fut*, etc.), and to the participles in *-ut*. The second and third conjugations developed as follows, with the Old Rumanian forms indicated parenthetically: *tăcui (tăcuiŭ), făcui, -usi, -u, urăm (-umu), -urăți (-utu), ură*. The modern first and second persons plural, like those of the first and fourth conjugations, are analogical to the third persons plural of their respective paradigms.

(f) Other strong preterites having become weak (see par. 85(*e*), above), the only strong preterites to remain were those in *-si*, and in the latter, the first person singular became weak by analogy to the corresponding form of the first conjugation: *zisei, zisești, zise, ziserăm, ziserați, ziseră*.

(g) The future tense developed as a periphrasis consisting of the present indicative of *volere* (*a vrea*) and the infinitive: thus, *voi cînta, vei cînta, va cînta, vom cînta, veți cînta, vor cînta*. Colloquially, the future is also expressed by the present indicative of *a avea* or *o* plus the present subjunctive of the verb concerned: thus, *am (o) să cînt, ai (o) să cînți*, etc.

(h) Like the future tense (see par. 85(*g*), above), the conditional also developed as a periphrasis consisting of an auxiliary plus the infinitive, but in the latter tense, the sequence of auxiliary-infinitive might be reversed: thus, *aș cînta (cîntare-aș), ai cînta (cantare-ai), ar cînta (cîntare-ar), am cînta (cîntare-am), ați cînta (cîntare-ați), ar cînta (cîntare-ar)*. The etymon of the auxiliary in this case is not certain, although it would seem most reasonable to assume that it is the imperfect tense of *volere*.

(i) The present perfect indicative evolved as a periphrasis consisting of the present indicative of *a avea* and the past participle. The pluperfect developed anomalously from the Latin pluperfect subjunctive, with the equally anomalous intrusion of the past participle: *cîntasem, tăcusem, făcusem, dormisem, -sesi, -se, -sem, -seți, -se*. The *-m* of the first person singular has been attributed to the analogical influence exerted by the corresponding form of the imperfect indicative, and to the Slavic adstratum. Colloquially, Modern Rumanian shows instrusion of the preterite forms in the plural: thus *cîntaseram, tăceserăm, vindeserăm, dormiserăm, '-serăti, '-seră*. The future and conditional perfect evolved as periphrases consisting, respectively, of the future or conditional of the auxiliary *a fi* plus the past participle of the verb concerned: thus, *voi fi cîntat, vei fi cîntat*, etc.; *aș fi cîntat, ai fi cîntat*, etc.

(j) The present subjunctive, except for the third persons singular and plural (*cînte, taca, vinda, doarma*), became analogically identical to the present indicative.

(k) A periphrasis consisting of *să fi* plus the past participle, for all persons (*să fi cîntat, tăcut, vindut, dormit*) replaced the etymological present perfect subjunctive of Old Rumanian (*cîntare, tăcere, vindere, dormire, -ri, -re, -rem, -ret, -re*). An analogical pluperfect subjunctive developed in which the *să fi* of the present perfect subjunctive was replaced by *să fi fost*, again for all persons (*să fi fost cîntat, tăcut,* etc.).

(l) The singular affirmative command developed etymologically in the first conjungation (*canta* > *cînta*), but vacillated between etymological and analogical forms in the other conjugations: thus, *tacĭ* and *umplă* in the second conjugation; *trecĭ* and *cere* in the third conjugation; and *fugĭ* and *simte* in the fourth conjugation. The plural affirmative imperatives were borrowed from the second person plural of the present indicative: thus, *cîntați, taceți, faceți, dormiți*. The singular imperative is negated by negating the derived infinitive (see par. 85(*a*), above): *nu cînta, nu tace,* etc. The plural imperative is negated by merely negating the affirmative: *nu cîntați, nu taceți,* etc.

(m) The passive voice is expressed by a periphrasis consisting of the auxiliary *a fi* and the past participle. The tense and mood of the principal verb are expressed by the auxiliary.

## Vulgar Latin Pronominal System

86. (a) The personal pronouns of Vulgar Latin differed from those of Classical Latin in the following respects: (1) they included forms for all three persons; (2) they were declined in only the nominative, dative, and accusative cases; (3) they assumed different forms in stressed and unstressed positions; (4) they vacillated between dative and accusative functions; (5) they adopted new, analogical forms. In the nominative singular, *ego*, except at first in Sardinia, became *eo*, stressed on the first or second vowel; *tu* remained unchanged; and the demonstratives *ille, illa, illu(d)* (to a lesser extent, *ipse, ipsa, ipsu*) were used to express the third person. In the nominative plural, *nos* and *vos* survived, and were complemented in the third person by the plural demonstratives. The accusative singular forms were *me, te,* and reflexive *se,* and the demonstrative accusatives, *illu-a, ipsu-a;* the corresponding plural forms were *nos, vos, se,* and the demonstrative plurals, *illos-as, ipsos,-as.* The dative singular contraction *mi* (< *mihi*) gave rise to the analogical forms *ti, si* and, conversely, in some regions, *mihi* developed as *mibi,* by analogy to *tibi, sibi.* The third person datives *illi,* \**ille* (< \**illae*) were rivaled by the new forms \**illui,* \**illei* (< \**illaei*), the first of which was probably analogical to the corresponding relative pronoun *cui.* The dative plurals *nobis, vobis* were largely replaced by *nos, vos,* which assumed multiple functions. The third person dative *illis* was rivaled by the genitive *illoru(m),* which assumed the dative function. *Cum* was often

prefixed and/or appended to first and second person, as well as reflexive, forms (*mecu, cum mecu*). Finally, *nos* and *vos* were often reinforced by *alteri, -e* (< *-ae*), *alteros-as*.

(b) The possessive pronouns of Vulgar Latin differed from those of Classical Latin in the following respects: (1) they were declined in only the nominative and accusative cases; (2) they often assumed different forms for stressed and unstressed position; (3) they replaced *vester* with *voster*, by analogy to *noster*; (4) they substituted the genitive plural demonstrative *illoru(m)* in some regions, in others *ipsoru(m)*, for third person plural *suus* and its related forms.

(c) The demonstrative pronouns of Vulgar Latin differed from those of Classical Latin in the following respects: (1) they were very often reinforced by prefixation (*ecce-, *eccu- *accu-*) or combination; (2) they did not maintain the schema *hic, iste, ille*, the first element of which survived only in such expressions as *ecce hic* (> Fr. *ici*), *hoc anno* (> Sp. *hogaño*), *hac hora* (> Sp. *ahora*), and the second and third as markers of proximity and remoteness, respectively, of person, time, and space; (3) *is* survived only in a few, rare expressions, such as *id ipsu* (> It. *desso*); (4) *idem* never came into use, both identity and self being expressed by *metipse, *metipsimu* (> Pr. *mezeis*, Sp. *mismo*).

(d) The relative and interrogative pronouns of Classical Latin were gradually reduced in Vulgar Latin to the nominative *qui*, dative *cui*, and accusative *quem*, all three signifying masculine and feminine gender, singular and plural number; and to the neuter *qued* (< *quid*). The genitive *cuius* survived as *cuiu, -a, -os, -as* in some regions; in others, it was replaced by the periphrasis *de unde* (> Fr. *dont*). *Qualis* replaced *qui* in some regions and, in others, prefixed by a demonstrative, was used concurrently as a reinforced form (*ille quale* > Fr. *lequel*, Sp. *el cual*). *Qui(s)na(m)* survived only in Lusitania.

(e) The indefinite pronouns of Vulgar Latin differed drastically from those of Classical Latin, in both form and meaning. *Alter* replaced *alius*, the latter surviving only in certain regions, as neuter *alid* (> OFr. *el*, OSp. *al*). *Omnis, quisque*, and *unusquisque* survived only in certain regions (It. *ogni*, Pr. *quecs, usquecs*, OSd. *kis, uniskis*), and were otherwise rivaled or replaced by (1) the Greek loan word *cata* reinforced by *unus* and its related forms (*cata unu* > Sp. *cada uno*), and (2) the hybrid *cascunu* (< *catunu* X *quisque*) (> Fr. *chacun*, It. *ciascuno*). *Quidam* was replaced by *certu, certanu* (> It. *certo*, Sp. *cierto*; Fr. *certain*). *Aliquis* survived as *aliquem, aliquid, aliquod* (> Sp. *alguien*, OFr. *alques* [with adverbial *-s*], Sp. *algo*), which were rivaled by the pleonastic *alicunus* (< *aliquis unus*) and its related forms (*alicunu* > Fr. *aucun*, It. *alcuno*, Sp. *alguno*); the negative meaning of Fr. *aucun* is a strictly modern development. Of the negatives *nemo* and *nihil*, only the former survived, albeit sporadically (OIt. *nimo,* Rm. *nime, nimenĭ*); it was rivaled by (1) *nullus* and its related forms (*nullu* > Fr. *nul,* OIt. *nullo,* OSp. *nullo*), (2) periphrases such as *nec unu* (> OFr. *negun,* Sp. *ninguno*) and *nec ipsu unu* (> It. *nessuno*), (3) (*homine*) *natu* (X *qui*) > OSp. *nadi* (X *alguien*) > MSp. *nadie. Nihil* was replaced by (1) *rem* (> Fr. *rien*) or *nata* (> Sp. *nada*) of *rem nata,* (2) such periphrases as *ne mica* (> Rm. *nimic*) and *nec ente* (> It. *niente*). Finally, *homo* (> Fr. *on*) was used in certain regions as an impersonal subject pronoun.

(f) The adverbs *inde, ibi* (> Fr. *en, y;* It. *ne;* OSp. *i, y*) assumed pronominal functions.

## The Pronoun in Gallo-Romance

87. (a) The personal pronouns of Vulgar Latin (see 86(*a*), above) developed in Old French as a stressed and unstressed series governed by case and gender, as well as person and number. In Modern French, personal subject pronouns became prefixed to their respective verb forms, occupying an invariably unstressed position: *je, tu, il* (< *illi* < *ille* X *qui*), *elle, nous, vous, ils* (OFr. *il* + anal. *-s*), *elles.* This development was accompanied by the following concomitants: (1) OFr. stressed *jo, gié* were lost; (2) *nous, vous* (< *nos, vos*) failed to become *\*neus, \*veus,* as they would have been expected to do in stressed position. (OFr. *el* [see par. 86(*a*), above] did not survive.) Accusative and dative pronouns remained identical in the first and second persons, and the reflexive: unstressed *me, te, se, nous, vous,* and stressed *moi, toi, soi, nous, vous.* The accusative third person forms evolved as unstressed *le, la, les,* and stressed *lui, elle, eux* (< *eus* < *els* < *illos*), *elles,* the corresponding dative forms being the invariable *lui, leur.* Old French distinguished between the masculine and feminine singular of the dative and accusative in stressed position (*lui* vs. *li*), but used *li* for both genders in the corresponding unstressed position.

(b) The personal pronouns of Vulgar Latin (see par. 86(*a*), above) developed in Old Provençal as a stressed and unstressed series governed by case and gender, as well as person and number: (Stressed) (1) nom. *eu, ieu;* dat. *mi, me;* acc. *me, mi;* nom., dat., acc. *nos;* (2) nom. *tu,* dat. *ti, te;* acc. *te, ti;* nom., dat., acc. *vos;* (3) (masc.) nom. *el,* dat. *lui,* acc. *lui;* nom. *il;* dat. *lor, els;* acc. *els, lor;* (fem.) nom. *ela;* dat. *lei, leis;* acc. *ela, lei, leis;* nom. *elas;* dat. *lor, elas;* acc. *elas, lor;* (4) (refl.) dat. *si, se;* acc. *se, si.* (Unstressed) (1) dat. *mi, me;* acc. *me, mi;* dat., acc. *nos;* (2) dat. *ti, te;* acc. *te, ti;* dat., acc. *vos;* (3) (masc.) dat. *li,* acc. *lo,* dat.*lor,* acc. *los;* (fem.) dat. *li,* acc., *la,* dat. *lor,* acc. *las;* (4) (refl.) dat. *si, se;* acc. *se, si.* Especially noteworthy is the concurrence of dative and accusative forms in stressed and unstressed positions. The origin of *-s* in *leis* is obscure. Finally, *lei, leis* had diphthongized variants (*liei, lieis*).

(c) The possessive pronouns of Vulgar Latin (see par. 86(b), above) developed in Old French as several stressed and one unstressed series governed by case and gender, as well as person and number. The failure to distinguish between possessive pronoun and adjective in Vulgar Latin persisted in Old French only insofar as the stressed forms were concerned, the unstressed forms performing an exclusively adjectival function. In Modern French, the stressed forms, reinforced by the definite article, serve as absolute pronouns. Beginning with the thirteenth and fourteenth century, respectively, all masculine singulars and all feminine singulars of the stressed forms became analogues of *mien* (< *meum*): *tuen, suen* (< *tuum, suum*) > *tien, sien; moie* (< *meie* < *\*męa* [the *e* of *\*męa* having closed to dissimilate itself from final *a*]), *toe, soe* (< *tuam, suam*) > *mienne, tienne, sienne.* The masculine unstressed forms *tes, ses, ti, si* are analogues of *mes* (< *\*mos* < *\*meos* < *meus*), *mi* (< *mei*). The feminine unstressed forms (*ma, mes; ta, tes; sa, ses*) are phonetic reductions of their stressed counterparts in proclitic position (*mea* > *ma, meas* > *mes,* etc.). The possessive plurals in Modern French consist of (1) the pronouns *le nôtre, la nôtre, les nôtres* (OFr. *nostre, nostre, nostres*), *le vôtre, la vôtre, les vôtres* (OFr. *vostre, vostre, vostres*), *le leur, la leur, les leurs* (OFr. *lor* [*lour, leur*] < *illoru*), and (2) the adjectives *notre, nos* (OFr. *noz*), *votre, vos* (OFr. *voz*), *leur, leurs.* The *-s* of *leurs* is analogical. The neuter forms of Old French possessives (*mien, tien, sien*) did not survive.

(d) The possessive pronouns of Vulgar Latin (see par. 86(b), above) developed in Old Provençal as several stressed and one unstressed series governed by case and gender, as well as person and number. OPr. stressed *teus* (*tieus*), *seus* (*sieus*) and their related forms are analogues of *meus, mieus* (< *meus*). The variants of stressed *mia, toa, soa,* etc., namely, *mieua, tieua, sieua,* are analogues of the corresponding masculine forms. The masculine singular accusatives of the unstressed series are as follows: *mo* (*mon*), *to* (*ton*), *so* (*son*), etc. *Ma* of the corresponding feminine forms is an analogue of *ta, sa.* Plural possessives are as follows: *nostre, nostres, nostra, nostras; vostre, vostres, vostra, vostras; lor, lur* (rarely, *lors, lurs,* with analogical *-s*). Accompanied by their respective definite articles, stressed forms may be used as absolute pronouns or as possessive adjectives (*lo mieus, la mia,* etc.). Unstressed forms invariably perform an adjectival function. In Modern Provençal, *lur* is most often replaced by *so, sa.* The anomalous *mi* in such fixed expressions as *midons, sidons* (*ma dame, sa dame*) has been explained as a vestige of the nominative-vocative (*mi dominus*).

(e) The demonstrative pronouns of Vulgar Latin (see par. 86(c), above) developed in Old French as systemic, declined composites of prefix *ecce and iste* or *ille,* and as sporadic, undeclined composites of prefix *ecce* and *hoc.* Although Old French had made no distinction between demonstrative adjective and pronoun, *ecce iste* and *ecce ille* evolved in Modern French as adjective and pronoun, respectively, the latter reinforced by appended *-ci* or *-là*, to indicate proximity or distance of person, time, or space. Of the *ecce iste* forms, only the masculine and feminine accusatives *ce(t)*, *cette*, *ces* (OFr. *cest, ceste, cez*) survived, the corresponding nominatives (distinctively, *cist*), the neuter (*cest*), and the datives (*cestui, cestei*) having fallen into disuse. Of the *ecce ille* forms, only the masculine dative singular and accusative plural *celui*, *ceux* (OFr. *celui; cels, ceus*), reinforced by *-ci* or *-là*, and the feminine accusatives *celle*, *celles* (OFr. *cele, celes*), similarly reinforced by *-ci* or *-là*, survived, the masculine and feminine nominatives (distinctively, *cil*), the masculine accusative and the neuter (both *cel*), and the feminine dative (*celei*) having fallen into disuse. The Old French demonstratives had concurrent variants in *i-* (*icist, icest, icil, icel,* etc.), whose initial sound is a phonological anomaly, often explained as a vestige of prefixed *hic* or *ibi*. *Ecce hoc* is the etymon of *ce* (< *ço*), *ceci* (*ce-ci*), and *cela* (*ce-là*).

(f) The demonstrative pronouns of Vulgar Latin (see par. 86(*c*), above) developed in Old Provençal as systemic, declined derivatives of (1) *iste* and its related forms, and (2) *ecce*, or *\*accu* plus *iste* or *ille* and the latter's related forms; and as sporadic, undeclined composites of *ecce* (*\*accu-*) *hoc*: (*iste*, etc.) *est, est, ist, estz; esta, estas*; (*ecce iste*, etc.) *cest, cest, cist, cestz, cesta* (occasional intrusion of masculine; thus, *cista*), *cestas*; (*ecce ille*, etc.) *cel, cel, cil, cels, cela, celas*; (*accu ille*, etc.) *aquel, aquel, aquil, aquels, aquela, aquelas*; (*ecce, accu hoc*) *so, aisso*.

(g) The interrogative and relative pronouns of Vulgar Latin (see par. 86(*d*), above) developed in Old French as follows: (interrogative) masculine and feminine nominative *qui*, dative and accusative *cui*, neuter nominative-accusative *quei* > *quoi* (stressed) and *que* (unstressed); (relative) masculine and feminine nominative *qui*, dative *cui*, and accusative *cui*, *que*. *Qualis*, which survived as *quels* and its related forms, served as an interrogative adjective and, reinforced by a prefixed article (*lequels*, etc.), as an interrogative or relative pronoun. In Modern French, *cui* has fused with *qui*.

(h) The interrogative and relative pronouns of Vulgar Latin (see par. 86(*d*), above) developed in Old Provençal as follows: (interrogative) masculine and feminine nominative *qui*, *que*, dative *cui*, and accusative *cui*, *que*. *Qualis*, which survived as *quals* and its related forms, served as an interrogative adjective and, reinforced by a prefixed article (*lo quals*, etc.), as an interrogative or relative pronoun. Peculiar to Old Provençal were *quina*, *quinha* (< *\*quiniam*), *quinas*, *quinhas*, and their masculine analogues *quin*, *quinh*, *quins*, *quinhs*, which could serve as interrogative adjectives or pronouns, and as relative pronouns.

(i) The indefinite pronouns of Vulgar Latin (see par. 86(*e*), above) developed in Old French as follows: *aliquid* + adverbial -*s* > *alques*; *aliquis unus* > *\*alicunus* > *alcuns, aucuns*, accusative *aucun*, etc.; *ali(u)d* > *el*; *alter* > *altre, autre*, dative *autrui*, etc.; *cata unus* > *\*caduns* > *cheüns*, accusative *cheün*, etc.; *cata unus* X *quisque* > *\*cascuns* > *chascuns*, accusative *chascun*, etc.; *homo* > *on*; *multu, -i, -os, -as* > *molt* (*mout*), *moltz* (*mouts*), *moltes* (*moutes*); *\*metipsimu* > *medesme* > *meesme* > *même*; *nec unus* > *neguns*, accusative *negun*; *nullus* > *nuls*, accusative *nul*, etc.; *\*pluriores* X *plus* > *\*plusiores* > *plusiors*; *paucu* > *pou* > *peu*; *rem* (*nata*) > *rien*; *talis* > *tels*, accusative *tel*, etc.; *tantus, -a, -u*, etc. > *tanz, tante, tant*, etc.; *totus* (*\*tottu*?), *-i, -os, -a, -as* > *toz, tot, tuit, toz, tote, totes*. In Modern French, *aucun* with its original, positive meaning, is replaced by *quelqu'un* and, having assumed negative meaning, replaces *negun, nesun; alques* is replaced by *quelque chose, un peu; el* is replaced by *autre chose*; and *molt* (*mout*) and its related forms are replaced by *beaucoup*.

(j) The indefinite pronouns of Vulgar Latin (see par. 85(*e*), above), developed in Old Provençal as follows: *aliquis unus* > *\*alcunus* > *alcus*, accusative *alcun*, etc.; *aliquid* + adverbial -*s* > *alques*; *ali(u)d* + adverbial -*s* > *als*, accusative *al, au; alter* > *altre, autre*, dative *autrui*, etc.; *cata unus* > *\*cadauns* > *cadaïns*, accusative *cadaïn*, etc.; *cata unus* X *quisque* > *\*cascuns* > *cascus*, accusative *cascun*, etc.; *multu* > *molt, mont, mot; \*metipse* > *mezeis; nec unus* > *negus*, accusative *negun, neün, degun* (by dissimilation); *nullus* > *nuls*, accusative *nul*, etc.; *omnis* > *om, hom, homs; quisque, unusquisque* > *quecs, usquecs*, accusatives *quec, usquec*, etc.; *res* > *re, res*, 'anybody, nobody' vs. OFr. 'anything, nothing'; *talis, tals*, accusative *tal*, etc. (also composites, such as *aitals, altretals*, and hybrids, such as *aitretals*); *tantu* > *tant, tam, ta*, etc. (also composites, such as *aitan, atretant*); *totus* (*\*tottus*?) *totz*, accusative *tot*, etc.

(k) The adverbial pronouns of Vulgar Latin, *inde* and *ibi* (see par. 86(*f*), above), survived in French and Provençal as *en, y* and *en* (*ne*), *i*, respectively.

*The Pronoun in Ibero-Romance*

88. (a) The personal pronouns of Vulgar Latin (see par. 86(*a*), above) developed in Spanish as a stressed and an unstressed series, governed by case and gender, as well as person and number: (Stressed) (1) Nominative *yo* (< *\*eo* < *ego*) and dative-accusative (post-prepositional) *mí* (< *mihi*), also OSp. *mive*, by analogy to *tive* (see below, this paragraph); nominative and dative-accusative (post-prepositional) *nosotros, -as* (< *nos alteros, -as*), originally emphatic variants of OSp. *nos*, which became normative, the latter form surviving as an archaism used in elevated and formulaic language, e.g.,

*Venga a nos el tu reino*; pleonastic *conmigo* and OSp. *connusco* (< *cum mecum, cum noscum*), the unetymological, stressed *i* and *u* being explained, respectively, as an analogue of *mí*, and a dissimilation from initial *o*. (2) Nominative *tú* and dative-accusative (post-prepositional) *ti*, by analogy to *mí*, also OSp. *tive* < *tĭbī*, with inflected stressed vowel due to final *ī*; nominative and dative-accusative (post-prepositional) *vosotros, -as* (< *vos alteros, -as*), originally emphatic variants of OSp. *vos* (cf. *nosotros, -as*, above, this paragraph); pleonastic *contigo* and OSp. *convusco* (< *cum tecum, cum voscum*), cf. *conmigo*, OSp. *connusco*, above, this paragraph. (3) Nominative and dative-accusative (post-prepositional) *él* (< OSp. *el[le], el[li]* < *ille*, *ille* X *qui*), *ella* (< *illa*), *ello* (< *illu[d]*); *usted* (< *vuestra merced*), which replaced *vos* as a pronoun of respect; and plurals *ellos, ellas, ustedes*. (4) Reflexive, dative-accusative (post-prepositional) *sí*, analogous to *mí*, which remains unchanged in the plural; pleonastic *consigo* (< *cum secum*), cf. *conmigo, contigo*, above, this paragraph. (Unstressed) (1) Dative-accusative *me, nos*. (2) Dative-accusative *te, (v)os* (the loss of the *v-* of *vos* occurred first in enclitic position with imperatives [*levantadvos* > *levantados* > *levantaos*], and later became generalized in proclitic, as well as enclitic, position). (3) Dative *le, les* (< [*il*]*li*, [*il*]*lis*, with loss of first syllable due to unstressed position), and accusative *lo(s), la(s)* (< [*il*]*los*, [*il*]*las*), with dative forms often used as accusatives (*leísmo*), and accusative *la, las* as datives (*laísmo*). The combination *illi illu* developed as follows: *illi illu* > *gello* (g=[dž]) > *gelo* (g=[ž]), with analogical reduction of *ll* to *l* > *se lo*, through identification of *ge* with reflexive *se*, which occurred in the same type of syntagma, and was similarly pronounced. The plural construction *illis illu* also became *se lo*, by analogy to the singular. In Early Old Spanish, unstressed pronouns ending in *-e*, in enclitic position with words ending in a vowel, lost their *-e*, and the unsupported consonants suffered the phonological consequences (*tengom* > *tengon*, *fu(i)stet* > *fusted*, *quem lo* > *quemblo*); by Late Old Spanish, final *-e* had been restored to avoid ambiguity, the apocopation of the third person pronouns being the most persistent. From Old Spanish through the Golden Age, enclitic pronouns often fused with verb forms through assimilation or metathesis (*serville=servirle, tornase=tornarse, dezildo=decirlo, dandos=dadnos*).

(b) The personal pronouns of Vulgar Latin (see par. 86(a), above) developed in Portuguese as a stressed and an unstressed series governed by case and gender, as well as person and number: (Stressed) (1) Nominative *eu* (< *\*eo* < *ego*), *nós*; dative-accusative (post-prepositional) *mim* (OPg. *mi*), with nasalization of *i* by initial *m*, *nós*; pleonastic *comigo, connosco* (OPg. *mego, comego* < *mecum, cum mecum*, also *migo, comigo*, analogues of *mi*; *nosco* < *noscum*). (2) Nominative *tu, vós*; dative-accusative (post-prepositional) *ti*, by

68

analogy to *mi, vós*; pleonastic *contigo, convosco* (OPg. *tego, contego < tecum, cum tecum*, also *tigo, contigo; vosco < voscum*). (3) Nominative *êle* (OPg. *el < ille*, final *e* falling because of proclisis), *ela* (< *illa*), and their plural analogues *êles* (OPg. *eis*), *elas*; dative-accusative (post-prepositional) *êle* (OPg. *el*), *ela*, OPg. *ello* (< *illu[d]*), and the analogous plurals *êles* (OPg. *eis*), *elas*. (4) Reflexive dative-accusative (post-prepositional) *si*, by analogy to *mi*, which remains unchanged in the plural; pleonastic *consigo* (OPg. *sego, consego < secum, cum secum*, also *sigo, consigo*). (Unstressed) (1) Dative-accusative *me, nos*. (2) Dative-accusative *te* (OPg. *che*), *vos*. (3) Dative *lhe* (< \**lhe[llo]* < \**[el]li ello < illi illu*) (OPg. *li < illi*), and analogical *lhes* (OPg. *lis < illis*); accusative *o, a, os, as* (the *l* of \**[el]lo, -a*, etc., fell when the pronouns were attached to verb forms or other pronouns ending in a vowel, e.g., *\*vejo-lo > vejo-o*, and the resultant *o, a*, etc., became generalized), *-lo, -la, -los, -las* (through the assimilation of final *r, s,* and *z* of verbs forms, and *s* of pronouns, to the *l* of attached \**[el]lo, -a*, etc.; e.g., \**fazer-lo > fazê-lo*), *-no, -na, -nos, -nas* (through the assimilation of the *l* of attached \**[el]lo, -a*, etc., to final *n* of verb forms; e.g., \**guardan-lo > \*guardan-no > guardam* [ʊ̃]-*no*). 4) Reflexive, dative-accusative *se* (OPg. *xe*, by analogy to *xo < \*se lo*).

(c) The personal pronouns of Vulgar Latin (see par. 86(*a*), above) developed in Catalan as a stressed and an unstressed series governed by case and gender, as well as person and number: (Stressed) (1) Nominative *jo* (< \**eo < ego*), *nosaltres* (< *nos alteros, -as*), and dative-accusative (post-prepositional) *mi, nosaltres*. (2) Nominative *tu, vós* (sing.), *vosaltres* (< *vos alteros, -as*), and dative-accusative (post-prepositional) *tu* (OCt. *ti*, by analogy to *mi*), *vós, vosaltres*. (3) Nominative *ell* (< *ille*), *ella* (< *illa*), *ells* (< *illos*), *elles* (< *illas*), MCt. *vostè* (< *vostra mercè*), which replaces *vós* as pronoun of respect, and dative-accusative (post-prepositional) *ell* (< *illu*), *ella, ells, elles, vostès*. (4) Reflexive dative-accusative (post-prepositional) *si*, by analogy to *mi*. (Unstressed) (1) Dative-accusative *me, nos*, reduced to *'m, 'ns* after a verb form ending in a vowel other than *u*, reduced to *m'* before a verb form beginning with a vowel or *h*, and converted to *em, ens* (supportive *e + 'm, 'ns*) before a verb form beginning with a consonant (*escolta'm, escolteu-me, m'inspira, em respecta*). (2) Dative-accusative *te* (cf. *me*, above, this paragraph), *vos*, the latter reduced to *us* in proclitic position (*us creiem*). (3) Dative *li* (< *[il]li*), *los* (< *[il]los*), the latter reduced to *'ls* after a verb form ending in a vowel other than *u*, and converted to *els* (supportive *e + 'ls*) before a verb form beginning with a consonant; accusative *lo, la, los, les, ho* (< *[il]lu, -a, -os, -as, hoc*), with the following modifications: *lo* and *la* elide to *l'* before a verb form beginning with a vowel or *h*; *lo* is reduced to *'l* after a verb form ending in a vowel other than *u*, and converts to *el* (supportive *e* + '*l*) before a verb form beginning with a consonant; *los* is reduced to '*ls* after a verb form ending in a vowel other than *u*, and converts to *els* before a verb form beginning with a consonant. (4) Reflexive dative-accusative *se* (cf. *me*, above, this paragraph).

(d) The possessive pronouns of Vulgar Latin (see par. 86(*b*), above) developed in Spanish in their accusative forms only, as nominative-accusative stressed forms, the unstressed forms (proclitic adjectives) being etymological apocopations in the feminine, and analogical apocopations in the masculine: (Pronouns) (1) (*el*) *mío* (OSp., also *mio*) < *\*mieo* < *měu*; (*la*) *mía* (< *\*mẹa*, [see par. 87(*c*), above]), and their plurals (*los*) *míos*, (*las*) *mías*; (*el*) *nuestro* (< *nostru*), (*la*) *nuestra* (< *nostra*), and their plurals (*los*) *nuestros*, (*las*) *nuestras*. (2) (*el*) *tuyo* (OSp. *to*), (*la*) *tuya* (OSp, *tua*, by dissimilation of the stressed *o* of *\*toa* < *tŭa* from final *a*), the feminine by analogy to the relative genitive *cuia*, and the masculine by analogy to the feminine, and their plurals (*los*) *tuyos*, (*las*) *tuyas*; (*el*) *vuestro* (< *vostru*), (*la*) *vuestra* (< *vostra*), and their plurals (*los*) *vuestros*, (*las*) *vuestras*. (3) (*el*) *suyo*, (*la*) *suya* (cf. *tuyo*, *tuya*, directly above), and their plurals (*los*) *suyos*, (*las*) *suyas*. (Adjectives) (1) *mi* (OSp., also *mío*, *mio*, for the masculine, and *míe* final *a* assimilating itself to stressed *i* for the feminine), the apocopation occurring etymologically in the feminine and analogically in the masculine, and plural *mis*; *nuestro*, -*a*, and their plurals *nuestros*, -*as* (cf. the corresponding pronouns, directly above). (2) *tu* (OSp. also *to* for the masculine, *tue* for the feminine [cf. the corresponding pronoun, directly above], the masculine being analogical to the etymological feminine), and its plural *tus*; *vuestro*, -*a* and their plurals *vuestros*, -*as* (cf. the corresponding pronouns, directly above) ; (3) *su* (cf. *tu*, directly above) and its plural *sus*.

(e) The possessive pronouns of Vulgar Latin (see par. 86(*b*), above) developed in Portuguese as stressed forms, performing also as adjectives: (Pronouns and Adjectives) (1) (*o*) *meu* (< *meu*, also OPg. *mou*), (*a*)*minha* (< *\*mẹa* [see par. 87(*c*), above]), and their plurals (*os*) *meus*, (*as*) *minhas*; (*o*) *nosso*, (*a*) *nossa* (< *\*nossu*, -*a*, also OPg. *nostro* [*nostru*], in *nostro Senhor*), and their plurals (*os*) *nossos*, (*as*) *nossas*. (2) (*o*) *teu*, by analogy to *meu* (OPg., also *tou*), (*a*) *tua* (< *\*toa*, stressed *o* in hiatus becoming *u*), and their plurals (*os*) *teus*, (*as*) *tuas*; (*o*) *vosso*, (*a*) *vossa* (< *\*vossu*, -*a*) and their plurals (*os*) *vossos*, (*as*) *vossas*. (3) (*o*) *seu*, by analogy to *meu* (OPg., also *sou*), (*a*) *sua* (cf. *tua*, directly above), and their plurals (*os*) *seus*, (*as*) *suas*.

(f) The possessive pronouns of Vulgar Latin (see par. 86(*b*), above) developed in Catalan as a stressed series, the proclitic, unstressed singulars of Old and Classical Catalan (*mon*, *ton*, *son*, etc.) having become obsolete: (Pronouns and adjectives) (1) (*el*) *meu*, (*la*) *meva* (OCt. *mia*), the feminine being an analogue of the masculine, and their plurals *(els) meus, (les) meves; (el) nostre, (la) nostra (< nostru, -a)*, and their plural *(els, les) nostres.* (2) *(el) teu*, by analogy to *meu, (la) teva* (cf. *meva*, directly above), and their plurals *(els) teus, (les) teves; (el) vostre, (la) vostra (< vostru, -a)* and their plural *(els, les) vostres.* (3) *(el) seu*, by analogy to *meu, (la) seva* (cf. *meva*, directly above), *llur (< [i]lloru)*, and their plurals *(els) seus, (les) seves, llurs.*

(g) The demonstrative pronouns of Vulgar Latin (see par. 86 *(c)*, above) developed in Spanish as follows: nominative-accusative (originally nominative) *este, -a, -o < iste, -a, -u[d]* (OSp., also *aqueste, -a, -o < \*ac[cu] iste, -a, -u[d]*), *ese, -a, -o < ipse, -a, -u* (OSp., also *aquese, -a, -o), aquel, -lla, -llo < \*ac(cu) il(le), illa, illu(d)*; their nominative-accusative (originally accusative) plurals *estos, -as, esos, -as, aquellos, -as. Este, ese, acquel* and their related forms assumed the functions of Classical Latin *hoc, iste, ille* and their related forms, respectively. The demonstratives perform as adjectives or pronouns, the latter being distinguished from the former, when necessary for clarity, by a written accent over stressed *e (éste, ése, aquél, etc.).* The pronoun of self developed as *mismo, -a,* etc. < *\*meismo, -a,* etc. < *\*medipsi(ssi)mu, -a,* etc.

(h) The demonstrative pronouns of Vulgar Latin (see par. 86 *(c)*, above) developed in Portuguese as follows: nominative-accusative (originally nominative) *êste, -a, -o* (OPg. *isto) < iste, -a -u*(d) (OPg., also *aqueste, -a -o < \*ac[cu] iste, -a, -o), êsse, -a, -o < ipse, -a, -u* (OPg., also *aquesse, -a, -o), aquele* (OPg. *aquel), -a, -o < \*ac(cu) ille, -a, -u(d)*, and the nominative-accusative, analogical plurals, *êstes, -as, êsses, -as, aqueles* (OPg. *aqueis), -as. Êste, êsse, aquele* and their related forms assumed the functions of Classical Latin *hoc, iste, ille*, respectively. The demonstratives perform as adjectives or pronouns, the distinction between the two grammatical categories being syntactic-contextual in nature. The pronoun of self developed as *mesmo, -a,* etc. < *meesmo, -a,* etc. < *\*medips(iss)imu, -a,* etc.

(i) The demonstrative pronouns of Vulgar Latin (see par. 86 *(c)*, above) developed in Catalan as follows: nominative-accusative (originally nominative) *aquest, -a < \*ac(cu) iste, -a* (OCt. *est, -a), aqueix, -a < \*ac(cu) ipse, -a* (OCt. *eix, -a), aquell, -a < \*ac(cu) ille, -a,* their plurals *aquests, -es, aqueixos, -es, aquells, -es,* and the neuters *açó, aixó, allò,* and OCt. *ço.* The pronunciation of *aquests* was simplified to *aque(s)ts*, and, by analogy, the singular *aquest* came to be pronounced *aque(s)t*, except when followed by a vowel. *Aquest, aqueix, aquell* and their related forms assumed the functions of Classical Latin *hoc, iste, ille* and their related forms, respectively, but in modern usage the functions of *aqueix* are being totally usurped by *aquest,* and the former is rapidly becoming obsolete. The demonstratives perform as adjectives or pronouns, the distinction between the two grammatical categories being of a syntactic-contextual nature. The pronoun of self developed as *mateix, -a*, etc. < *\*met-tipsu, -a*, etc.

(j) The relative and interrogative pronouns of Vulgar Latin (see par. 86(*d*), above) developed in Spanish as follows: (Pronouns) Nominative-accusative *que* < *quid* became the invariable relative for persons and things. Nominative-accusative *quien* < *quem* and its analogical plural *quienes* (OSp. invariable *quien, qui*) became alternate relatives for persons, especially after prepositions. Nominative-accusative *el, la cual* < *quale(m)*, *los, las cuales* < *quales* became alternate relatives for *que* and *quien*, especially to avoid ambiguity. *Qué, quién, -es, cuál, -es* became interrogative pronouns. (Adjectives) *Cuyo, -a*, etc. <*cuiu, -a*, etc.. became relative possessive adjectives, and *qué* came to be used adjectivally in questions and exclamations.

(k) The relative and interrogative pronouns of Vulgar Latin (see par. 86(*d*), above) developed in Catalan as follows: (Pronouns) Nominative-accusative *que* < *quid* became the normative relative for persons and things; in the literary language, it is occasionally replaced by *qui* for persons in the nominative, to avoid ambiguity; after prepositions, it is replaced by *què* for things and *qui* for people, with *el, la qual* < *quale(m)*, and *els, les quals* < *quales*, as weak, literary substitutes.

(l) The relative and interrogative pronouns of Vulgar Latin (see par. 86(*d*), above) developed in Portuguese as follows: (Pronouns) Nominative-accusative *que* < *quid* became the invariable relative for persons and things. Nominative-accusative *quem* < *quem* became an alternate relative for persons, especially after prepositions. Nominative-accusative *o, a qual* < *quale(m)*, *os, as quais* < *quales* became alternate relatives for *que* and *quem*, especially to avoid ambiguity. *Que, quem, qual, quais* became interrogative pronouns. (Adjectives) *Cujo, -a*, etc. < *cuiu, -a*, etc. became relative possessive adjectives, and *que* came to be used adjectivally in questions and exclamations. *El qual* and its related forms may replace *que* in non-restrictive clauses only, to avoid ambiguity. *Qui (quis)* and *que* became the normative interrogative pronouns for people and things, respectively, and 'which' was expressed by a declension built on *quinam*: *quin, quins, quina, quines*. (Adjectives) *Quin* and its related forms became interrogative adjectives. *El qual* and its related forms became relative adjectives, which have fallen into disuse.

(m) The indefinite pronouns of Vulgar Latin (see par. 86(*e*), above) developed in Spanish as follows: OSp. *al* < *ali(u)d*; *algo* < *aliquod*; *alguien* < *aliquem* X *quien*; *alguno, -a*, etc. < *\*alcunu, -a*, etc. < *aliqu(em) unu, -a*, etc.; *cada uno, -a*, < *cata unu, -a*; *cierto, -a*, etc. < *certu, -a*, etc.; *cualquiera* < *\*qual(em) quaerat*; *cuanto, -a*, etc. < *quantu, -a*, etc.; *mucho, -a*, etc. < *multu, -a*, etc.; *nada* < *(rem) nata; nadie* < *(omne) nado* X *quien* (OSp., also *nadi, nadien, naide*); *ninguno, -a*, etc. < *nec unu, -a*, etc. X *non*; OSp. *nul, nulla* < *nul(lu)*,

-a; *otro, -a,* etc. < *alteru, -a,* etc.; (OSp. also *otri, otrie* < *alteru* X
*qui, quien*); *poco, -a,* etc. < *paucu, -a,* etc.; *quienquiera* < *\*quem
quaerat*; *tanto, -a,* etc. < *tantu, -a,* etc.; *todo, -a,* etc. < *totu, -a,* etc.,
*uno, -a,* etc. < *unu, -a,* etc. The indefinites also perform as adjectives,
with the following exceptions: *algo, alguien, nada, nadie, quienquiera.*
The indefinite adjectives *alguno, ninguno,* and *uno* are apocopated
in the masculine singular only (*algún, ningún, un*), whereas *cualquiera* is apocopated in both the masculine and feminine singular
(*cualquier*).

(n) The indefinite pronouns of Vulgar Latin (see par. 86(*e*),
above) developed in Catalan as follows: *algú, algun, -a,* etc. < *\*alcunu, alcunu, -a,* etc. < *aliqu*(*em*) *unu, unu, -a* etc.; *altre, -a, -es*
< *alteru, -a, -os, -as; altri* < *altrui; cada u, cadascú, cadascún* < *cata
u*(*nu*), *cata* (*qui*)*sq*(*ue*) *u*(*nu*); *cap* < *\*capu; hom* < *homo; ningú*
(OCt. *negú, negun, nengú, nengun*) < *ne*(*c*) *unu* X *non*; *qualsevol* <
*\*quale se volet, qualsevulla* < *\*quale se voleat; quelcom* < *\*quale
quod homo; res,* OCt. *re* < *res, rem; tal, -s* < *tale, tales; tot, tot, -a*
< *totu, totu, -a; tothom* < *totu homo; un, -a* < *unu, -a.* The declinable
pronouns also perform as adjectives, with the feminines and plurals
indicated, except that the plurals of *qualsevol, qualsevulla* are purely
orthographic (*qualssevol, qualssevulla*).

(o) The indefinite pronouns of Vulgar Latin (see par. 86(*e*),
above) developed in Portuguese as follows: OPg. *al* < *ali*(*u*)*d; algo*
< *aliquod; alguém* < *aliquem* X *quem; algum, -a,* etc. < *\*alcunu, -a,*
etc. < *aliqu*(*em*) *unu, -a* etc.; *cada um, -a,* etc. < *cata unu, -a,* etc.;
OPg. *homem, ome* < *homine, homo; nada* < (*em*) *nata;* OPg.
*nenguem* < *ne*(*c*) *quem*; OPg. *nẽ hum, -a,* etc., OPg. *nengum, ningum,
-a,* etc., *nenhum, -a,* etc. < *ne*(*c*) *unu -a,* etc.; *ninguém,* by analogy
to *alguém*; OPg. *nulho* (borrowed from OSp. *nullo* < *nullu*); *outro-a,*
etc. < *alteru, -a,* etc.; OPg. *rem* < *rem; tal, tais* < *tale, tales; tudo*
< *totu; uns, umas* < *unos, -as.* The declinable pronouns also perform
as adjectives, *cada* of *cada um, -a* serving the same purpose. The
declinable adjective *todo* replaces the invariable *tudo.* The *-m-* of *uma*
and its derivatives intrudes normatively between stressed *u* and
final *a.*

(p) The adverbial pronouns of Vulgar Latin (see par. 86(*f*),
above) developed in Ibero-Romance as follows: *hic, ibi* > OSp. *i, y,*
OPg. *hi, i, y,* Cat. *hi* (OCt. *hic*); *inde* > OSp. *en, end, ende,* Cat. *en*
(*ne*).

## The Pronoun in Rheto-Romance

89. (a) The personal pronouns of Vulgar Latin (see par. 86(*a*),
above), with the exception of the reflexive, survived in Surselvan
as stressed forms only: (1) Nominative *jeu* < *\*eo* < *ego,* accusative
*mei* < *me,* dative (*a*) *mi* < *mi* < *mihi,* and nominative-accusative-

dative *nus* (*a nus*) < *nos*; (2) Nominative *ti* < *tu*, accusative *tei* < *te*, dative (*a*) *ti* (by analogy to *mi*), and nominative-accusative-dative *vus* (*a vus*) < *vos*; (3) Nominative-accusative-dative *el* (*ad el*) < *illu* (also *agli* < *a*[*d*] [*i*]*lli*), *ella* (*ad ella*) < *illa*, their plurals *els*, *ellas* (< *illos*, -*as*), and neuter-nominative *igl* (before vowels), *ei* (before consonants), borrowed from the Italian and used in impersonal expressions; (4) Reflexive *sei*, (*a sei*) < *se*, also unstressed *se*.

(b) The possessive pronouns of Vulgar Latin (see par. 86(*b*), above) survived in Surselvan as stressed pronoun-adjectives, the pronoun being marked by a preceding definite article, except when serving as a predicate: (1) (*il*) *miu*, (*la*) *mia*, (*ils*) *mes*, (*las*) *mias* (< *meu*, -*a*, *meos*, -*as*); (*il*) *nies* (< *\*nossu*, see par. 24, above), (*la*) *nossa*, (*ils*) *nos*, (*las*) *nossas* (< *\*nossu*, -*a*, *nossos*, -*as*); (2) (*il*) *tiu* (by analogy to *miu*), (*la*) *tia* (*tua*), (*ils*) *tes* (< *tuos*), (*las*) *tias* (< *tuas*); (*il*) *vies*, (*la*) *vossa*, (*ils*) *vos*, (*las*) *vossas* (< *\*vossu*, -*a*, *vossos*, -*as*); (3) (*il*) *siu* (by analogy to *miu*), (*la*) *sia* (< *sua*), (*ils*) *ses* (< *suos*), (*las*) *sias* (< *suas*); (*il*, *la*, *ils*, *las*) *lur* (< [*il*]*loru*). The masculine singular adjectives, like the corresponding nouns, are derived from the Latin nominative when they serve as predicates: (1) *mes*, *nos*; (2) *tes*, *vos*; (3) *ses* (*lur* does not perform the same function).

(c) The demonstrative pronouns of Vulgar Latin (see par. 86(*c*), above) developed in Surselvan as a dual system corresponding to CL (1) *hic*, *iste* and (2) *ille*; (1) *quest*, -*a quests*, -*as* (< *eccu iste*, -*a*, *istos*, -*as*), (2) *quel*, -*lla*, *quels*, -*llas* (< *eccu ille*, -*a*, *illos*, -*as*), *tschel*, -*lla*, *tschels*, -*llas* (< *ecce ille*, -*a*, *illos*, -*as*. The neuter demonstrative is *quei*. *Quei* replaces *quel*, and *tschei* replaces *tschel*, -*lla* as demonstrative adjectives.

(d) The relative and interrogative pronouns of Vulgar Latin (see par. 86(*d*), above) developed in Surselvan as follows: (Relative Pronouns) Nominative-accusative, originally accusative, *che* (< *que*[*m*]), which serves for masculine and feminine, singular and plural, and its alternates, used principally to avoid ambiguity: *il qual*, *ils quals* (<*il*[*lu*] *quale*, *il*[*lo*]*s quales*), and the analogous *la quala*, *las qualas*. (Interrogative Pronouns) Nominative-accusative, masculine-feminine *tgi* (< *qui*, *que*[*m*]) and neuter *tgei* (< *quid*); *qual*, -*a*, *quals*, -*llas*, and their alternates: *tgeinin*, -*a*, *tgeinins*, -*as* (<*quid unu*, -*a*, -*os*, -*as*). (Interrogative Adjectives) *Tgei*, *qual* and its related forms, *tgeinin* and its related forms.

(e) The indefinite pronouns of Vulgar Latin (see par. 86(*e*), above) developed in Surselvan as follows: *con*, -*ta*, etc. < *quantu*, -*a*, etc.; *enzatgei* < *\*unus non sapit quid*, *enzatgi* < *\*unus non sapit qui*; *ins* < *unus*; *negin* < *nec unu*; *nuot* (*nuotta*) < *ne*(*c*) (*g*)*ut*(*ta*); *scadin* < *cata unu* X *quisque*; *tut* < *\*tottu tuts*, *tuttas* < *\*tottos*, -*as*).

90. (a) The personal pronouns of Vulgar Latin (see par. 86(a), above) developed in Italian in a stressed and an unstressed series: (Stressed) (1) Nominative *io* < *\*eo* < *ego*, *noi* < *nos* (OIt., also *nui*, *noialtri* [< *nos alteri*]), and accusative (post-prepositional) *me*, *nos*, which combined with *cum* in *meco*, OIt. *nosco* (< *noscum* vs. CL *nobiscum*); (2) Nominative *tu*, *voi* < *vos* (OIt., also *vui*, *voialtri* [< *vos alteri*], and accusative (post-prepositional) *te*, *voi*, which combined with *cum* in *teco*, OIt. *vosco* (< *voscum* vs. CL *vobiscum*); (3) Nominative, principally *lui*, *lei*, *loro* < *illui*, *\*illei*, *illoru*, also *egli* < OIt. *elli* (< *ille* X *qui*) + vowel, *esso*, *-a*, etc. < *ipsu*, *-a*, etc. (OIt., also *ello*, *-a*, etc. < *illu*, *-a*, etc., pl. *egli* [cf. sing. *egli*], *ellino*, *eglino*, *elleno* [by analogy to the corresponding verbal endings]). Accusative, principally *lui*, *lei*, *loro*, also *esso*, *-a*, etc. (OIt., also *ello*, *-a*, etc.); (4) (Reflexive) Accusative (post-prepositional) *se*, which combined with *cum* to form *seco*. (Unstressed) (1) Nominative OIt. *i* < *i(o)*. Dative-accusative *mi* < *mi* < *mihi* and *ci* < *ecce hic*, by analogy to *vi* (see (2) following) (OIt., also *no*, *ne* < *nos*); (2) Dative-accusative *ti*, by analogy to *mi*, and *vi*, a reduction of *voi* which fused with *vi* < *ibi* (OIt., also *vè*); (3) Nominative OIt. (masc. sing.) *el*, *ei*, *e*, (fem. sing.) *la*, (masc. pl.) *gli*, *ei*, *e' i'* (fem. pl.) *le* (neut.) masculine forms or *la*. Dative *gli* < *illi* (OIt., also *li*, *igli*), *le* < *\*illei*, *loro* < Fr. *leur* < *illoru* (OIt. *li*, *lli*, *gli*). Accusative *lo*, *la* (< *illu*, *-a*), *li* < *illi* (OIt., also *gli*), *le* < *\*ille* < *illae*, also neut. *lo*, *la* (the latter now limited to fixed expressions). (4) (Reflexive) Dative-accusative *si*, by analogy to *mi*. In combinations of two unstressed pronouns, if the second is *ne* (see par. 90(k), below) or begins with *l*, the first opens its final *i* to *e*, possibly by analogy to *ello* < *illu* (*me lo*, *te ne*, *gliene*, *gliela*, etc.).

(b) The personal pronouns of Vulgar Latin (see par. 86(a), above) developed in Sardinian as a stressed and an unstressed series: (Stressed) (1) Nominative *(d)eo* (OSd. *e[g]o* ⪤ *ego*), dative (*a*) *mmie* < *mi* + paragogic *e*, accusative *me*, which combines with *cum* to form *kumme[g]us* (final *s* by analogy to OSd. *noscus*, directly below); nominative-accusative *nois* (OSd. *nos*) borrowed from the dative *nois* < *nobis*. *Nos* combined with *cum* to form OSd. *noscu*, *noscus* (final *s* to indicate plurality). *Noi[š]ateros* < *nobis alteros* often replaces *nois* as a more explicit form. (2) Nominative *tue* < *tu* + paragogic *e*, dative (*a*) *ttie* < *ti* + paragogic *e*, accusative *te*; nominative-accusative *bois* (OSd. *bos* < *vos*), borrowed from the dative *bois* < *vobis*. *Cum* combined with *te* to form *kunte[g]us* (cf. *kumme[g]us*, directly above). *Boi[š]ateros* (cf. *noi[š]ateros*, directly above) often replaces *bois* as a more explicit form. (3) Nominative-accusative (post-prepositional) *isse* (MSd., also *issu* < *ipsu*), *-a*, *issos*, *-as* < *ipse*, *-a*, *ipsos*, *-as*, genitive (also post-prepositional) *issoro* < *ipsoru*. In Old Sardinian, *cum* and prepositions ending in a vowel were followed, respectively, by *ille, -a, -u,* etc., and *'lle, -a, -u,* etc. (*cum ille, super 'lla, pro 'llos*). (4) (Reflexive) Accusative (post-prepositional) *se.* (Unstressed) (1) Dative-accusative *mi* (accusative *mi* through influence of the corresponding Italian form; OSd. accusative *me*), *nos.* (2) Dative-accusative *ti* (cf. *mi,* directly above), *bos.* (3) Dative *li, lis* (< *illi, illis*), accusative *lu, la, los, las* (< *illu, -a, illos, -as*). When followed by another pronoun, MSd. *li, lis* become *bi* < *ibi.* In enclitic position, when preceded by a consonant, the longer forms *ilu, ila, ili,* etc. are used, and, by analogy, *imi* replaces *mi.*

(c) The possessive pronouns of Vulgar Latin (see par. 86(*b*), above) developed in Italian as stressed forms, unstressed apocopations being old and/or colloquial: (1) (*il*) *mio, nostro,* (*la*) *mia, nostra,* (*i*) *miei, nostri,* (*le*) *mie, nostre* (< *meu, -a, mei, -e, nostru, -a, nostri, -e*), OIt., also such apocopations as *me, mi, ma,* the last becoming invariable (*madonna, madonne*). (2) (*il*) *tuo, vostro,* (*la*) *tua, vostra,* (*i*) *tuoi, vostri,* (*le*) *tue, vostre* (< *tuu, -a, tui, -e; vostru, -a, vostri, -e*). (3) (*il*) *suo, loro* (OIt. also *su*[*o*]), (*la*) *sua, loro* (OIt., also *su*[*a*]), (*i*) *suoi, loro* (OIt., also *su*[*oi*]), (*le*) *sue, loro* (OIt., also *su*[*e*]) < *suu, -a, sui, -e,* Fr. *leur* < *illoru.* In Late OIt., *mia, tua, sua* were used to express the plural of both genders.

(d) The possessive pronouns of Vulgar Latin (see par. 86(*b*), above) developed in Sardinian as stressed forms: (1) *meu, mia, mios, -as* (OSd., also *mio, meos*); *nostru, -a nostros, -as* (< *meu, -a, meos, -as; nostru, -a, nostros, -as*). (2) *tuo* (final *u* of *\*tuu* dissimilating itself from stressed *u*), *tou* (through metathesis of the *u* and *o* of *tuo*), *tua, tuos, -as* (< *tuu, -a; tuos, -as*) ; *bostru, -a, bostros, -as* (< *vostru, -a; vostros, -as*). (3) *suo, sou* (cf. *tuo, tou,* directly above), *sua; issoro* (< *suu, -a; ipsoru*).

(e) The demonstrative pronouns of Vulgar Latin (see par. 86(*c*), above), developed in Italian as follows: (Pronouns-adjectives, originally adjectives only) *questo, -a,* etc. (OIt., also *esto, chesto, -a,* etc.) < *eccu istu, -a,* etc., obsolete *codesto* (*cotesto*), *-a,* etc. < *eccu tibi istu, -a,* etc., *quel, quei* < *eccu il(lu), i(ll)i, quello, quegli* < *eccu illu, illi, quella, -e* < *eccu illa, \*ille* (< *illae*). (Pronouns) Nominative-accusative (originally nominative) *questi,* obsolete *codesti* (*cotesti*), *quelli* (*quegli*) ; nominative-accusative (originally accusative) *costui, costei, costoro* (now pejoratives), obsolete *codestui* (*cotestui*), *codestei, codestoro; colui, colei, coloro.* Neuter: *ciò* < *ecce hoc. Quel, quei* are used when a consonant other than impure *s* follows ; *quello, quegli* are used when a vowel, impure *s,* or *z* follows. The schema *questo, codesto, quello* originally corresponded to CL *hic, iste, ille;* when *codesto* and its related forms became obsolete, their functions were assumed by *quello.*

(f) The demonstrative pronouns of Vulgar Latin (see par. 86(*c*), above) developed in Sardinian as follows: *(i)kuste, (i)kustu, -a,* etc.

76

(OSd., also [*e*]*custe,* [*e*]*custu,* -*a,* etc.) < *eccu iste, istu,* -*a,* etc., (*i*)*kusse,* (*i*) *kussu,* -*a,* etc. < *eccu ipse, ipsu,* -*a,* etc., (*i*) *kuḍḍe,* (*i*) *kuḍḍu,* -*a,* etc. (OSd. [*e*]*culle,* [*e*]*cullu,* -*a,* etc. < *eccu ille, illu,* -*a,* etc.). The long forms in *i*- are used after prepositions and conjunctions ending in a consonant, the intervocalic [k] then becoming [ɡ]. The -*e* forms refer to persons only. All forms except neuter -*u* also perform as adjectives. The *hoc, iste, ille* relationship of *kuste, kusse, kulle* is no longer rigorous.

(g) The relative and interrogative pronouns of Vulgar Latin (see par. 86(*d*), above) developed in Italian as follows: (Relative) Nominative-accusative *che* (OIt., *ched* before vowels) < *quid* for singular and plural, masculine and feminine; nominative-accusative *il, la quale, i, le quali,* as alternates of *che,* especially for purposes of clarity; genitive-dative-accusative (principally dative) *cui* (*di cui, a cui*); nominative *chi,* used independently as the equivalent of *colui* (*colei*) *che.* (Interrogative) Nominative-accusative *chi* < *qui,* referring to persons; nominative-accusative *che* (OIt. *ched* before vowels) < *quid,* referring to things, also used adjectivally; nominative-accusative *quale,* -*i* (OIt., also *chente* < *quid* + adv. *mente*), also used adjectivally. Interrogative *che cosa* and *cosa* are concurrents of *che.* Interrogatives are also used to introduce exclamations.

(h) The relative and interrogative pronouns of Vulgar Latin (see par. 86(*d*), above) developed in Sardinian as follows: (Relative) Nominative-accusative *ki* (OSd., accusative *ken* < *quem*) < *qui,* for persons and things, singular and plural, masculine and feminine; nominative-accusative *su, sa* [ɡ]*uale, sos, sas* [ɡ]*uales* < *ipsu,* -*a quale, ipsos,* -*as quales,* referring to persons or things, used as concurrents of *ki,* especially for purposes of clarity; OSd. genitive, adjectival *cuiu,* -*a,* etc. (Interrogative) Nominative- accusative *kie* (< *qui* + paragogic *e,* possible influence of ·-*e* of *kuste, kusse,* etc.) for persons and things, singular and plural, masculine and feminine; nominative-accusative *quale,* -*es* for persons and things, masculine and feminine, as concurrents of *kie,* also used adjectivally; *cuiu,* -*a,* etc., used as genitives in 'Whose is (are)?' constructions; interrogative-exclamatory *bitte, it*(*t*)*e* (< *quid Deu*), also used adjectivally (*ite,* -*a,* etc.).

(i) The indefinite pronouns of Vulgar Latin (see par. 86(*e*), above) developed in Italian as follows: pronominal-adjectival *alcuno,* -*a* < \**alicunu* -*a* < *aliq(uem) unu,* -*a*; nominative singular *altri* and corresponding dative-accusative *altrui*; pronominal-adjectival *altro,* -*a,* etc. < *alteru,* -*a,* etc.; pronominal-adjectival *certo,* -*a,* etc.; *chechè* < *quid quid* (*chechessia,* OIt. *cheunque*), and analogous *chi che* (*chicchessia, chiunque*), *qual che* (*qualchessia, qualunque*); *ciascuno* < OFr. *chascun* < *cata unu* X *quisque* (OIt. *catuno, cescaduno, cescheduno*); *nessuno* < *ne ipse unu* (OIt. *neuno, niuno* < *ne*[*c*] *unu, nimo* < *nemo, nullu,* -*a*); *niente* < *ne(c) gente,* and *nulla* < *nulla*

77

(*rem*); adjectival *ogni* < *omne* (*homo*) and its pronominal derivative *ognuno*; adjectival *qualche* and pronominal *qualcuno, qualcheduno*; pronominal-adjectival *quanto, -a*, etc., and *tanto, -a*, etc.; pronominal *tutto* < *\*tottu* and pronominal-adjectival *tutto, -a*, etc.; OIt. *uomo, on* < *homo*, and *uno* < *unu; veruno* < *vere unu*.

(j) The indefinite pronouns of Vulgar Latin (see par. 86(*e*), above) developed in Sardinian as follows: pronominal-adjectival *atteru*, (cf. OIt. *atro* for *altro*) and pronominal *atere*, with final *e* by analogy to *kuste, kusse*, etc.; *dogni, dondzi* (OSd. *onnia, ogna, dogna* < *omnia, cada* < *cata*); *kalki* (cf. It. *qualche*) and *kalkiunu* (cf. It. *qualcheduno*), OSd. *alikis, unukis, kis* < *aliquis, unu quis(que), quis(que)*, pronominal-adjectival *kantu, -a*, etc., *tantu, -a*, etc. (cf. It. *quanto, tanto*); *nemos* < *nemo* + analogical *s* (*alikis*) and *niunu, ni[s]unu* < *ne(c) unu, ne(c) ipse unu*, and *niune, ni[s]une*, with analogical final *e* (*kuste, kusse*, etc.).

(k) The adverbial pronouns of Vulgar Latin (see par. 86(*f*), above) developed in Italian as *ne* < *inde, vi* < *ibi*, and *ci* < *ecce hic*.

*The Pronoun in Balkan Romance*

91. (a) The personal pronouns of Vulgar Latin (see par. 86(*a*), above) developed in Rumanian as a stressed and an unstressed series, governed by case and gender, as well as person and number: (Stressed) (1) Nominative *eu*[*ięu*] < *\*eo* < *ego*, accusative *mine* (ORm. *mene*) < *me* + echo of interrogative enclitic particle *-ne* (*que(m)ne: mene*), and dative *mie* < *mi* (<*mihi* + paragogic *e*); nominative-accusative *noi* < *nos*, and dative *nouă* (ORm. *noao*) < *nobis*. (2) Nominative *tu*, accusative *tine* (ORm. *tene*, cf. *mene*, directly above), and dative *ţie*, by analogy to *mie*; nominative-accusative *voi* < *vos*, and dative *vouă* (ORm. *voao*) < *vobis*. (3) Nominative-accusative *el* [*iel*] < *illu, ea* < *illa*, and dative *lui* < *\*illui, ei* < *\*illei* (< *\*illaei*); nominative-accusative *ei* < *illi, ele* < *\*ille* (*illae*), and dative *lor* < *illoru*. (4) (Reflexive) Accusative *sine* (ORm. *sene*, cf. *mene*, directly above), and older concurrent *sineşi;* dative *şie* (by analogy to *mie*, directly above), *sieşi*, and older concurrents *şie, şieşi*. Third person accusatives are preceded by the preposition *pe* (< *per*). Third person pronouns have the following modern concurrents: Nominative-accusative *dînsul, dînsa, dînşii, dînsele* < *ad ipsu illu, -a*, etc., and dative *dînsului, dînsei, dînşilor, dînselor* (cf. *lui, ei, lor*, directly above). After the prepositions *întru* (*într'*), *dintru* (*dintr'*), *printru* (*printr'*), the older forms *însul, însa, înşii, însele* are used: thus, *într-însul, dintr-însa, printr'-înşii*, etc. (Unstressed) (1) Accusative *ma* (ORm. *me*), *m'* < *me*, and dative *mi, îmi* < *mi* < *mihi*; accusative *ne* (ORm. *na*) < *nos*, and dative *ne, ni* < *nos*. (2) Accusative *te* and dative *ţi, iţi* (by analogy to *mi*, directly above); accusative *va, v'* < *vos*, and dative *va, v', vi* < *vos*. (3) Accusative masculine *l, îl* < *illu*, feminine *o* < *illa*, and dative *i, îi* < *illi* for both

78

genders; accusative masculine *i, îi* < *illi*, feminine *le* < *\*ille* (< *illae*), and dative *le, li* <*illis* for both genders. (4) (Reflexive) Accusative *se, s'* and dative *şi, îşĭ*, by analogy to *mi,* directly above. The use of the alternate forms of pronouns is determined by the phonetic and syntactic context: the elided forms are usually used before an unstressed vowel, and the strengthened forms (*îmĭ, îţĭ,* etc.) before a consonant or a stressed vowel, or when in sentence-initial position.

(b) The possessive pronouns of Vulgar Latin (see par. 86(*b*), above) developed as a stressed series of pronouns and adjectives, the former being preceded by a possessive article: (1) (*al*) *meu,* [*mieŭ*], (a) *mea,* (*ai*) *mei,* (*ale*) *mele* (cf. *stee/stele,* par. 97, below) : (*al*) *nostru,* (*a*) *noastra* < *nostra,* (*ai*) *noştri,* (*ale*) *noastre* < *nostre.* (2) (al) *tău* < *\*tou* (dissimilated form of *\*tuu*), (a) *ta* < *\*tua* (by analogy to *tau*), (*ai*) *tăi* < *\*tui,* (*ale*) *tale* (by analogy to *mele,* directly above); (al) *vostru* (a) *voastra* < *vostra,* (*ai*) *voştri,* (*ale*) *voastre* < *vostre.* (3) (*al*) *său* < *\*sou* (cf. *tău,* directly above), *lui* < *\*illui,* (a) *sa* (cf. *ta,* directly above), *ei* < *\*illei* (*\*illaei*), (*ai*) *săi* < *\*sui,* (*ale*) *sale* (cf. *tale,* directly above), *ei;* (*al*) *lor* < *illoru,* (*a*) *lor,* (*ai*) *lor,* (ale) *lor.* The forms *lui* and *ei,* originally used in opposition to *său, sa,* etc., to signify independence of the subject of the main clause, are now used, for the sake of clarity, to signify the gender of the possessor.

(c) The demonstrative pronouns of Vulgar Latin (see par. 86(*c*), above) developed in Rumanian as a pronominal-adjectival system of personal, spatial, and temporal proximity, corresponding semantically to Latin *hic* and *ille,* and morphologically to Latin *iste* and *ille:* (Pronouns) (1) Nominative-accusative, masculine-neuter *acesta* < *accu + iste* + paragogic *a,* masculine plural *aceştia,* feminine *aceasta* < *accu + ista,* and feminine-neuter plural *acestea* < *accu + \*iste* (< *istae*) + paragogic *a;* genitive-dative, masculine-neuter *acestuia* < *accu + \*istui* + paragogic *a,* masculine plural *acestora* < *accu + \*istoru* + paragogic *a,* feminine *acesteia* < *accu + \*istei* + paragogic *a,* and plural *acestora.* (2) Nominative-accusative, masculine-neuter *acela* < *accu + ille* + paragogic *a,* masculine plural *aceia* ·< *accu + illi* + paragogic a, feminine *aceea* < *accu + illa,* and feminine-neuter plural *acelea* < *accu + \*ille* (< *illae*) + paragogic *a;* genitive-dative, masculine-neuter *aceluia* < *accu + illui* + paragogic *a,* masculine plural *acelora* < *accu + illoru* + paragogic *a,* feminine *aceleia* < *accu + \*illei* + paragogic *a,* and feminine-neuter plural *acelora.* (Pronouns-Adjectives) (1) Nominative-accusative, masculine-neuter *(a)cestălalt, celălalt* < *(a)ccu + iste (ille) + alter,* masculine plural (a)*ceştilalţi, ceilalţi,* feminine (a)*ceastălaltă, cealaltă,* and feminine-neuter plural *(a)cestelalte, celelalte;* genitive-dative, masculine-neuter *(a)cestuilalt, celuilalt,* masculine plural *(a)cestorlalţi, celorlalţi,* feminine *(a)cesteilalte, celeilalte,* and feminine-neuter plural *(a)cestorlalte, celorlalte.* (2) (Colloquial) Nominative-accusative, masculine-neuter *ăsta, ăla* < *iste, ille* + paragogic *a*, masculine plural *ăştia, ăia*, feminine *asta, aia*, and feminine-neuter *astea, alea*; genitive-dative, masculine-neuter *ăstuia, ăluia*, masculine plural *ăstora, ălora*, feminine *ăsteia, asteia, ăleia*, and feminine-neuter plural *ăstora, ălora*. (Adjectives) (1) Nominative-accusative, masculine-neuter *acest, acesta*, masculine plural *aceşti, aceşti*, feminine *aceasta*, and feminine-neuter plural *aceste, acestea*; genitive-dative, masculine-neuter *acestui, acestuia*, masculine plural *eceşti, aceştia*, feminine *acestei, acesteia*, and feminine-neuter plural *acestor, acestora*. (2) Nominative-accusative, masculine-neuter *acel, acela*, masculine plural *acei, aceia*, feminine *acea, aceea*, and feminine-neuter plural *acele, acelea*; genitive-dative, masculine-neuter *acelui, aceluia*, masculine plural *acelor, acelora*, feminine *acelei, aceleia*, and feminine-neuter plural *acelor, acelora*. (3) (*Colloquial*) Nominative-accusative, masculine-neuter *ăst, ăl*, masculine plural *ăşti, ăi*, feminine *astă, a*, feminine-neuter plural *aste, ale*; genitive-dative, masculine-neuter *ăstui, ălui*, masculine plural *ăstor, ălor*, feminine *ăstei, astei, ălei*, and feminine-neuter plural *ăstor, ălor*. Identity is expressed by (1) the forms *dintr'* (*intr', print'*) *însul, însa, însii, însele* (see par. 91(*a*), above), (2) composites of *însu* and unstressed reflexive pronouns, gender being differentiated only when reinforcing personal accusatives: (with nominatives) *însumi, însuţi, însuşi, însine, însivă, înşişi;* (with accusatives) the preceding forms for the masculine, and the feminine forms *însami, însaţi, însaşi, însene, înseva, înseşi*, and (3) composites of the demonstrative *acela* and the unstressed reflexive *şi*: (nominative-accusative *acelaşi, aceeaşi, aceiaşi, aceleaşi;* (genitive-dative) *aceluiaşi, aceleiaşi, aceloraşi*.

(d) The relative and interrogative pronouns of Vulgar Latin (see par. 86(*d*), above) developed in Rumanian as relative-interrogative pronouns, and interrogative adjectives: (pronouns) nominative-accusative *cine* < *que(m)ne* (cf. *mine, ţine*, par. 91(*a*), above); *ce* < *quid; care* < *quale; cât. -a, câţi, -e* < *quantu, -a, -i, -e;* genitive-dative *cui; caruia, careia, carora* < *quale* + *\*illui, \*illei* (*\*illaei*); *illoru* + paragogic *a; câtor* < *quanti* + *illoru;* (adjectives) nominative-accusative *care; cât, -a*, etc.; genitive-dative *carui, carei, caror*. Accusatives except *ce* are preceded by the preposition *pe*, genitives by *al* (*a, ai, ale*). The genitive of *ce* is preceded by *de, din*, or *despre*, and the dative by *la*.

(e) The indefinite pronouns of Vulgar Latin (see par. 86(*e*), above) developed in Rumanian as pronouns and pronominal adjectives: declined pronouns *altul, alta*, etc., and their corresponding adjectives *alt, alta*, all derived from *alter, -a*, etc.; *atare, atari* < *\*accu tale, -i;* declined *atâta* < *accu tantu, -a;* declined *carevă* < *quale volet, câtva, ceva, cineva; destul, -a*, etc. < *de satulu, -a*, etc.; declined *cutare* < *\*eccu tale;* declined *fiecare* < *fieri quale, fiecât, fiecine*, and invariable *fiece;* declined *nescine* < *nescio que(m)ne, niştecare*, and

80

invariable *nişte*; invariable *nimeni* < *nemine*, *nimic* < *ne mica*; declined pronouns *niciunul*, *niciuna* < *nec unu illu*, *nec una illa*, and their corresponding adjectives *niciun*, *nicio* < *nec unu*, *-a*; declined *oarecare* < *hora quale*, *oarecine*, and invariable *oarece;* declined *orcine*, *oricare*, *oricât*, and invariable *orice*; declined *tot*, *toata* < *totu*, *-a*; declined pronouns *unul* (*vre'unul*), *una* (*vre'una*), and their corresponding adjectives *un* (*vre'un*), *o* (*vre'o*).

## The Article in Vulgar Latin

92. The definite and indefinite article, which were alien to the morphology of Classical Latin, emerged, respectively, in Vulgar Latin, in the guise of (1) the demonstrative pronouns *ille*, *ipse* and their related forms, and (2) the numerical adjective *unus*, *-a*, *-u(m)*.

## The Article in Gallo-Romance

93. (a) The articles of Vulgar Latin (see par. 92, above) developed in Old French as a two-case system: Nominative *li* < *ille* X *qui*, *li* < *illi*, *la* < *illa*, *les* < *illas*; *uns* < *unus*, *un* < *uni*, *une* <*una*, *unes* < *unas*. Accusative *lo* (< *illu*) > *le*, *les* < *illos*, *la* < *illa*, *les* < *illas*; *un* < *unu*, *uns* < *unos*, *une* < *una*, *unes* < *unas*. Prepositions and articles combined to form the following contractions: *a* + *lo*, *le* (+ cons.) > *au*; *a* + *les* > *as* (later, *aus*, and orthographic variant *aux*, by analogy to *au*); *de* + *lo*, *le* > *del* (+ cons.) > *dëu*, *du*; *de* + *les* > *des*; *en* + *le* (+ cons.) > *el*; *en les* > *es*. *Lo*, *le*, *la*, when followed by a vowel, elided to *l'*. In Modern French, the accusative forms *le* (*l'*), *la* (*l'*), *les* survive as nominative-accusatives; the contractions *au*, *aux*, *du*, *des*, *ès* also survive, the last only in stereotyped expressions, e.g., *bachelier ès lettres*.

(b) The articles of Vulgar Latin (see par. 92, above) developed in Old Provençal as a two-case system: Nominative *lo* < *illu* (less frequently, *le* < *ille*, and rarely *el* < *ille*, or possibly by analogy to contractions *del*, *pel*, etc.), *li*, *lhi* [*ti*] < *illi*, *la* < *illa* (sporadically, also *li* < *illa* X *qui*), *las* < *illas*; *uns* < *unus*, *un* < *uni*, *una*, *unas*. Accusative *lo* < *illu*, *los* < *illos*, *la*, *las*; *un* <*unu*, *uns* < *unos*, *una*, *unas*. Prepositions and articles combined to form the following contractions: *a* + *lo(s)* > *al(s)*, *de* + *lo(s)* > *del(s)*, *per* + *lo(s)* > *pel(s)*, *\*vers* + *lo(s)* > *vel(s)*, *\*sus* + *lo(s)* > *sul(s)*. *Lo*, *la*, *li*, when followed by a vowel, elided to *l'*. As enclitics, *li* becomes *'lh*, *'ill*, or *'il* (*et li* > *e'lh*, *e'ill*, *e'il*), *lo* becomes *'l* (*si lo* > *si'l*, *fa lo* > *fa'l*), and *los* becomes *'ls* (*entre los* > *entre'ls*, *meiron los* > *meiro'ls*). The articles *so*, *sa* < *ipsu*, *-a* and their related forms appear very sporadically. In some dialects of Modern Provençal, *lo* has developed as *lou*.

94. (a) The articles of Vulgar Latin (see par. 92, above) developed in Spanish as a one-case, nominative-accusative system, deriving all of its forms except *el* from the accusative: masculine *el* < *ille*, *los* (OSp., also *elos*) < *illos*, feminine *la, las* (OSp., also *ela, elas*) < *illa, illas*, neuter *lo* (OSp., also *elo*) < *illu(d)*; *un* < *un(u)*, *unos*, *una, unas*. In Old Spanish, *ela* became *el* or *ell* when followed by the initial vowel of a noun or adjective, particularly *a*; in Modern Spanish, *el* survives in this context, but only before the initial, stressed *a* of a noun. In Old Spanish, moreover, the initial *l* of *la, los, las* often assimilated itself to the final *n* of directly preceding *en* or *con*, e.g., *enna, connas*; and *el* became enclitic *l* after prepositions ending in a vowel, e.g., *al, del, paral, contral*, only *al* and *del* surviving in Modern Spanish.

(b) The articles of Vulgar Latin (see par. 92, above) developed in Old Catalan as *lo, la, los, les* < *illu, -a, illos, -as; so, sa, sos, ses* < *ipsu, -a, ipsos, -as; uno, -a, unos, -es* < *unu, -a, unos, -as*. *Lo, la* and *so, sa* became *l'* and *s'* before vowels. From enclitic *lo, los*, reduced to *l, ls* after final vowels, and specifically from the contractions *del, dels*, originated the Modern Catalan articles *el, els*, the other forms being *la, les*. *So, sa*, and related forms have become dialectal. In Modern Catalan, *el* and *la* become *l'* before vowels or mute *h*, e.g., *l'home, l'ombra*, except that *la* does not change (1) before atonic *i* and *u*, e.g., *la idea, la unitat*, (2) before the letters of the alphabet, e.g., *la e, la o*, and (3) if change would result in semantic clash, e.g., *la una* vs. *luna, la anormalitat* vs. *la normalitat*. The prepositions *a, de*, and *per* combine with *el* and *els* to form the contractions *al(s), del(s)*, and *pel(s)*. Neuter *el*, for reasons of clarity, is being replaced in certain instances by Spanish *lo*.

(c) The articles of Vulgar Latin (see par. 92, above) developed in Portuguese as *o, a, os, as* < *\*lo, \*la, \*los, \*las* < *illu, -a, illos, -as*, and *um, -a, ums, -as* < *unu, -a, unos, -as*. The *l* of *\*lo, \*la*, etc., was lost in intervocalic position, and the resultant *o, a*, etc., became generalized. Final *r* and *s* assimilated themselves to the *l* following *\*lo, \*la*, etc., the resultant *-ll-* simplifying to *-l-*; the only vestige of this assimilation in Modern Portuguese is in *pelo, -a*, etc. < *pello, -a*, etc. < *per \*lo, \*la*, etc. The *l* of *\*lo, \*la*, etc., assimilated itself to the preceding *n* of *en*, the resultant *-nn-* later simplifying to *-n-*, with the nasalization of *e*, which later denasalized and disappeared: thus, *en \*lo* > *enno* > *ēno* > *eno* > *no*. The contractions *num, numa*, etc., are analogical to *no, na*, etc. The prepositions *a* and *de* combine with *o, a*, etc., to form the contractions *ao, à, aos, às*, and *do, da, dos, das*. Anomalously, the article *el* (< *ille*), which may have been borrowed from Spanish, is used only before *rei*, and principally when referring to kings of Portugal.

95. The articles of Vulgar Latin (see par. 92, above) developed in Surselvan as *il* < *ille* X *qui, igl* (before vowels) < *\*illi* + vow., *la* < *illa, l'* (before vowels), *ils, igls, las; in, -a* (see par. 27, above) < *unu, -a.*

## The Article in Italo-Romance

96. The articles of Vulgar Latin (see par. 92, above) developed in Italian as follows: *il* < OIt. *el* < *il(le),* before consonants other than *gn,* impure *s,* and *z* (OIt., also *lo* < *(il)lu,* especially in initial position and after final *r*), *lo* before *gn,* impure *s,* and *z* (OIt., also *il*), *l'* before vowels, *la* < *il(la), l'* before vowels, *i* (OIt., also *li, ei* [*e'*] < *illi;* also *gli* < *illi* + vow., especially in initial position), *gli* before vowels, *gn,* impure *s,* and *z, le* < *\*ille* (< *illae*), *l'* when followed by *e; un, uno* (before *gn,* impure *s,* and *z*), *una, un'* (before *a*) < *unu, -a.* The prepositions *a, con, di, in,* and *per* combined with articles to form the contractions *al, allo,* etc., *col, collo,* etc., *del, dello,* etc., *nel, nello,* etc., *pel, pello,* etc. The modern language tends to avoid contractions with *con* and *per.*

(b) The articles of Vulgar Latin (see par. 92, above) developed in Sardinian as *(is)su, -a, (is)sos (-us), -as* < *ipsu, -a, ipsos, -as; unu, -a.* In Old Sardinian, the long forms of the definite article were used after prepositions and conjunctions ending in a consonant, a practice which has survived only in the rural regions, e.g., *in issa me[š]a.*

## The Article in Balkan Romance

97. The articles of Vulgar Latin (see par. 92, above) developed in Rumanian as an enclitic, two-case system: (Nominative-Accusative) masc. *-l* (after *u*), *-(u)l* (after a consonant) < *illu, -le* (after *e*) < *ille, -i* < *illi;* fem. *-a* (replacing final *ă*), *-(u)a* (after *a* or *i*) < *illa, -le* < *\*ille (< illae);* masc. *un,* fem. *o* < *unu, -a.* (Genitive-Dative) masc. *-lui* < *\*illui, -lor* < *illoru,* fem. *-ei* < *\*illei* (< *\*illaei*), *-lor.* The masculine article *-l* is not pronounced. Thus, nominative-accusative *socrul, lupul, fratele, socrii, lupii, fraţii; sora, steaua, sorele, stelele; un om, o casa;* and genitive-dative *socrului, lupului, fratelui, socrilor, lupilor, fraţilor; sorei, stelei, sorelor, stelelor; unui om, unei case.* Enclitic articles are also appended to adjectives which precede the nouns they modify, the nouns remaining undeclined.

## The Adjective in Vulgar Latin

98. The morphology of the adjective in Vulgar Latin was almost identical to that of the noun (see par. 74, above). With the fusion

of the neuter singular noun with its masculine counterpart, and the neuter plural with the identical feminine singular, the neuter adjective was reduced in usage to describing a concept or action, rather than a person or thing. Adjectives fell into one of two principal classes, according to whether they did or did not differentiate between the masculine and feminine gender, corresponding, respectively, to the following Classical Latin declensions: (1) *bonus, -a, -um*; *liber, -a, -um*; *acer, acris, -e*; and (2) (m. & f.) *tristis*, (n.) *triste*; (m., f., & n.) *felix*; (m. & f.) *melior*, (n.) *melius*. The same two-case declensional system prevailed as for the nouns. Comparatives were expressed by periphrases consisting of *plus* or *magis* and the adjective, and superlatives by a demonstrative pronoun-article, *plus* or *magis*, and the adjective: *plus (magis) bellus, ille plus (magis) bellus*. A small number of the organic comparatives and superlatives of Classical Latin survived, including the following: (comparatives) *major, minor, melior, pejor*; (superlatives) *optimus, pessimus, proximus*. Superlatives in *-issimus* survived as learned forms and were used principally as intensives.

*The Adjectives in Gallo-Romance*

99. (a) The Vulgar Latin adjectives (see par. 98, above) developed in Old French as follows: (Trimorphic Vulgar Latin nominatives) (1) (M.) *bons, bon, bon, bons*; (f.) *bone, bone, bones, bones*; (n.) *bon, bon*. (2) *tiedes, tiede, tiede, tiedes*; *tiede, tiede, tiedes, tiedes*; *tiede, tiede*. (3) *tendre, tendre, tendre, tendres*; *tendre, tendre, tendres, tendres*; *tendre, tendre*. (Dimorphic Vulgar Latin nominatives) *granz, grant, grant, granz*; *granz* (later, *grant*), *grant, granz, granz*; *grant, grant*. Of the first group, *bons* represents all adjectives which lose final *u*; *tiedes*, all adjectives which retain final *u* as *e*; and *tendre*, all adjectives which retain final *e* of *-er* in the masculine singular. Masculine plural *grant* is an analogue of the corresponding forms of the first group, which are identical to their accusative singulars. The loss of final *s* in feminine singular *granz* [ts] is attributable to a desire to distinguish between genders: *grant* vs. *granz*. Phonological factors such as final *a* and *s* caused disparities between (1) genders and (2) cases: (1) *blanc < blancu, blanche < blanca*; *sec < siccu, seche < sicca*; *beaus < bellus, belle < bella*; *vieus < veclus, vieille < vecla*, etc. (2) *ses < siccus, sec < siccu*; *vis < vivus, vif < vivu*; *beaus < bellus, bel < bellu*; *vieus < veclus, vieil < veclu*; *nues < novus, nuef < novu*, etc. The Latin comparatives and superlatives which survived in Old French include the following: (1) (comparatives) *maire, maiour < major, majore*; *mendre* (later, *meindre, moindre*, on the analogy of *meins, moins < minus*), *menor < minor, minore*; *mieldre, meillour < melior, meliore*; *pire, peiour < pejor, pejore*; *graindre, graignour < grandior, grandiore*; *joindre, joignour*

< *junior, juniore*, etc. (2) (superlatives) *maismes* < *maximus*, *mermes* < *minimus, pesmes* < *pessimus, prüismes* < *proximus*, and such learned forms as *altismes* < *altissimus, fortismes, grandismes*, etc. Except for Latin survivals, the comparative came to be expressed by *plus* + *adj.*, and the superlative by *très* < *trans* + *adj.* or *def. art.* + *plus* + *adj.* In Modern French, with few exceptions, only the accusative forms of the Old French adjectives survive; *beau, nouveau, vieux*, etc., are analogues of the corresponding etymological plurals, e.g., *beaux* = *beaus* < *bellos*, the etymological singulars (*bel, nouvel, vieil*, etc.) being used only before nouns beginning with a vowel or mute *h* (*un bel homme, un vieil ami*). Adjectives which belonged to the second Old French group, modeled by *granz, grant*, above, have modeled themselves after the *bon, bone* adjectives of the first group; thus, *grand, grands, grande, grandes* (the etymological feminine singular survives in *grand'mère, grand'messe, grand'rue*); *fort, forts, forte, fortes*, etc. Since -*e* and -*es* are merely orthographic, feminine gender in these cases is marked only by the pronunciation of an otherwise muted occlusive (m. *fort* [fɔ:r] vs. f. *forte* [fɔrt]). Finally, there is a considerable number of adjectives in -*e*, -*es* which are not marked for gender: *rouge(s), large(s), triste(s)*, etc.

(b) The Vulgar Latin adjectives developed in Old Provençal as follows: (Trimorphic Vulgar Latin nominatives) (1) (m.) *bons, bon, bon, bons*; (f.) *bona, bona, bonas, bonas*; (n.) *bon, bon.* (2) *paubre(s), paubre, paubre, paubres; paubra, paubra, paubras, paubras; paubre, paubre.* (Dimorphic Vulgar Latin nominatives) (1) *fortz, fort, fort, fortz; fortz* (also, analogical *forta*), *fort* (also, *forta*), *fortz* (also, analogical *fortas*), *fortz* (*fortas*); *fort, fort.* Nominative masculine plural *boni, mali, soli*, etc., which were used sporadically in lieu of normative *bon, mal, sol*, etc., have been variously attributed to (1) the survival of the -*i* of the corresponding Latin form, and (2) the analogical influence exerted by the article *li.* The neuter forms were used only in such expressions as *m'es bel, m'es greu.* The Latin comparatives and superlatives which survived include the following: (1) (comparatives) *majer, maire* < *major, major* < *majore; menre* < *minor, menor* < *minore; melher* < *melior melhor* < *meliore; pejer, piejer* < *pejor, pejor* < *pejore; ausser* < *altior, alzor, auzor* < *altiore.* (2) (superlatives) *pesme* < *pessimu, prosme, pruesme* < *proximu*, and such learned forms as *altisme* < *altissimu* and *santisme* < *sanctissimu.* Except for the Latin survivals, comparatives were expressed by *plus* + *adj.*, and superlatives by *mout* + *adj.*, and *def. art.* + *plus* + *adj.*

### The Adjective in Ibero-Romance

100. (a) The Vulgar Latin adjectives (see par. 98, above) developed in Spanish in their accusative forms only, which reduced tri-

morphic adjectives to two forms (-*o*, -*a*), and dimorphic adjectives to one (-*e*). The neuter forms disappeared through atrophy, there being no neuter nouns to give them purpose, and the neuter concept was expressed by *lo* + *masc. sing.* The following forms are apocopated when followed by masculine nouns: *algun(o)*, *buen(o)*, *cien(to)*, *mal(o)*, *ningun(o)*, *primer(o)*, *postrer(o)*, *san(to)* [except when the proper noun begins with *Do-* or *To-*], *tercer(o)*, *un(o)*; *much(o)*, *tod(o)*, and *nul(lo)* were similarly apocopated in Old Spanish. Monomorphic adjectives often lost final *e* in Old Spanish (*amanecient*, *fuert*, *grant*, *semejant*, etc.); the only vestige of this apocopation in Modern Spanish is *gran(de)*, which loses its final syllable before nouns of either gender. Adjectives in -*or* and -*és*, which were monomorphic in Early Old Spanish, later developed analogical feminines in -*a* (*señora*, *burguesa*); -*ora* has become the rule, but -*esa* is used only with adjectives of nationality or origin (*francesa*, *holandesa*, *burgalesa*, but *cortés*). Latin comparatives and superlatives which survived include the following: (comparatives) *mayor* < *majore*, *menor* < *minore*, *mejor* < *meliore*, *peor* < *pejore*; (superlatives) *máximo* < *maximu*, *mínimo* < *minimu*, *óptimo* < *optimu*, *pésimo* < *pessimu*, and learned forms in -*ísimo*. Except for Latin survivals, the comparative came to be expressed by *más* + *adj.*, and the superlative by *muy* + *adj.*, or *def. art.* + *más* + *adj.*

(b) The Vulgar Latin adjectives (see par. 98, above) developed in Catalan in their accusative forms, which reduced trimorphic adjectives to two forms (-*e*, -*a* [both pronounced like French mute *e*]), and dimorphic adjectives to one (-*e*). The neuter forms disappeared through atrophy, there being no neuter nouns to give them purpose, and the neuter concept was expressed by *el* + *masc. adj.*, or by the Hispanicism *lo* + *masc. adj.* Latin -*u*, -*a* adjectives whose masculine forms became oxytonic in Catalan formed their feminines in accordance with the masculine endings: (1) (m.) -*c*, -*t*, (f.) -*ga*, -*da* (*mut*, *muda*; *groc*, *groga*). (2) (m.) -*s* (< -*ssu*, -*tiu*, -*rsu*), (f.) -*ssa* (*espès*, *espessa*; *postís*, *postissa*; *escàs*, *escassa*. (3) (m.) *vow.* (< *vow. n*), (f.) -*na* (*humà*, *humana*). (4) (m.) -*u*, (f.) -*va* (*nou*, *nova*). (5) (m.) -*ig* (*boig*, *roig*), -*ig* (*mig*, *lleig*), (f.) -*ja* (*boja*, *roja*), -*tja* (*mitja*, *lletja*, but OCt. *mija*, *lleja*). (6) (m.) all other endings, (f.) -*a*. Some adjectives which were derived from the Latin third declension developed analogical feminines in -*a*: *dolça*, *forta*, *trista*, *verda*, etc. Latin comparatives and superlatives which have survived in Catalan include the following: (comparatives) *major* < *majore*, *millor* < *meliore*, *menor* < *minore* (OCt. *mills* < *melius*, *forçor* < *fortiore*); (superlatives) learned forms in -*íssim* (OCt., also -*isme*) < -*issimu*. Except for Latin survivals, the comparative is expressed by *més* + *adj.*, and the superlative by *molt* + *adj.*, or *def. art.* + *més* (OCt. *pus*) + *adj.*

(c) The Vulgar Latin adjectives (see par. 98, above) developed in Portuguese in their accusative forms only, which reduced the trimorphic adjectives to two forms (-o, -a), and the dimorphic adjectives to one (-e, which was lost after c, l, n, r, or s). Neuter forms disappeared through atrophy, there being no neuter nouns to give them purpose, and the neuter concept was expressed by *masc. def. art.* + *adj.* The endings -o, -a, and their plurals, -os, -as, in hiatus with a preceding tonic vowel, were affected as follows: (1) They fused with tonic [ã] into -ão, -ã, -ãos, -ãs. (2) The masculine endings changed to -u and -us when the tonic vowel was a or e (*malu* > *mau*, *reos* > *reus*); they fused with tonic u into -ú and -ús (*nudu*, *nudos* > *nú*, *nús*); and they fused with tonic o into -om and -ons (*bonu*, *bonos* > *bom*, *bons*). (3) The feminine endings fused with tonic a into -á, -ás (*mala*, *malas* > *má*, *más*); and assimilated to tonic e and o (*rea* > *ree*, *sola* >*só*). Monomorphic plurals (-es) of words whose stem ended in l lost the l (which had become intervocalic), and their ending changed to -is (*personales* > *personais*). Some monomorphic adjectives, especially those of nationality and those (other than comparatives) ending in -or, developed analogical feminines in -a (*espanhola*, *inglêsa*, *encantadora*). The Latin comparatives and superlatives which survived in Portuguese include the following: (comparatives) *mór*, *maior* (OPg. *meor*) < *majore*, *menor* (OPg. *meor*) < *minore*, *melhor* < *meliore*, *pior* (OPg. *peior*) < *pejore*; (superlatives) *máximo*, *mínimo*, *óptimo*, *péssimo*, and the learned forms in -*íssimo*. Except for the Latin survivals, the comparative came to be expressed by *mais* + *adj.*, and the superlative by *muito* + *adj.*, or *def. art.* + *mais* + *adj.*

## The Adjective in Rheto-Romance

101. The Vulgar Latin adjectives (see par. 98, above) developed in Surselvan in their accusative forms only, except for the anomalous nominative forms of the masculine singular predicate adjective and the masculine singular and plural participial adjectives (see par. 83 (a), above). Trimorphic adjectives were reduced to two forms (attributive, -cons., -a; predicative, -s, -a); dimorphic forms retained etymological masculines (attributive, -cons., predicative, -s) and developed an analogical feminine in -a (*gronda*, *verda*). Feminine forms were derived from the corresponding masculine predicative forms (*buns:buna*). Attributive and predicative forms of the masculine singular often developed quite differently because of phonological considerations: thus, *bien* vs. *buns*, *bi* vs. *bials* (*in bien affon*, *igl affon ei buns*; *in bi marcau*, *quei marcau ei bials*). Latin comparatives which survived include the following: *mèglier* < *melior*, *pir* > *pejor*. Except for the Latin survivals, the comparative is expressed

87

by *pli* + *adj.*, and the superlative by *fetg* (*fictu*) + *adj.*, and *def. art.* + *pli* + *adj.*

## The Adjective in Italo-Romance

102. (a) The Vulgar Latin adjectives (see par. 98, above) developed in Italian in their accusative singular and nominative (or accusative, see par. 72 (*a*), above) plural forms. Trimorphic adjectives were reduced to two forms (*-o, -a*), and dimorphic adjectives to one (*-e*); thus, *buono, -a, buoni, -e; forte, -i*. Some adjectives in *-o* developed apocopated forms when followed by nouns other than those with initial *gn*, impure *s*, or *z* (thus, *bel, buon*, and *san*), and *grande* became *gran* before masculine or feminine nouns. Latin comparatives and superlatives which survived include the following: (comparatives) *maggiore* < *majore, minore* < *minore, migliore* < *meliore, peggiore* < *pejore*, (superlatives) *massimo* < *maximu, minimo* < *minimu, ottimo* < *optimu, pessimo* < *pessimu*. Except for Latin survivals, the comparative came to be expressed by *più* + *adj.*, and the superlative by *molto* + *adj.*, and *def. art.* + *più* + *adj.*

(b) The Vulgar Latin adjectives (see par. 98, above) developed in Sardinian in their accusative forms only, which reduced the trimorphic adjectives to two forms (*-u, -a*), and the dimorphic adjectives to one (*-e*). The Latin comparatives which survived include *ma[ž]ore* (also, *ma[ž]ori*) < *majore*, and *minore* (also, *minori*) < *minore*. Except for the Latin survivals, the comparative is expressed by *prus* (*plus*) + *adj.*, and the superlative by *def. art., prus* + *adj.*

## The Adjective in Balkan Romance

103. The Vulgar Latin adjectives (see par. 98, above) developed in Rumanian without their neuter forms, which reduced trimorphic adjectives to two forms, (*-cons.* or *-u, -ă*), and dimorphic forms to one (*-e*): thus, *bun, bună, buni, bune*, and *dulce, dulci*. Adjectives whose masculines ended in *-iu* or *-tor* developed feminines in *-ie* and *-toare*, respectively: thus, *târziu, târzie*, and *folositor, folositoare*. Masculine diminutives in *-el* developed feminine counterparts in *-ica* and *-ea*: thus, *frumuşel* and *frumuşica, frumuşea*. The adjective is declined when it precedes its noun, which remains undeclined (see par. 97, above). The comparative is expressed by *mai* + *adj.*, and the superlative by *foarte* + *adj.*, or by a form of the *dem. art. cel* + *mai* + *adj.*

## The Adverb in Vulgar Latin

104. The Classical Latin adverbs in *-o* and *-e* (*cito, bene*) survived sporadically in Vulgar Latin; the adverb derived from the

neuter accusative of the corresponding adjective was similarly sporadic in the West, but became the norm in the East; and the periphrases with *modo* were reduced to the single *quo modo*. The adverbial innovations in the Vulgar Latin of the West were periphrases, principally the combination of a feminine adjective and the ablative *mente*, which originally must have indicated the state of mind which accompanied an action, rather than the manner in which it was performed (*modo*). Other periphrases included the combination of (1) preposition and adverb (*ad satis*), (2) *ecce* (*eccu, accu*) and pronoun (*ecce hic*), (3) *ad* and a noun or verbal stem in *-ones, -oni* (*\*ad genuculones*). Analogical adverbs in *-s* (*\*numquas, \*sempres*) were still another western feature. The adverbial innovation in the Vulgar Latin of the Balkans was the generalized form in *-isce*, the adverbial ablative of the ethnic adjectival ending *-iscus* (*\*veteranisce*). The adverbial comparative was expressed by *magis* or *plus* + *adv.*, and the superlative by *multu, trans*, or *forte* + *adv.*, or by *def. art.* + *magis* or *plus* + *adv.* A small number of Classical Latin comparatives persisted: *maius, minus, melius, pejus*.

## The Adverb in Romance

105. The Vulgar Latin adverbs (see par. 104, above) developed as follows in (1) Western and Italo-Romance, and (2) Balkan Romance: (1) Latin forms in *-o* and *-e*, the neuter accusative, and analogical forms in *-s* survived sporadically (Pg. *cedo*, Sp. *tarde*, It. *molto*, Sp. *entonces*), but the normative adverbial formation was the periphrasis of *fem. adj.* + *mente* (It., Pg., Sd., Sp. *-mente*, Ct., Fr. *-ment*, SS. *-mein*, Pr. *-men*). The organic comparatives survived as follows: *maius* > OIt. *maggio*; *minus* > Ct. *menys*, Fr. *moins*, It. *meno*, Pg. *ménos*, Sd. *minus*, Sp. *menos*, SS. *meins*; *melius* > Fr. *mieux* (OFr. *mieuz*), It. *meglio*, OCt. *mils*, Sd. *me[ž]us*; *pejus* > Fr. *pis*, It. *peggio*, Sd. *peyus*. The comparative is otherwise expressed by *magis* (Ct. *més*, Sp. *más*, etc.) or *plus* (Fr. *plus*, It. *più*, etc.) + *adv.*, and the superlative by *multu* (It. *molto*, Sp. *mucho*) or *trans* (Fr. *très*) + *adv.*, or by *def. art.* + *multu* or *trans* + *adv.* (2) Practically any part of speech may be used adverbially in Rumanian, but principally the noun (a vestige of the neuter accusative). The adverbial suffixes are *-eşte* < *-isce* (*\*veteranisce* > *bătrâneşte*) and *-iş* < *ice* (*\*crucice* > *crucis*). The comparative is expressed by *mai* + *adv.*, and the superlative by *foarte* + *adv.*, or by *cel* + *mai* + *adv.*

## The Numerals in Vulgar Latin

106. The first three cardinal numerals continued to be declined, with the following innovations: (1) *duo* developed an analogical masculine (*dui, doi*) and neuter (*dua, doa*), and (2) *tres* developed

a nominative *trei* on the analogy of *dui*. *Quattuor* and *quinque* developed phonologically as *quattor, quatro,* and *cinque* [ts]. In the West and Italy, *ūndecim* developed also as *ŭndecim; quattuordecim* became *\*quattordece; sedece* was also expressed periphrastically as *\*dece et (ac) sex;* and *septendecim, duodeviginti,* and *undeviginti* were replaced by the periphrases *\*dece et (ac) septe, octo,* and *nove,* respectively. In the Balkans, probably through Slavic influence, a new system evolved for *eleven* through *nineteen: unus super dece, dui super dece,* etc. In the West and Italy, all the ten's above *dece* lost their intervocalic *g; nona(g)inta* was rivaled by its analogical concurrent *nova(g)inta;* and there was generally a shift of stress from penult to antepenult. In Northern Gaul, possibly through the Celtic substratum, a vigesimal system evolved alongside the Latin decimal system, surviving only vestigially in Modern French, e.g., *quatre-vingts.* In the Balkans, the Latin system of ten's was replaced by a system of multiples of ten (*dui deci, trei deci,* etc.). The contracted hundred's of Classical Latin probably had segmental concurrents in Vulgar Latin: *dui centi, d(u)os centos; trei centi, tres centos,* etc. The plurals of *mille* were *mille* and *mil(l)ia,* the latter becoming a feminine singular in the East. In the West and Italy, the ordinal *primu* had *primariu* as a concurrent; in the Iberian peninsula, *tertiu* had *tertiariu* as a concurrent; and the new ordinal, originally distributive, suffix *-enu* was not uncommon (*novenu* for *nonu*). In the Balkans, *primu* was largely replaced by *\*antaneu,* and the rest of the Latin ordinals by a non-Latin system (see par. 111, below).

*The Numerals in Gallo-Romance*

107. (a) The cardinal numerals of Vulgar Latin (see par. 106, above) developed in French as follows: (1) *One, two, three* (MFr. *un, une, deux, trois*) continued to be declined in Old French: (m.) *uns, un* (f.) *une, une;* (m.) *dui (doi), dous (deus)* (f.) *dous (deux), dous (deus)*; (m.) *trei (troi), treis (trois)* (f.) *treis (trois), treis (trois).* (2) *Four* to *sixteen* conformed to the Classical-Vulgar Latin patterns, whereas *seventeen* to *nineteen* were distinctly Vulgar Latin in origin: *quatre, cinq, six, sept, huit, neuf, dix, onze, douze, treize, quatorze, quinze, seize, dix-sept, dix-huit, dix-neuf.* (3) The ten's, from *twenty* to *ninety,* show traces of a Vulgar Latin vigesimal system in *seventy, eighty,* and *ninety: vingt, trente, quarante, cinquante, soixante, soixante-dix* (CL *septuaginta*), *quatre-vingts* (CL *octoginta*), *quatre-vingt-dix* (CL *nonaginta*). OFr. *vint* was declinable: (m.) *vint* (later, *vins*), *vinz (vins),* (f.) *vinz (vins), vinz (vins).* (4) OFr. *cent* was declinable: (m.) *cent,* (later, *cens*), *cenz (cens),* (f.) *cenz (cens), cenz (cens).* The hundred's above *cent* were derived from the analytical forms of Vulgar Latin: *deux cents < \*dos centos* (CL *ducentos*), *trois cents < \*tres centos* (CL *trecentos*), etc.

(5) OFr. *mil* and plurals *mil, mile, milie* fused into MFr. Latinized *mille*, the old spelling *mil* being reserved for dates. The ordinal numerals of Vulgar Latin, with the exception of *primariu, -a* (> *premier, -ière*), did not survive beyond Old French, in which all but indeclinable *terz* (*tierz*) were declined for case, gender, and number: *seconz, secont, secont, seconz* < *secundus, -u, -i, -os, seconde, seconde, secondes, secondes* < *secunda, -as; terz* (*tierz*), *terce* (*tierce*), etc. < *tertius, -a,* etc.; *quarz, quarte,* etc. < *quartus, -a,* etc.; *quinz, quinte,* etc. < *quintus, -a,* etc.; *sistes, siste,* etc. < *sextus, -a,* etc.; *sedmes, sedme,* etc. < *septimus, -a,* etc.; *uitmes, uitme,* etc., *nuefmes, nuefme,* etc.; (CL *octavus, nonus*), on the analogy of *sedmes,* above, and *dismes, disme,* etc. < *decimus, -a,* etc. The MFr. ordinal suffix *-ième* (*deuxième, troisième,* etc.) has been explained as a Norman dialectal variant of OFr. *-ime, -isme* (< *-ecimu*).

(b) The cardinal numerals of Vulgar Latin (see par. 106, above) developed in Provençal as follows: (1) *One, two,* and *three* continued to be declined: (m.) *uns, un* (f.) *una, una;* (m.) *dui* (*doi*), *dos* (f.) *doas, doas;* (m.) *trei, tres* (*treis*). (2) *Four* to *sixteen* conformed to Classical-Vulgar Latin patterns, whereas *seventeen* to *nineteen* were of distinctly Vulgar Latin origin: *quatre, cinq, seis* (*sieis*), *set, oit* (*ueit, ueg*), *nou, detz, onze, dotze, tretze, quatorze, quinze, setze* (*sedze*), *detz e set, detz e oit, detz e nou.* (3) The ten's, from *twenty* to *ninety,* show a single vestige of a Vulgar Latin vigesimal system, namely, the form for *eighty: vint, trenta, quaranta, cinquanta, seissanta, setanta, quatre vint, nonanta* (*noranta*). (4) *Cent* was invariable, but its multiples were declined: (m.) *docent, docens,* (f.) *docentas, docentas* (< *ducenti, -os, -as*); *trecent, trecens* (< *trecenti,* etc.); *quatre cent, cens* (< *\*quattor centi, centos*); *cinq cent, cens,* etc. All hundred's above *three hundred* are derived from Vulgar Latin analytical forms. (5) The plurals of *one thousand* (*mil*) were *mil(l)ia* and its variants *melia, miria.* The ordinals, which, except for indeclinable *tertz,* were declined for case, number, and gender, were expressed, beginning with the variants for sixth (*seizens, seizena*), with the originally distributive suffix *-enus, -ena* (> *ens, -ena*): *premiers, premiera* < *primarius, -a; segons, segonda* < *secundus, -a; tertz, tersa* < *tertius, -a; quartz, quarta* < *·quartus, -a; quintz, quinto* < *quintus, -a; sest, sesta* < *sextus, -a,* (*seizens, seizena* < *\*sexenus, -a*); *setens, setena* < *\*se(p)tenus, -a; ochens, ochena* < *\*octenus, -a; novens, novena* < *\*novenus, -a; detzens, detzena* < *\*decenus, -a.*

## The Numerals in Ibero-Romance

108. (a) The cardinal numerals of Vulgar Latin (see par. 106, above) developed in Spanish as follows: (1) Of *one, two,* and *three,* only *one* and *two* continued to be declined, the latter not beyond Old

91

Spanish: *un(o)*, *una*; *dos* (OSp. *duas*, *dues*); *tres*. (2) *Four* to Old
Spanish *sixteen* followed the Classical-Vulgar Latin patterns, but
Modern Spanish *sixteen*, and *seventeen* to *nineteen*, were derived
from the analytical forms of Vulgar Latin: *cuatro*, *cinco* (*-o* on the
analogy of *cuatro*), *seis*, *siete*, *ocho*, *nueve*, *diez*, *once*, *doce*, *trece*,
*catorce*, *quince*, *dieciséis* (also *diez y seis*, OSp. *sedze*, *seze* < *\*sedece*
< *sedecim*), *diecisiete* (also *diez y siete*), *dieciocho* (also *diez y
ocho*), *diecinueve* (also *diez y nueve*). (3) The ten's, beginning with
*twenty*, were derived from their Vulgar Latin etyma, with pretonic
*a* assimilating to tonic *e* in the forms for *forty* to *ninety*, e.g.,
*quadra(g)inta* > OSp. *cuaraenta* > MSp. *cuarenta*: *veinte* (OSp.
*veínte*), *treinta* (OSp. *treínta*, with stressed *i* on the analogy of
*veínte*), *cuarenta* (OSp. *cuaraenta*), *cincuenta* (OSp. *cinquaenta*,
with *c-* on the analogy of *cinco*), *sesenta* (OSp. *sesaenta*, with *-s-* on
the analogy of *seis*), *setenta* (OSp. *setaenta*), *ochenta* (OSp. *ocha-
enta*), *noventa* (OSp. *novaenta*, with *nov-* on the analogy of *nove*;
also *nonaenta* < *nona(g)inta*). (4) Of the multiples of *one hundred*
(*ciento*, *cien*, OSp. *cient*), Old Spanish *two*, *three*, *five*, and *six hundred* were derived from Classical Latin compounds which·survived
in Vulgar Latin, whereas *four*, *seven*, *eight*, and *nine hundred* were
derived from the analytical forms of Vulgar Latin: *doscientos*, *-as*
(OSp. *dozientos*, *-as* < *ducentos*, *-as*), *trescientos*, *-as* (OSp. *trezien-
tos*, *-as* < *trecentos*, *-as*), *cuatrocientos*, *-as*, *quinientos*, *-as*
(< *quin(g)entos*, *-as*), *seiscientos*, *-as* (< *sexcentos*, *-as*), *setecientos*,
*-as*, *ochocientos*, *-as*, *novecientos*, *-as*. (5) Multiples of *one thousand*
(*mil*) came to be expressed by *mil*, through the Old Spanish periphrases *dos* (*vezes*) *mil*, *tres* (*vezes*) *mil*, etc. Of the ordinal numerals from *first* to *tenth*, only *first* to *fifth* survived as popular forms,
the others having disappeared or become substantivized (*siesta*,
*ochavo*, *diezmo*); from *eleventh* on, the ordinals had no popular development, and the learned forms were modeled directly on their Latin
counterparts (*vigésimo*, *trigésimo*, etc., exception made for substantivized *quadragesima*, *quinquagesima* > *\*cuaresima*, *\*cinquesima*
> *cuaresma*, OSp. *cincuesma*): *primero*, *-a*, etc. < *primariu*, *-a*, etc.;
*segundo*, *-a*, etc. < *secundu*, *-a*, etc.; *tercero*, *-a*, etc. < *tertiariu*, *-a*,
etc.; *cuarto*, *-a*, etc. <*quartu*, *-a*, etc.; *quinto*, *-a*, etc. < *quintu*, *-a*,
etc.; *sexto*, *-a*, etc. < *sextu*, *-a*, etc.; *séptimo*, *-a*, etc. < *septimu*, *-a*,
etc.; *octavo*, *-a*, etc. < *octavu*, *-a*, etc.; *noveno*, *-a*, etc. < *\*novenu*, *-a*,
etc., and *nono*, *-a*, etc. < *nonu*, *-a*, etc.; *décimo*, *-a*, etc. < *decimu*, *-a*,
etc.

(b) The cardinal numerals of Vulgar Latin (see par. 106, above)
developed in Catalan as follows: (1) Of *one*, *two*, and *three*, only
*one* and *two* continued to be declined: *un* (*u*, to signify the numeral
itself, and in such contexts as *u i dos fan tres*), *una*; *dos*, *dues* (also,
popular *dugues*, and the Hispanicism *dos*); *tres*. (2) *Four* to *sixteen*
followed the Classical-Vulgar Latin patterns, but *seventeen* to *nine-*

*teen* were derived from the analytical forms of Vulgar Latin: *quatre, cinc, sis, set, vuit, nou, deu, onze, dotze, tretze, catorze, quinze, setze, disset, divuit, dinou.* (3) All of the ten's, beginning with *twenty,* are contractions of the corresponding Latin forms, and *forty* to *ninety* show shift of stress as well: *vint, trenta, quaranta, cinquanta, seixanta* (also, popular *xixanta*), *setanta, vuitanta, noranta.* (4) *One hundred* and its multiples were inflected for number and gender, the multiples having been derived from the corresponding analytical forms of Vulgar Latin: *cent(s), -es; dos-cents, dues-centes; tres-cents, tres-centes,* etc. (5) *One thousand* and its multiples were expressed by the invariable *mil.* All ordinal numerals were inflected for number and gender and, beginning with the form for *fifth,* were expressed by suffixed cardinals, the originally distributive *-enus, -a, -os, -as* (> *-è, -ena, -ens, -enes*) serving the purpose: *primer, -a,* etc. < *primariu, -a,* etc.; *segon. -a,* etc. < *secundu, -a,* etc.; *tercer, -a,* etc. < *tertiariu, -a,* etc. (also, *terç* < *tertiu*); *quart, -a,* etc. < *quartu, -a,* etc.; *cinquè, -ena,* etc. < *\*cinquenu, -a,* etc. (also, learned *quint, -a,* etc. < *quintu, -a,* etc.) ; *sisè, -ena,* etc. < *\*sexenu, -a,* etc. (also, learned *sext, -a,* etc. < *sextu, -a,* etc.); *setè, -ena,* etc. < *\*se(p)tenu, -a,* etc. (also, learned *sèptim, -a,* etc. < *septimu, -a,* etc.); *vuitè, -ena,* etc. < *\*octenu, -a,* etc. (also, learned *octau, -ava,* etc. < *octavu, -a,* etc.; *novè, -ena,* etc. < *\*novenu, -a,* etc.; *desè, -ena,* etc. < *\*decenu, -a,* etc. (also, learned *dècim, -a,* etc. < *decimu, -a,* etc.); *onzè, dotzè, tretzè,* etc.

(c) The cardinal numerals of Vulgar Latin (see par. 106, above) developed in Portuguese as follows: (1) Of *one, two,* and *three,* only *one* and *two* continued to be declined: *um, uma; dois* (< *dous,* through dissimilation), *duas; tres.* (2) *Four* to Old Portuguese *sixteen* followed the Classical-Vulgar Latin patterns, but Modern Portuguese *sixteen,* and *seventeen* to *nineteen,* were derived from the analytical forms of Vulgar Latin: *quatro, cinco* (*-o* on the analogy of *quatro*), *seis, sete, oito, nove, dez, onze, doze, treze, catorze, quinze, dezasseis* (< *\*dece ac sex,* OPg. also *seze* < *\*sedece* < *sedecim,* and *dez e seis* < *\*dece et sex*), *dezassete* (OPg. *dez e sete*), *dezóito* (< *dezaoito,* through assimilation, OPg. *dez e oito*), *dezanove* (OPg. *dez e nove*). (3) The ten's, beginning with *twenty,* were derived from their Vulgar Latin etyma, with pretonic *a* assimilating to tonic *e* in the forms for *forty* to *ninety,* e.g., *quadra(g)inta* > OPg. *quaraenta* > MPg. *quarenta: vinte, trinta* (< *\*triinta* < *tri(g)inta,* with tonic *i* on the analogy of *vinte*); *quarenta, cinqüenta* (with *-c* on the analogy of *cinco*); *sessenta* (< *sessaenta* < *sexa(g)inta,* with *-ss-* on the analogy of *seis*); *setenta, oitenta* (< *oitaenta* < *\*octaginta,* with *octa-* on the analogy of *quadra-, q(u)inqua-,* etc.); *noventa* (< *novaenta* < *\*novaginta,* with *nova-* in lieu of etymological *nona-,* on the analogy of *nove*). (4) Of the multiples of *one hundred* (*cem* < *centu*), *two, three* and *five hundred* were derived from Classical Latin compounds which survived in Vulgar Latin, whereas *four, six, seven, eight,* and *nine hundred* were derived from analytical Vulgar Latin forms: *duzentos, -as* (< *ducentos, -as*), *trezentos, -as* (< *trecentos, -as*), *quatrocentos, -as* (< \**quattro centos*), *quinhentos, -as* (< *quingentos, -as*), *seiscentos* (< \**sex centos*), *setecentos* (< \**sette centos*), *oitocentos* (< \**octo centos*), *novecentos* (< \**nove centos*). (5) Multiples of *one thousand* (*mil*) came to be expressed by *mil* through the Old Portuguese periphrases *dous* (*vezes*) *mil, tres* (*vezes*) *mil,* etc. The ordinal numerals from *sixth* to *tenth* had very little popular development, and those from *eleventh* on, no popular development at all, with the possible exception of *quaresma* < \**quaraesima* < *qua(d)ra(g)esima,* which may be a Hispanicism (cf. Sp. *cuaresma*): *primeiro, -a,* etc. < *primariu, -a,* etc.; *segundo, -a,* etc. < *secunda, -a,* etc.; *terceiro, -a,* < *tertiariu, -a,* etc. (*têrço -a,* etc. < *tertiu, -a,* etc., only in *têrça-feira*); *quarto, -a,* etc. < *quartu, -a,* etc. (OPg., also *quarteiro, -a,* etc. < \**quartariu, -a,* etc.); *quinto, -a,* etc. < *quintu, -a,* etc. (OPg. also *quinteiro, -a,* etc. < *quintariu, -a,* etc.); *sexto, -a,* etc. < *sextu, -a,* etc. (OPg., also *seisto, -a,* etc., on the analogy of *seis*); *seistimo, -a,* etc., on the analogy of *seitimo, -a,* etc. [which follows]; and *seismo, sesmo, -a,* etc. < \**seximu, -a,* etc., on the analogy of *septimu, -a,* etc. [which follows]; *sétimo, -a,* etc. < *septimu, -a,* etc., on the analogy of *sete* (OPg. *seitimo, -a,* etc.); *oitavo, -a,* etc. < *octavu, -a,* etc. (OPg., also *outavo, -a,* etc.); *nono, -a,* etc. < *nonu, -a,* etc. (OPg., also *noveo, -a,* etc. < *novenu, -a,* etc.); *décimo, -a,* etc. < *decimu, -a,* etc.

*The Numerals in Rheto-Romance*

109. The cardinal numerals of Vulgar Latin (see par. 106, above) developed in Surselvan as follows: (1) Of *one, two,* and *three,* only *one* and *two* continued to be declined: *in, ina; dus, duas; treis.* The Latin neuter plurals *dua* and *tria* survived in collectives and multiples: *dua pèra, bratscha; trei pèra, bratscha; duatschien, treitschien; duamelli, treimelli.* (2) *Four* to *sixteen* followed Classical-Vulgar Latin patterns, whereas *seventeen* to *nineteen* were derived from the analytical forms of Vulgar Latin: *quater, tschun, sis, siat, otg, nov, diesch, endisch, dudisch, tredisch, quitordisch, quendisch, sedisch, gissiat* (< \**dece sette*), *șchotg* (< \**dece octo,* with loss of first syllable), *șcheniv* (< \**dece nove,* with loss of first syllable). (3) The ten's, beginning with *twenty,* were derived from their Vulgar Latin etyma, with contraction and shift of stress in each case: *vegn, trenta, curonta, tschunconta, sissonta, siatonta, otgonta, navonta* (< \**novaginta,* on the analogy of *nove*). (4) The multiples of *one hundred* (*tschien* < *centu*) were derived from analytical Vulgar Latin forms, the neuter plurals *dua, tria* (> *dua, trei*) being used to express *two* and *three hundred: duatschien, treitschien, quatertschien, tschun-*

94

*tschien*, etc. (5) Multiples of *one thousand* (*melli*) were also expressed by *melli*, the neuter plurals *dua, tria* (> *dua, trei*) being used to express *two* and *three thousand*: *duamelli, treimelli, quatermelli, tschunmelli*, etc. The ordinal numerals from *fifth* on are expressed by suffixed cardinals, the purpose being served by the suffixes *-avel, -avla*, etc., analogues of *otgavel, otgavla*, etc. (< *octavu, -a*, etc. + *ille, -a*, etc.) : *emprem, -a*, etc.; *secund, -a*, etc.; *tierz, tiarza*, etc.; *quart, -a; tschunavel, -avla; sisavel, -avla; siatavel, -avla*, etc. The only vestiges of the Latin ordinals above *fifth* are *cuareisma* (Lent) < *\*quaresima* < *quadragesima*, and *tschuncheismas* (Pentecost), *tschuncheisma* (a unit of measure) < *\*cinquesima* < *quinquagesima*.

## The Numerals in Italo-Romance

110. (a) The cardinal numerals of Vulgar Latin (see par. 106, above) developed in Italian as follows: (1) Of *one, two*, and *three*, only *one* continued to be declined: *un(o), una; due* (OIt., also *duo, dui, dua*, used indiscriminately); *tre*. (2) *Four* to *sixteen* followed the Classical-Vulgar Latin patterns, whereas *seventeen* to *nineteen* were derived from the analytical forms of Vulgar Latin: *quattro, cinque, sei, sette, otto, nove, dieci* (*-i*, perhaps on the analogy of *venti*, see (3), directly below), *undici, dodici, tredici, quattordici, quindici, sedici, diciassette* (< *\*dece ac sette*), *diciotto* (< *\*dece otto*), *diciannove* (< *\*dece ac nove*). (3) The ten's show contraction beginning with *twenty*, and shift of stress beginning with *forty*: *venti* (tonic *e* on the analogy of *trenta*), *trenta, quaranta, cinquanta, sessanta, settanta, ottanta, novanta* (< *\*novaginta*, on the analogy of *nove*). (4) Multiples of *one hundred* (*cento*) were derived from the analytical forms of Vulgar Latin, with the exception of *three hundred*, which was derived from the corresponding Latin compound: *duecenti, trecenti, quattrocenti, cinquecenti*, etc. (5) Multiples of *one thousand* (*mille*) were expressed by *mila* (*milia* X *mille*). Ordinal numerals beyond *tenth* were expressed by suffixed cardinals, the learned suffix *-esimo, -a*, etc., serving the purpose: *primo, -a*, etc. < *primu, -a*, etc., *secondo, -a*, etc. < *secundu, -a*, etc.; *terzo, -a*, etc. < *tertiu, -a*, etc.; *quarto, -a*, etc. < *quartu, -a*, etc.; *quinto, -a*, etc. < *quintu, -a*, etc.; *sesto, -a*, etc. < *sextu, -a*, etc.; *settimo, -a*, etc. < *septimu, -a*, etc.; *ottavo, -a*, etc. < *octavu, -a*, etc.; *nono, -a*, etc. < *nonu, -a*, etc.; *decimo, -a*, etc. < *decimu, -a*, etc.; *undicesimo, dodicesimo, tredicesimo*, etc.

(b) The cardinal numerals of Vulgar Latin (see par. 106, above) developed in Sardinian as follows: (1) Of *one, two*, and *three, one* and *two* continued to be declined: *un(u), una; duos, duas; tres*. The neuter plural *dua* survived in the expression of *two thousand* (*dua milia* > *dua mi*[ž]*a*). (2) *Four* to *sixteen* followed the Classical-Vulgar Latin patterns, with occasional syncope of *-di-* < *\*de(ce)*, whereas *seventeen* to *nineteen* were derived from the analytical forms of Vulgar Latin: *battoro, kimbe, ses, sette, otto, noe, deghe, undighi, doighi, treighi, battordighi, bindighi, seighi, deghesette* (< *\*dece sette*), *degheotto, deghenoe*. (3) The ten's, beginning with *twenty*, show contraction and shift of stress in each case: *binti, trinta, baranta, kimbanta, sessanta, settanta, ottanta, noranta* (< *\*nonanta* < *nonaginta*, through dissimilation). (4) Multiples of *one hundred* (*kentu*) were derived from the analytical forms of Vulgar Latin, exception made for *two* and *three hundred*, which were derived from Latin compounds: *dughentos* < *ducentos, treghentos* < *trecentos*. Neither *kentu* nor its multiples had feminine forms. (5) Multiples of *one thousand* (*milli*, with *-i* through assimilation to the tonic vowel) were expressed by *mi[ž]a* < *milia*. The neuter plural *dua* (see (1), directly above) was used to express the multiple *dua mi[ž]a*. Although Italian ordinals (see (*a*), directly above) with *-u* were used (*primu, segundu, terzu, kuartu*, etc.), they were largely replaced by periphrases consisting of *def. art.* + *de* + *card. num.*; thus, *su de unu, su de duos, su de tres*, etc.

*The Numerals in Balkan Romance*

111. The cardinal numerals of Vulgar Latin (see par. 106, above) developed in Rumanian as follows: (1) Of *one, two*, and *three, one* and *two* continued to be declined: *un, unui, o* (< *\*ua* < *una*), *unei; doi, doŭa; trei*. (2) *Four* to *ten* followed the Classical-Vulgar Latin patterns, whereas *eleven* to *nineteen* were expressed by periphrases consisting of *un* (*doi, doŭa, trei, patru*, etc.) + *spre* (< *super*) + *zece*: *patru, cinci, şase, şapte, opt, noŭa, zece, unsprezece, doisprezece* (*doŭasprezece*), *treisprezece, patrusprezece*, etc. (3) The ten's, beginning with *twenty*, were expressed as multiples of substantivized, feminine *zece*: *doŭazeci, treizeci, patruzeci, cincizeci*, etc. (4) The hundred's, beginning with *two hundred*, were expressed as multiples of Slavic, feminine *suta*, which replaced Latin *centum*: *doŭa sute, trei sute, patru sute*, etc. (5) Multiples of *one thousand* (*mie*, ORm. plural derived from *milia* and carried over to the singular) were expressed by analogical *mii*: *doŭa mii, trei mii*, etc. The Latin ordinals were replaced by periphrases consisting of *def. art.* + *card. num.* + *def. art.*, exception made for *first* (*întîiul, întîia* < *\*antaneu* + *ille, \*antanea* + *illa*): *al doilea* (*a doŭa*), *al treilea* (*a treia*), *al patrulea* (*a patra*), *al cincilea* (*a cincia*), etc. The only survival of the Latin ordinals is substantivized *păresimi* (Lent) < *\*quaresima* < *quadragesima*.

# APPENDIX A
## LINGUISTIC TEXTS
### I. GALLO-ROMANCE

a. *Old French*
(Luke, XV, 11-24)

11. . . . Uns hom avoit II filz. 12. Li plus juenes dist a son pere: Pere, done moi ma porcion del chatel qui m'afiert. Et il peres devisa sa substance, et dona a celui sa part. 13. Et dedenz brief tens, toutes choses assemblées ensemble, li plus juenes filz ala fors del païs en loingtiene region, et despendi iluec sa substance en vivant luxurieusement o les foles femes. 14. Et apres ce qu'il ot tout folement despendu, il fu famine en cele region. Lors comença il a avoir sofrete. 15. Et il ala et s'acovenança a I des citoiens de cele region, et il l'envoia en sa vile por pestre les porceaus. 16. Et il convoitoit a emplir son ventre de ce que li porcel menjoient, et nus hom li donoit. 17. Et il, reperant a soi meismes, dist: O, tant de serjanz ont habondanment del pain en la meson mon pere, et ge peris ici de faim! 18. Ge m'en partirai d'ici, et irai a mon pere, et li dirai: Pere, ge ai pechié devant Deu et devant toi, 19. ge ne sui pas dignes que ge soie apelez tes filz, mes fai moi come a un de tes serjanz mercenneres (Serjanz mercenneres est serjanz qui est acovenancié a servir desi a terme nommé, por le loier qu'il en doit recevoir). 20. Et cil se leva et vint a son pere. Quant il estoit encore loing, son pere le vit, et fuz meuz de misericorde (ce est a dire, il ot pitié de lui, et fu meuz de cuer a fere li misericorde), et il acorut, et li chaï sor le col, et le besa. 21. Lors li dist li filz: Pere, je ai pechié devant Deu et devant toi, ne ge ne sui ja mie dignes d'estre apelez tes filz. 22. Lors dist li peres a ses serjanz: Aportez tost avant la plus chiere vesteure, et le vestez, et li metez anel en sa main, et chaucemente en ses piez, 23. et amenez le veel engressié, et l'ociez, et menjons et fesons feste. 24. Car icist mien filz avoit esté mort, et il est revescuz, et il estoit perduz, et or est retrovez. Et tuit comencierent a mengier.

b. *Modern French*
(Luke, XV, 11-24)

11. . . . Un homme avait deux fils. 12. Le plus jeune dit à son père: "Père, donne-moi la part de fortune qui me revient." Et le

père leur partagea son bien. 13. Peu de jours après, le plus jeune fils, rassemblant tout son avoir, partit pour un pays lointain et y dissipa son bien dans une vie de prodigue. 14. Quant il eut tout dépensé, une grande famine survint en ce pays et il commença a sentir la privation. 15. Il alla se mettre au service d'un des habitants de la contrée, qui l'envoya dans ses champs garder les cochons. 16. Il aurait bien voulu se remplir le ventre des caroubes que mangeaient les cochons, mais personne ne lui en donnait. 17. Rentrant alors en lui-meme, il se dit: "Combien de journaliers de mon père ont du pain en abondance, et moi je suis ici à mourir de faim. 18. Je veux partir, retourner vers mon père et lui dire: 'Père, j'ai péché contre le Ciel et contre toi; 19. je ne mérite plus d'être appelé ton fils, traite-moi comme l'un de tes journaliers.' " 20. Il partit donc et s'en retourna vers son père. Comme il était encore loin, son père l'aperçut et fut touché de compassion; il courut se jeter à son cou et l'embrassa longuement. 21. Le fils alors lui dit: "Père, j'ai péché contre le Ciel et contre toi; je ne mérite plus d'être appelé ton fils." 22. Mais le père dit à ses serviteurs: "Vite, apportez la plus belle robe et l'en revêtez, mettez-lui un anneau au doigt et des chaussures aux pieds. 23. Amenez le veau gras, tuez-le, mangeons et festoyons, 24. car mon fils que voilà était mort et il est revenu à la vie; il était perdu et il est retrouvé!" Et ils se mirent à festoyer.

### c. *Old Provençal*
### (John, XIV, 1-16)

1. E dix a sos decipols. No sia turbatz lo uostre cor ni s'espauent. crezetz en deu. et a mi crezetz. — 2. e la maiso del meu paire so moutas estaias. Si d'autra guiza eu agues dig a uos. Quar uau aparelhar a uos loc. — 3. E si eu anarei. et aparelarei a uos oc. de rescaps uenrei e recebrei uos ab mi meteiss. et aqui on eu so e uos siatz. — 4. Et on eu uau sabetz e la uia sabetz. — 5. Dix a lui Tomas. senher no sabem on uas e cum podem la uia saber? — 6. Dix a lui Jhesu. eu so uia e ueritatz e uida. negus no ve al paire, sino per mi. — 7. Si aguessetz conogut mi, el meu paire a certas agratz conogut. e d'aici enant conoisseretz lui. e uisz lui. — 8. Dis a lui Phelips. senher demostra a nos lo paire. et auonda a nos. — 9. Dix a lui Jhesu. tant de temps so ab uos. e no me conogues Phelip? qui ue mi ue neiss lo paire. en qual maneira dizes tu. demostra a nos lo paire? — 10. No cres que eu so el paire el paire e mi es? Las paraulas que eu parli a uos de mi meteis no parli. mais lo paire e mi estantz. el fa las obras. — 11. No crezetz. quar eu so el paire. el paire es e mi? d'autra guiza per las obras meteissas crezetz. — 12. Verament uerament dic a uos. qui cre e mi las obras que eu fasz et el fara e mairos d'aquestas ne fara. quar eu uau al paire. — 13. E qualque causa queretz al paire el meu nom. el uos o donara que sia glorificatz lo paire el fil. — 14. Si

alcuna causa me queretz el meu nom aisso farei. — 15. Si mi amatz los meus mandamentz gardatz. — 16. Et eu pregarei lo paire, et autre cofortador dara a uos. que estia ab uos en durableta.

### d. *Modern Provençal*
### (Matthew, XX, 1-16)

1. Lou rouyaoume doou cièl' es parié '-n-un pèro de famïo, que sourté de gran matin, pèr louga d'ouvriè pèr travaya ' sa vigno. 2. Estèn d'acor emé leis ouvriè d'un deniè cadun pèr la journado, lei mandé à sa vigno. 3. Sourté 'ncaro su la tresièm' ouro doou jou, e n'aguèn vi d'aoutre que si tenièn su la plac' à rèn faire, 4. Li digué: Anà-v'en aoussi à ma vigno, e vou dounarai ce que sera resounable; 5. E l'anéroun. Sourté 'ncaro su la sièsièm' e su la noouvièm' ouro doou jou, e fagué la memo caouvo. 6. Enfin estèn sourti su la vounzièm' ouro, nen trouvé d'aoutre qu'èroun aqui tou lou lon doou jou sènço rèn faire, en cu digué: Pèrqu'istà 'qui sènço rèn faire? 7. Es, li diguéroun, que degun nous a louga, e li digué: Anà-v'en tambèn vaoutr' à ma vigno. 8. Lou tremoun estèn vengu, lou mèstre de la vigno digué 'n aqueou qu'aviè souin de seis afaire: Souènà leis ouvriè, e pagà-lei, en coumençàn desempuèi lei darniè finqu'ei proumiè. 9. Aquelei doun qu'èroun vengu à la vigno qu'aperaqui vounz' ouro, s'estèn avança, reçubéroun cadun un deniè. 10. Aquelei qu'èroun louga lei proumiè venèn à soun tour, creséroun que li dounarièn de mai; mai reçubéroun tambèn qu'un deniè cadun: 11. E en lou reçubèn repepiávoun contro lou pèro de famïo, 12. E li disièn: Aquestei darniè au travaya qu'un' ouro, e lei rendè 'gaou à naoutre, qu'avèn pourta lou fai doou jou e de la calour. 13. Mai pèr responso digué à-n-un d'elei: Moun ami, vou foou je de tor: sian pa counvengu d'un deniè pèr vouèsto journado? 14. Prenè ce qu'es vouèstre, e en-anà-v'en: Pèr iou, vouèli douna 'n aqueou darniè aoutan qu'à vou. 15. M'es-t-i pa pèrmé, de faire ce que vouèli? e vouèst uèi es-t-i marri, parço que siou bouèn? 16. Ensin lei darniè seran lei proumiè, e lei proumiè seran lei darniè: parço que n'a fouèsso de souèna, mai gaire d'elu.

## II.  IBERO-ROMANCE

### a. *Spanish*
### (Luke, XV, 11-24)

1. . . . Cierto hombre tenía dos hijos: 12. y el menor de ellos dijo a su padre: Padre, dame la parte que me toca de tus bienes. Y él les partió la hacienda. 13. Y no muchos días después, juntándolo todo

el hijo menor, partió para una región lejana; y allí desperdició su caudal, viviendo disolutamente. 14. Y cuando lo hubo gastado todo, sucedió una grande hambre en aquel país; y él comenzó a padecer necesidad. 15. Y fue, y arrimóse a uno de los ciudadanos de aquel país; el cual le envió a sus campos para apacentar los puercos. 16. Y deseaba hartarse de las algarrobas que comían los puercos; y nadie le daba nada. 17. Mas cuando volvió en sí, dijo: ¡Cuántos jornaleros de mi padre tienen sobreabundancia de pan, y yo aquí perezco de hambre! 18. Me levantaré, e iré a mi padre y le diré: Padre, he pecado contra el cielo y delante de ti; 19. ya no soy digno de ser llamado hijo tuyo; haz que yo sea como uno de tus jornaleros. 20. Y levantóse, y fue a su padre. Y estando todavía lejos, le vio su padre; y conmoviéronsele las entrañas; y corrió, y le echó los brazos al cuello, y le besó fervorosamente. 21. Y el hijo le decía: Padre, he pecado contra el cielo, y delante de ti: ya no soy digno de ser llamado hijo tuyo. 22. Mas el padre dijo a sus siervos: Sacad al momento la ropa más preciosa, y vestidle con ella; y poned un anillo en su mano, y zapatos en sus pies; 23. y traed el becerro cebado, y matadle y comamos, y regocijémonos; 24. porque este mi hijo muerto era, y ha vuelto a vivir; habíase perdido, y ha sido hallado. Y comenzaron a regocijarse.

### b. *Catalan*
### (Luke, XV, 11-24)

11. . . . Un home tenia dos fills. 12. I digué el mès jove d'ells al pare: Pare, doneu-me la part que em toca del patrimoni; i els repartí els béns. 13. I, passats no gaires dies, el fill més jove, aplegant-ho tot, se n'anà lluny a país estranger, i allí malversà el seu patrimoni, vivint disbauxadament. 14. I quan s'ho havia gastat tot, hi hagué forta fam per a aquell país, i ell començà de freturejar. 15. I anà a acollir-se a un dels habitants d'aquell país, el qual l'envià a les seves terres a pasturar porcs, 16. i desitjava omplir el seu ventre de les garrofes que menjaven els porcs, i ningú no li'n donava; 17. i, havent entrat en si, digué: Quants jornalers del meu pare tenen pa de sobres, i jo aquí en moro de fam! 18. M'alço, i me'n vaig al meu pare, i li diré: Pare, he pecat contra el cel i envers vós, 19. ja no só digne d'ésser anomenat fill vostre; feu-me com un dels vostres jornalers. 20. I, alçant-se, vingué al seu pare. I, essent encara ell un tros lluny, el veié el seu pare i s'enterní i corrent se li tirà al coll, i el besava. 21. I li digué el fill: Pare, he pecat contra el cel i envers vós, ja no só digne d'ésser anomenat fill vostre. 22. I digué el pare als seus servents: De pressa, traieu la roba millor i vestiu-l'en, i poseu-li anell a la mà i calçat als peus, 23. i porteu el vedell gras, mateu-lo, i fem un àpat de festa, puix aquest fill meu era mort i ha reviscut, era perdut i s'és trobat. I començaren la festa.

## c. *Portuguese*
## (Luke, XV, 11-24)

11. . . . Um certo homem tinha dois filhos; 12. e o mais moço deles disse ao pai: Pai, dá-me a parte da fazenda que me pertence. E ele repartiu por eles a fazenda. 13. E, poucos dias depois, o filho mais novo, ajuntado tudo, partiu para uma terra longínqua, e ali desperdiçou a sua fazenda, vivendo dissolutamente. 14. E, havendo ele gastado tudo, houve naquela terra uma grande fome, e começou a padecer necessidades. 15. E foi, e chegou-se a um dos cidadãos daquela terra, o qual o mandou para os seus campos, a apascentar porcos. 16. E desejava encher o seu estômago com as bolotas que os porcos comiam, e ninguém lhe dava nada. 17. E, tornando em si, disse: Quantos jornaleiros de meu pai têm abundância de pão, e eu, aqui, pereço de fome! 18. Levantar-me-ei, e irei ter com meu pai, e dir-lhe-ei: Pai, pequei contra o céu e perante ti; 19. já não sou digno de ser chamado teu filho; faze-me como um dos teus jornaleiros. 20. E, levantando-se, foi para seu pai; e, quando ainda estava longe, viu-o seu pai, e se moveu de íntima compaixão, e, correndo, lançou-se-lhe ao pescoço e o beijou. 21. E o filho lhe disse: Pai, pequei contra o céu e perante ti, e já não sou digno de ser chamado teu filho. 22. Mas o pai disse aos seus servos: Trazei depressa o melhor vestido, e vesti-lho, e ponde-lhe um anel na mão, e alparcas nos pés; 23. e trazei o bezerro cevado, e matai-o; e comamos, e alegremo-nos; 24. porque este meu fiho estava morto, e reviveu; tinhase perdido, e foi achado. E começaram a alegrar-se.

## III. RHETO-ROMANCE

### (Luke, XV, 11-24)

11. . . . In um haveva dus fegls. 12. Ed il giuven de quels ha getg al bab: Bab, dai a mi la part della rauba che tucca a mi! E qual ha partigiu siu fatg denter els. 13. Paucs gis suenter ha il fegl giuven priu tut ed ei tilaus naven en ina tiara lontana, e leu ha el sfatg sia rauba cun viver slaschadamein. 14. Cu el ha giu consumau tut, ha ei dau en lezza tiara in grond fomaz, ed el ha entschiet a pitir basegns. 15. Cheu eis el ius e sefultschius tier in vischin de lezza tiara, e qual ha tarmess el sil funs a pertgirar ses pors. 16. Ed el giavischava d'emplenir siu venter culla panetscha ch'ils pors maglia-van, mo negin deva quella ad el. 17. Cheu eis el ius en sesez ed ha getg: Cons luvrers de miu bab han paun en abundonza, mo jeu stosel cheu pirir della fom! 18. Jeu vi sefar si ed ir tier miu bab e vi gir ad el: Bab, jeu hai fatg puccau encunter il tschiel ed avon tei 19. e sun buca vengonts pli de vegnir numnaus tiu fegl; fai esser mei sco in de tes schurnaliers. 20. Ed el ei sefatgs si ed ius tier siu bab.

Cu el era aunc dalunsch, ha siu bab tscherniu el. Ed el ha giu compassiun, ei currius, ha pegliau entuorn culiez ad el e bitschau el. 21. Ed il fegl ha getg ad el: Bab, jeu hai fatg puccau encunter il tschiel ed avon tei; jeu sun buca vengonts pli de vegnir numnaus tiu fegl! 22. Mo il bab ha getg a ses fumegls: Spert, purtei il meglier vestgiu e targei en ad el, e dei in ani per siu maun e calzers per ses peis! 23. E menei il vadi engarschau e mazzei el, e nus lein magliar e star de buna veglia; 24. pertgei quest miu fegl era morts ed ei turnaus en veta, era pers ed ei vegnius anflaus. Ed els han entschiet a star si legher!

# IV. ITALO-ROMANCE

## a. *Italian*
(Luke, XV, 11-24)

11. . . . Un uomo aveva due figli, 12. e il più giovane di essi disse al padre: Padre, dammi la parte dei beni che mi spetta. E il padre divise tra loro i beni. 13. Pochi giorni dopo, il figlio più giovane, messa insieme ogni cosa, se n'andò in un paese lontano y quivi dissipò la sua sostanza, menando vita dissoluta. 14. Quand'ebbe consumato ogni cosa, una gran carestia colpì quel paese; ed egli cominciò a sentire la miseria. 15. E messosi in cammino, si pose al servizio d'uno di quegli abitanti, che lo mandò ne' suoi campi a custodire i porci. 16. Ed egli desiderava ardentemente di cavarsi la fame con le ghiande che mangiavano i porci, ma nessuno gliene dava. 17. Allora, rientrato in sè, disse: Quanti servitori in casa di mio padre hanno pane a volontà, mentre io qui muoio di fame! 18. M'alzerò e andrò dal padre mio e gli dirò: Padre, ho peccato contro il cielo e contro te; 19. non son più degno d'esser chiamato tuo figlio, trattami pure come uno de' tuoi servitori. 20. Levatosi, andò da suo padre; e mentre egli era ancora lontano, il padre suo lo vide e n'ebbe pietà; gli corse incontro e gli si gettò al collo e lo baciò. 21. Gli disse il figliuolo: Padre, ho peccato contro il cielo e contro te; non sono più degno d'esser chiamato tuo figliuolo! 22. Ma il padre commandò a suoi servi: Presto, portate quà la veste più bella, e metteteglila addosso; ponetegli un anello al dito e calzari ai piedi; 23. menate il vitello ingrassato ed ammazatelo e si mangi e si banchetti; 24. perchè questo mio figliuolo era morto ed è tornato in vita; era perduto ed è state ritrovato. E cominciarono a far gran festa.

## b. *Sardinian*
(Luke, XV, 11-24)

1. . . . Unu certu homine tenìat duos fizos: 12. Su minore de ipsos nesit ad su babbu: Babbu, dami sa parte de sos benes qui mi toccant.

Et ipse lis dividèsit s'heredidade. 13. Et pustis de pagas dies, congregadas totu sas cosas, su fizu minore si partèsit a logu lontanu, et in caddàe dissipèsit totu su sou vivende luxuriosamente. 14. Et pustis qui haìat consummadu ogni cosa, occurret una grande carestia in cussu paesu, et ipse principièsit a tenner bisonzu. 15. Et andèsit, et s'addirit ad unu de sos cittadinos de cussu paesu, su quale lu mandèsit in sos campos pro li paschere sos porcos. 16. Et bramaìat de si pienare sa bentre sua de sas tilibas qui mandigaìant sos porcos: et niunu ndeli daìat. 17. Ma intradu in se matepsi nesit: Quantos teraccos in domo de babbo meu abbundant de pane, et eo inhòghe morzo de fàmine! 18. M'hapo alzare, et querzo andare ad inue est babbu meu, et l'hapo a narrer: Babbu, hapo peccadu contra ad su Chelu et contra ad tie. 19. Ja non so dignu de mi jamare plus fizu tou: tràctami que unu de sos servidores tuos. 20. Et alzèndesi, benit ad su babbu sou. In su mentres qui fit ancòras allargu, lu bidet su babbu, et si movèsit a piedade, et currende si li bettèsit in brazzos, et si lu basèsit. 21. Et i su fizo nesit ad ipsu: Babbu, hapo peccadu contra su Chelu et contra ad tie; non so dignu d'essere jamadu fizu tou. 22. Et nesit instantu su babbu ad sos servidores suos: Prestu, battide sa veste plus pretiosa, et bestidebìla, et ponìdeli s'aneddu in sa manu sua, et i sas iscarpas in sos pees suos. 23. Et portàdemi unu bitellu rassu, et boccidelu, et mandighemus et iscialemus. 24. Proìte custu fizu meu fit mortuu, et est torradu a vida; fit pèrdidu, et s'est incontradu. Et cominzèsint ad iscialare.

# V. BALKAN-ROMANCE

## (Luke, XV, 11-24)

11. . . . un om aveà doi fii. 12. Şi cel mai tânăr dintre ei zise tatălui său: tată, dă-mi partea de avuţie ce-mi cade. Şi le împărţi averea. 13. Şi nu după multe zile fiul mai tânăr, strângând toate, se duse într'o ţară depărtată, şi acolo risipì avuţia sa, vieţuind destrămat. 14. Şi după ce dânsul cheltuì tot, se întâmplă foamete mare prin aceea ţară, şi el începù să fie in lipsă. 15. Şi ducându-se, se lipì de unul dintre locuitorii acelei ţări, şi-l trimise la câmpul său să păzească porcii; 16. Şi dorià să-şi umple pântecile din roşcovii pe care îi mâncau porcii, dar nimenea nu-i dà. 17. Şi venindu-şi în minţi zise: câţi simbriaşi ai tatălui meu, au prisos de pâne, iar eu pier aci de foame. 18. Sculându-mă, voiu merge la tatăl meu şi-i voiu zice: tată, am greşit în faţa cerului şi înaintea ta. 19. Nu mai sunt vrednic a fi numit fiul tău; fă-mă ca pe unul dintre simbriaşii tăi. 20. Şi sculându-se, venì la tatăl său. Şi fiind el încă departe, tatăl său îl văzù şi i-se făcù mila, şi alergând se plecă pe gâtul lui şi-l sărută. 21. Iar fiul îi zise: tată, am greşit în faţa cerului şi înaintea ta, nu

mai sunt vrednic a fi numit fiul tău. 22. Şi tatăl zise către slugile sale: aduceţi curând un vestmânt lung, cel dintâiu, şi îmbrăcaţi-l, şi daţi inel î mâna lui şi încălţăminte în picioare. 23. Şi aduceţi viţelul cel îngrăşat, înjunghiaţi, şi mâncând să ne veselim. 24. Că acest fiu al meu mort era şi înviè, pierdut erà şi se află. Şi începură a se veselì.

# APPENDIX B

## *GLOSSARY OF LINGUISTIC TERMINOLOGY*

*Adstratum*: the language of one of two contiguous speech communities which exerts an influence upon the language of the other. The influence is often a mutual one.
Ex.: Bulgarian, as related to Rumanian.

*Affricate*: a sound which is produced by the immediately successive articulation of an *occlusive* (*q.v.*) and a *fricative* (*q.v.*).
Ex.: [tš], as in Sp. mu*chacho*.

*Analogue*: a form which assumes one or more of the phonetic characteristics of a dissimilar form which performs a similar or identical grammatical function.
Ex.: Fr. *chantAIS* [ɛ], as related to *devAIS* [ɛ].

*Analogy*: the process whereby *analogues* (*q.v.*) originate and take shape.

*Apheresis*: the loss of the initial sound of a word, which is most often absorbed originally by the identical final vowel of a preceding article.
Ex.: *illa apotheca* > Sp. *la bodega*.

*Apocope* (*Apocopation*): the shortening of a word or form by the loss or omission of its final vowel.
Ex.: Sp. *BUENO* vs. *un BUEN hombre*.

*Articulation*: the production of a speech sound by means of the vocal organs.

*Aspirate*: to pronounce like the [h] of Eng. *how*.
Ex.: OSp. *Fambre* (*Hambre*) during the fifteenth, and most of the sixteenth century.

*Assimilation*: process whereby one of two phonemes within a word assumes one, several, or all of the phonetic features of the other.
Ex.: *dIrEctu* > Sp. *dErEcho*.

*Atonic*: unstressed.

*Balkan System*: vocalic system of the Vulgar Latin spoken in the Balkans, which differs principally from the *Italic System* (*q.v.*) in that the stressed ŭ of Classical Latin becomes [u] rather than [ọ], and from the *Sardinian System* (*q.v.*) in that stressed ĭ becomes [ẹ] rather than [i].

*Cacuminal*: (a sound) produced by the tip of the tongue curled back in retroflex fashion against the front of the hard palate.
 Ex.: [ḍ], as in Sd. *kaddu.*
*Checked (Closed) Syllable*: one which ends in a consonant.
*Close (d) Vowel:* one which is articulated with mouth less open than for an *open vowel (q.v.)*, and with tongue raised.
 Ex.: Fr. *chantÉ* [e].
*Dialect*: a homogeneous variant of the language of a speech community, which is restricted to a geographic area.
 Ex.: Fr. *picard (Picardie), normand (Normandie).*
*Dimorphic*: having two distinct forms.
*Dissimilation*: process whereby one of two similar or identical phonemes within a word loses one, several, or all of the phonetic features it has in common with the other, or disappears altogether.
 Ex.: *fOrmOsu, aRboRe* > Sp. *hErmOso, áRboL.*
*Distributive Suffix:* one which is appended to a numeral, serving to signal a group consisting of as many components as are indicated by the numeral.
 Ex.: CL *-enus.*
*Duration of Articulation*: length of time that vocal organs retain the position they assume for the production of a speech sound; phonemically significant when it serves to differentiate two otherwise phonetically identical forms.
 Ex: CL ōs (long *o*), *'mouth'* vs. ŏs (short o), *'bone.'*
*Enclitic*: an unstressed element in a *syntagma (q.v.)* which is appended to the stressed form it follows; the syntactic position occupied by such an element.
 Ex.: Sp. *dígaME.*
*Fricative*: (a sound) produced with only partial occlusion of the air passage, accompanied by audible or inaudible friction, and possibly by the vibration of the vocal chords.
 Ex.: Sp. [ƀ], [đ], [g̶] in *haBa, laDo, laGo.*
*Gemination*: the doubling of consonants.
*Guttural = Velar (q.v.).*
*Haplology*: loss or omission of one of two consecutive, similar or identical sounds or sound clusters within a word or form.
 Ex.: CL *metipsissimus* > VL *metipsimus.*
*Hiatus*: the phonetic circumstance of consecutive vowels which do not combine to form a diphthong; the pause which separates such vowels.
 Ex.: CL *folia (fo-li-a), vidua (vi-du-a).*
*Imparisyllabic*: not having the same number of syllables in all case forms of a declension.
 Ex.: CL *ars, artis.*
*Impure s*: initial *s* followed a consonant, or consonantal group, which gives rise to *prosthesis (q.v.).*

106

*Inchoative*: expressing the beginning of an action or state of being; said of Latin verbs with *infix* (*q.v.*) *-sc-*, and of Romance verbs which derive this infix etymologically or adopt it analogically, usually with phonological modifications.

Ex.: Fr. *finiSSons*, It. *finiSCe, finSCono*.

*Infix*: an unetymological sound or sound cluster which is inserted in a word or form to modify its meaning, and serves as a source of analogical forms with no modification of meaning.

Ex.: *inchoative* (*q.v.*) *-sc-*.

*Inflection*: a systematized modification of the stem or ending of a form, to signal one or more grammatical facts.

*Intervocalic*: (a consonant or consonantal group) immediately preceded and followed by a vowel.

*Intrusive*: describes an unetymological vowel or consonant which serves to facilitate the articulatory transition from one phoneme to another.

Ex.: *teNeRu* > *\*teN'Ru* > *teNDRe*.

*Italic System*: vocalic system of the Vulgar Latin spoken in Italy and the western provinces of the Roman Empire, which differs principally from the *Balkan System* (*q.v.*) in that CL stressed *ŭ* becomes [ǫ], not [u], and from the *Sardinian System* (*q.v.*) in that CL stressed *ĭ* becomes [ẹ], not [i].

*Labial*: a consonant whose articulation involves one or both lips, or a vowel whose articulation involves the rounding of the lips.

Ex.: [f], which involves one lip and the teeth (labio-dental); [m], which involves both lips (bilabial); [o], which involves lip rounding.

*Latent z*: the [z] in French which is pronounced only in *liaison* (*q.v.*).

*Learned Influence*: influence of the school and/or church, which partially or totally impeded the popular development of a word or form.

Ex.: Sp. *espíritu*, in which, contrary to popular development, the *post-tonic vowel* (*q.v.*) survives, the *intervocalic surd* (*q.v.*) fails to become *sonorous* (*q.v.*), and final *u* does not become *o*.

*Liaison*: the pronunciation of an otherwise silent final consonant when followed by a vowel.

Ex.: French *les* [le] vs. *les arbres* [lezárbr].

*Long Syllable*: in Classical Latin words or forms of three or more syllables, a *penult* (*q.v.*) which contained a *long vowel* (*q.v.*) or a diphthong, or ended in a consonant, and therefore carried the stress.

*Long Vowel*: in Classical Latin, a vowel whose *duration of articulation* (*q.v.*) distinguished it from the corresponding *short vowel* (*q.v.*); marked by a macron, *e.g.*, ā.

*Manner of Articulation*: the disposition of the vocal organs involved in the articulation of a speech sound.

107

*Metathesis*: the process whereby two phonemes within a word exchange position.

Ex.: *peRicuLu* > Sp. *peLigRo*.

*Monomorphic*: having only one form.

*Morpheme*: the smallest unit of speech which has an identifiable meaning of its own.

*Morphology*: the study of the constituents of systematic grammatical forms.

*Mute e*: a neutral vowel to which certain unstressed vowels in Catalan, French, and Portuguese are reduced; also known as *shwa*; represented phonetically as [ə].

*Nasal*: (a sound) produced by lowering the velum, and thus permitting the partial or total flow of air through the nose, with the mouth serving as a resonance chamber.

*Nasalize*: to articulate with the velum lowered, so as to produce a *nasal* (*q.v.*).

*Neutralization*: in certain phonetic environments, the fusion of the phonetic features which otherwise serve to distinguish between two or more phonemes in a given language.

Ex.: Sp. *oBtener* [p], *eN vano* [m].

*Occlusive*: an oral consonant whose articulation requires the momentary stoppage of the flow of air through the mouth.

Ex.: [t], [d], [p], [b], [k], [g].

*Open Syllable*: one which ends in a vowel.

*Open Vowel*: one which is articulated with the mouth opened much wider than for a *close* (*d*) *vowel* (*q.v.*).

Ex.: Fr. *chantAIS, mEttre* [ɛ] ; *dOnne*, botte[ɔ].

*Oxytone*: a word which is stressed on the last syllable.

*Palatal*: (a sound) produced by the blade of the tongue against the hard palate.

*Palatalize*: to articulate with a following *yod* (*q.v.*).

Ex.: VL *ce, ci* [kje, kji], *ge, gi* [gje, gji], which develop into the affricates [tš], [dž].

*Paradigm*: the forms which constitute a conjugation or declension.

*Paragoge*: the addition to a word or form of an unetymological sound or sound group in final position, for purposes of pattern conformity.

Ex.: It. *amanO*.

*Paroxytone*: a word which is stressed on the next to the last syllable.

*Patois*: the colloquial speech of a local area; usually a variant of a provincial dialect.

*Penult*: the next to the last syllable of a word.

*Perfective Verb*: one which denotes an action which can be completed.

*Periphrasis*: a construction consisting of two or more words which performs the same syntactic function as a single, inflected form.

*Personal Infinitive*: an infinitive which is conjugable, being inflected for person and number.

*Phoneme*: in a given language, a minimal unit of distinctive sound, whose phonetic contours vary predictably in accordance with the phonetic environments in which it occurs.

*Phonemic Differential*: the difference in sound which results in a difference in meaning.

*Phonology*: the study of the *phonemes* (*q.v.*) of a given language.

*Pleonasm*: a form or construction characterized by its redundancy.

*Plosive = Occlusive (q.v.)*.

*Post-tonic Vowel*: one which follows the stressed vowel of a word, usually exclusive of the final vowel.
    Ex.: It. *povEro*.

*Pretonic Vowel*: one which precedes the stressed vowel of a word, usually exclusive of the initial vowel.
    Ex.: CL *bonItatem*.

*Proclitic*: an unstressed constituent of a *syntagma* (*q.v.*) which combines with the stressed form it precedes to form a phonetic and syntactic unit; the position occupied by such a constituent in sentence phonetics.
    Ex.: Fr. (*Jean*) *ME LE donne*.

*Proparoxytone*: a word which is stressed on the second from the last syllable.
    Ex.: Sp. *pájaro*.

*Prosthesis*: prefixing of Classical Latin *impure s* (*q.v.*) with Vulgar Latin [i] to facilitate pronunciation, the prosthetic [i] surviving in Romance as [e] or [i], with related phonological consequences.
    Ex.: *spatha* > Fr. *épée*, Sp. *espada*.

*Quality*: the distinctive character of the Vulgar Latin vocalic system, in which *open* and *close* (*d*) *vowels* (*q.v.*) correspond to the *long* and *short vowels* (*q.v.*), respectively, of the Classical Latin vocalic system.
    Ex.: CL ō, ŏ = VL [ọ], [ǫ].

*Quantity*: the distinctive character of the Vulgar Latin vocalic system, in which *long* and *short vowels* (*q.v.*), which were otherwise identical, were distinguished by *duration of articulation* (*q.v.*).

*Rigor*: the degree of predictability with which a linguistic phenomenon occurs.

*Sardinian System*: the vocalic system of the Vulgar Latin spoken in Sardinia, which differs principally from the *Balkan System* (*q.v.*) in that CL stressed ĭ becomes [i], not [ẹ], and from the *Italic System* (*q.v.*) in that CL stressed ŭ becomes [u], not [ọ].

*Semantic*: concerned with the meaning conveyed by language.

*Semi-Consonant*: [i̯] or [u̯] as the first element of a rising diphthong (unstressed—stressed).
    Ex.: It. *pIede*, Sp. *pUeblo*.

109

*Semi-Vowel*: [i̯] or [u̯] as the second element of a falling diphthong (stressed—unstressed).

Ex.: Sp. *peIne, caUdal.*

*Short Vowel*: in Classical Latin, one whose *duration of articulation* distinguishes it phonemically from its corresponding *long vowel* (*q.v.*); marked by a breve, as in ă.

*Sonorous*: articulated with the accompanying vibration of the vocal chords.

*Stop* = *Occlusive* (*q.v.*).

*Strong Form*: a verb form which is stressed on the stem, rather than the ending.

*Substratum*: a language which was superseded by another, by reason of military conquest, colonization, cultural superiority, etc., but which had a perceptible effect upon the language which superseded it.

*Superstratum*: a language which was introduced into a speech community by reason of military conquest, colonization, cultural superiority, etc., and which had a perceptible effect upon the native language before disappearing.

*Supportive Vowel*: an unetymological final vowel which was appended to a word or form whose development had resulted in an anomalous final consonant or consonantal cluster.

Ex.: *teneru* > Fr. *tendrE.*

*Surd*: (a sound) whose articulation is not accompanied by the vibration of the vocal chords.

Ex.: [f], [k], [p], [t].

*Syncope*: the loss of a *pretonic* or *post-tonic vowel* (*q.v.*).

*Syntagma*: a construction whose component forms (tagmemes), in the order in which they occur, constitute a syntactic unit.

*Syntax*: the study of the arrangement of forms into phrases, clauses, and sentences, with the attendant changes required by the effect of one constituent on another.

*Tonic*: stressed.

*Trilled R*: one which is produced by the vibration of the tip of the tongue against the hard palate.

Ex.: Sp. *Rojo, peRRo.*

*Unchecked Syllable, Vowel* = *Open Syllable, Vowel* (*q.v.*).

*Unvoiced* = *Surd* (*q.v.*).

*Uvular R*: one which is produced by the vibration of the uvula against the back of the tongue.

*Velar*: (a sound) produced by the back of the tongue against the soft palate (velum).

*Velarize*: to pronounce an originally non-velar sound in velar fashion, i.e., by raising the back of the tongue toward the soft palate (velum).

*Vocalization*: process whereby a consonant becomes a vowel or *semi-vowel* (q.v.).

> Ex.: *aL(teru)* > [aU] > [oU] > [o] (Fr. *autre*, Sp. otro).

*Voiced* = *Sonorous* (q.v.).

*Weak Form*: a verb form which is stressed on the inflected ending, rather than on the stem.

*Yod*: the *semi-consonant* (q.v.) and *semi-vowel* (q.v.) [i], which occurs as the unstressed element of a rising and falling diphthong, respectively.

# BIBLIOGRAPHY

## 1. Latin

Díaz y Díaz, Manuel C. *Antología del latín vulgar.* 2nd ed. Madrid: Ed. Gredos, 1962.

Grandgent, Charles H. *An Introduction to Vulgar Latin.* Boston, 1907; New York: Hafner, 1962.

Heraeus, E. *Silviae vel potius Aetheriae Peregrinatio ad Loca Sancta.* 4th ed. Heidelberg, 1939.

Herman, Joseph. *Le latin vulgaire.* Collection Que sais-je? Paris, 1967.

Hofmann, J. B. *Lateinische Umgangssprache.* 2nd ed. Heidelberg, 1936.

Lindsay, W. M. *The Latin Language.* Oxford, 1894.

Meillet, A. *Esquisse d'une histoire de la langue latine.* 5th ed. Paris, 1948.

Muller, H. F., and P. Taylor. *A Chrestomathy of Vulgar Latin.* New York, 1932.

Palmer, L. R. *The Latin Language.* London, 1954.

Rohlfs, Gerhard. *Sermo Vulgaris Latinis.* 2nd ed. Tübingen, 1956.

Stolz, F., and J. H. Schmalz. *Lateinische Grammatik,* ed. Leumann and Hofmann. Munich, 1928.

Väänänen, V. *Le latin vulgaire des inscriptions.* Helsinki, 1937.

Vossler, Karl. *Einführung ins Vulgärlatein,* ed. H. Schmeck. Munich, 1954.

## 2. General and Comparative Romance

*Archivum Romanicum.* Geneva, Florence, 1917-41.

*Boletim de filologia.* Lisbon, 1932—.

*Boletim de filologia.* Río de Janeiro, 1946—.

Bouciez, Édouard. *Éléments de linguistique romane,* ed. Jean Bourciez. 4th ed. Paris: Klincksieck, 1946.

Criado de Val, Manuel. *Fisonomía del idioma español: sus características comparadas con las del francés, italiano, portugués, inglés y alemán.* Madrid, 1954.

*Cultura neolatina.* Modena, 1941—.

Elcock, W. D. *The Romance Languages.* New York: Macmillan, 1960.

*Estudis Romànics.* Barcelona; 1947—.

*Filologia romanza.* Turin, 1954.

Gröber, G. *Grundriss der romanischen Philologie.* 2nd ed. Strassburg, 1904-1906.

Heatwole, Oliver W. *A Comparative Practical Grammar of French, Spanish and Italian.* New York: Vanni, 1949.

Iordan, Iorgu. *Introducere in studiul limbilor romanice.* Tr., ed., John Orr, *An Introduction to Romance Linguistics.* London, 1937.

Karlinger, Felix, ed. *Romanische Märchen.* Tübingen: Max Niemeyer, 1962.

Kuen, Heinrich. *Versuch einer vergleichenden Charakteristik der romanischen Schriftsprachen.* Erlangen: Universitätsbund Erlangen, 1958.

Kuhn, Alwin. *Romanische Philologie. Erster Teil: Die romanischen Sprachen.* Berne: Francke, 1951.

Lausberg, Heinrich. *Romanische Sprachwissenschaft. I. Einleitung und Vokalismus. II. Konsonantismus. III. Formenlehre: Erster Teil. IV. Formenlehre: Zweiter Teil.* Berlin: de Gruyter, 1956 (I, II), 1962 (III, IV).

Meyer-Lübke, Wilhelm. *Einführung in das Studium der romanischen Sprachen.* 4 vols. Leipzig, 1890-1902. Tr., ed., Américo Castro, *Introducción a la lingüística románica.* Madrid, 1926.

——————. *Romanisches etymologisches Wörterbuch.* Heidelberg, 1935.

*Modern Language Notes.* Baltimore, 1886—.

*The Modern Language Review.* Cambridge, 1906—.

*Modern Philology.* Chicago, 1903—.

Monteverdi, A. *Manuale di avviamento agli studi romanzi. Le lingue romanze.* Milan, 1952.

*Die neueren Sprachen.* Marburg, 1894—.

*Neuphilologische Mitteilungen.* Helsingfors, 1899—.

*Orbis.* Louvain, 1952—.

Posner, Rebecca. *The Romance Languages: A Linguistic Introduction.* Garden City, New York: Doubleday-Anchor, 1966.

*Revue de linguistique romane.* Paris, 1925—.

*Revue des langues romanes.* Montpellier, 1870—.

*Revue Romane,* Copenhagen, 1966—.

*Rivista di filologia romanza.* Imola (Roma), 1872-75.

Rohlfs, Gerhard. *An der Quellen der romanischen Sprachen.* Halle, 1952.

——————. *Romanische Philologie.* 2 vols. Heidelberg, 1950-52.

*Romance Philology.* Berkeley, 1948—.

*Romania.* Paris, 1872—.

*Romanische Forschungen.* Erlangen, Frankfurt am Main, 1882—.

*Romanistisches Jahrbuch.* Hamburg, 1947—.

*Romanische Studien.* Strassburg, 1875-95.

Ruggieri, R. M. *Testi antichi romanzi: 1. Facsimili, 2. Trascrizioni.* Modena, 1949.

*Studia neophilologica.* Uppsala, 1928—.

*Studi di filologia romanza.* Rome, 1885-1903.

*Studi romanzi.* Rome, 1903—.

113

Tagliavini, Carlo. *Le origini delle lingue neolatine.* Bologna, 1952.

Vidos, B. E. *Handboek tot de Romaanse Taalkunde.* 's Hertogenbosch, 1956. Tr., Francisco de B. Moll, *Manual de lingüística románica.* Madrid: Aguilar, 1963.

von Wartburg, Walter. *Die Ausgliederung der romanischen Sprachräume.* 2nd ed. Berne, 1950. Tr., *La fragmentación lingüística de la Romania.* Madrid, 1952.

————. *Die Entstehung der romanischen Völker.* Berne, 1950. Tr., Claude C. de Maupassant, *Les origines des peuples romans.* Paris: Presses universitaires, 1941.

Vossler, Karl. *Wesenszüge romanischer Sprache und Dichtung: Italienisch, Französich, Spanisch.* Munich, 1946.

*Vox Romanica.* Zürich, Berne, 1936—.

Zauner, Adolf. *Romanische Sprachwissenschaft.* Berlin, 1921.

*Zeitschrift für romanische Philologie.* Halle, 1877—.

### 3. Gallo-Romance

Anglade, Joseph. *Grammaire de l'ancien provençal.* Paris, 1921.

Appel, Carl. *Provenzalische Lautlehre.* Leipzig, 1918.

Bartsch, Karl. *Chrestomathie de l'ancien français,* ed. Leo Wiese. 12th ed. Münster, 1919; New York: Hafner, 1968.

Berthaud, P.-L. *Bibliographie occitane (1919-42).* Paris, 1946.

Bloch, O. and W. von Wartburg. *Dictionnaire étymologique de la langue française.* 2nd ed. Paris, 1950.

Bruneau, Charles. *Petite histoire de la langue française. I. Des origines à la Révolution.* Paris, 1955. *II. De la Révolution à nos jours.* Paris, 1958.

Brunot, F., and C. Bruneau. *Précis de grammaire historique de la langue française.* Paris, 1949.

Dauzat, Albert. *Dictionnaire étymologique de la langue française.* Paris: Larousse, 1938.

Ewert, A. *The French Language.* London, 1933.

Fouché, P. *Phonétique historique du français. I. Introduction.* Paris, 1952. *II. Les voyelles.* Paris, 1958.

Gamillscheg, Ernst. *Etymologisches Wörterbuch der französischen Sprache.* Heidelberg, 1928.

Henry, Albert. *Chrestomathie de la littérature en ancien français.* 3rd ed. Berne: Francke, 1965.

Nyrop, K. *Grammaire historique de la langue française.* 6 vols. Copenhagen, 1899-1930.

Pope, Mildred K. *From Latin to Modern French, with Especial Consideration of Anglo-Norman.* 2nd ed. Manchester, 1952.

Raynaud de Lage, Guy. *Manuel pratique d'ancien français.* Collection Connaissance des Langues, II. Paris: Picard, 1964.

Regula, M. *Historische Grammatik des Französischen.* 2 vols. I. *Lautlehre.* II. *Formenlehre.* Heidelberg: 1955, 1956.

Rheinfelder, H. *Altfranzösische Grammatik.* 2nd ed. Munich, 1953-55.

Rohlfs, Gerhard. *Vom Vulgärlatein zum Altfranzösischen.* Tübingen: Niemeyer, 1963.

Schultz-Gora, O. *Altprovenzalisches Elementarbuch.* Heidelberg, 1924.

Schwan, E., and D. Behrens. *Grammatik des Altfranzösischen.* 2 vols. Leipzig, 1925. Tr., O. Bloch, *Grammaire de l'ancien français.* Leipzig, 1932.

von Wartburg, W. *Évolution et structure de la langue française.* 6th ed. Berne, 1962.

Voretzch, C. *Einführung in das Studium der altfranzösischen Sprache.* 6th ed. Halle, 1932.

Wagner, Robert-Léon. *Introduction à la linguistique française.* Lille, Geneva, 1947.

—————. *Supplément bibliographique à la linguistique française, 1947-1953.* Lille, Geneva, 1955.

### 4. Ibero-Romance

Alarcos Llorach, Emilio. *Fonología española.* 4th ed. Madrid: Ed. Gredos, 1965.

Alonso, Amado. *De la pronunciación medieval a la moderna en español.* 2 vols. Vol. I: Madrid: Ed. Gredos, 1955. Vol. II, in press.

Badía Margarit, Antonio. *Gramática histórica catalana.* Barcelona, 1951.

Boléo, M. de Pavia. *Introdução ao estudo da filologia portuguesa.* Lisbon, 1946.

Corominas, Juan (Coromines, Joan). *Diccionario crítico-etimológico de la lengua castellana.* 4 vols. Berne, 1954-57.

—————. *El que s'ha de saber de la llengua catalana.* Palma de Mallorca, 1954.

Entwistle, W. J. *The Spanish Language, together with Portuguese, Catalan and Basque.* London, 1951.

Ford, Jeremiah D. M. *Old Spanish Readings.* Boston, 1906.

Fotitch, Tatiana. *An Anthology of Old Spanish.* Washington: The Catholic University of America Press, 1962.

García de Diego, Vicente. *Gramática histórica catalana.* Madrid: Ed. Gredos, 1961.

Gifford, D. J., and F. W. Hodcroft. *Textos lingüísticos del medioevo español.* Oxford: Dolphin, 1959.

Gili, Joan. *Catalan Grammar.* 3rd ed. Oxford: Dolphin 1967.

Griera, A. *Gramàtica històrica del català antic.* Barcelona, 1931.

—————. *Bibliografía lingüística catalana.* Barcelona, 1947.

Hall, Pauline Cook. *A Bibliography of Spanish Linguistics*. Baltimore, 1956.

Hanssen, Friedrich. *Spanische Grammatik auf historischer Grundlage*. Halle, 1910. Tr., *Gramática histórica de la lengua castellana*. Buenos Aires, 1945.

Hoge, Henry W. *A Selective Bibliography of Luso-Brazilian Linguistics*. Milwaukee: University of Wisconsin Press, 1966.

Huber, J. *Altportugiesisches Elementarbuch*. Heidelberg, 1933.

Jungemann, Frederick H. *La teoría del sustrato y los dialectos hispano-romances y gascones*. Madrid, 1955.

Lapesa, Rafael. *Historia de la lengua española*. 4th ed. New York: Las Américas, 1959.

Menéndez Pidal, Ramón. *Cantar de Mio Cid: Texto, gramática y vocabulario*. 3rd ed. 3 vols. Madrid: Espasa-Calpe, 1954-56. Vols. I, II.

————. *Crestomatía del español medieval*, ed. Rafael Lapesa y María Soledad de Andrés. 2 vols. Madrid: Ed. Gredos, (I) 1965, (II) 1966.

————. *Manual de gramática histórica española*. 11th ed. Madrid: Espasa-Calpe, 1962.

————. *Orígenes del español*. 4th ed. Madrid: Espasa-Calpe, 1956.

Meyer-Lübke, Wilhelm. *Das Katalanische*. Heidelberg, 1925.

Moll, Francisco de B. *Gramática histórica catalana*. Madrid: Ed. Gredos, 1952.

Montesinos Abellán, José. *Gramática histórica latino-española*. Cádiz, 1954.

Neto, S. de Silva. *História da lingua portuguesa*. Río de Janeiro, 1952.

*Nueva Revista de Filología Hispánica*. México, 1947—.

Nunes, José J. *Compêndio de gramática histórica portuguesa*. 3rd ed. Lisbon, 1945.

*Revista de filología española*. Madrid, 1914—.

*Revista de filología hispánica*. New York, Buenos Aires, 1939-46.

*Revista portuguesa de filologia*. Coimbra, 1947—.

Rohlfs, Gerhard. *Manual de filología hispánica*, tr. Carlos Patiño Rosselli. Bogotá, 1957.

Russell-Gobbett, Paul. *Mediaeval Catalan Linguistic Texts*. Oxford: Dolphin, 1965.

Serís, Homero. *Bibliografía de la lingüística española*. Publ. del Inst. Caro y Cuervo, XIX. Bogotá, 1964.

Spaulding, Robert K. *How Spanish Grew*. Berkeley, Los Angeles: University of California Press, 1943. Paperbound edition, 1962.

Williams, Edwin B. *From Latin to Portuguese: Historical Phonology and Morphology of the Portuguese Language*. 2nd ed. Philadelphia: University of Pennsylvania Press, 1962.

Willis, R. Clive. *An Essential Course in Modern Portuguese*. London: Harrap, 1965.

Woodbridge, Hensley C., and Paul R. Olson. *A Tentative Bibliography of Hispanic Linguistics.* Urbana: University of Illinois Press, 1952.
Zauner, Adolf. *Altspanisches Elementarbuch.* 6th ed. Heidelberg, 1921.

## 5. Rheto-Romance

*Bibliografia Retoromontscha,* ed. Ligia Romontscha. Chur, 1938.
Gartner, Theodor. *Handbuch der rätoromanischen Sprache und Literatur.* Halle, 1910.
—————. *Rätoromanische Grammatik.* Heilbronn, 1883.
Maxfield, Elizabeth. *Raeto-Romance Bibliography: A Selected Bibliography of Works on Raeto-Romance, with Special Consideration of Romansch.* Chapel Hill: University of North Carolina Press, 1941.
Nay, Sep Modest. *Bien di, bien onn: Lehrbuch der rätoromanischen Sprache.* Chur, 1948.
Pult, Caspar, *et al. Dicziunari rumantsch grischun.* Cuoira, 1939—.

## 6. Italo-Romance

Atzori, M. T. *Bibliografia di linguistica sarda.* Florence, 1953.
Bartoli, M., and G. Braun. *Grammatica storica della lingua italiana e dei dialetti italiani.* Milan, 1906.
Battisti, C., and G. Alessio. *Dizionario etimologico italiano.* 5 vols. Florence, 1950-58.
Devoto, G. *Profilo di storia linguistica italiana.* Florence, 1953.
Dionisotti, C., and C. Grayson. *Early Italian Texts.* Oxford: Dolphin, 1949.
Grandgent, Charles H. *From Latin to Italian.* 3rd ed. Cambridge, Mass., 1940.
Hall, Robert H. *Bibliography of Italian Linguistics.* Baltimore, 1941.
Hubschmid, J. *Sardische Studien.* Bari, 1953.
*L'Italia Dialettale.* Pisa, 1925—. See Vol. I for Max Leopold Wagner's articles on Sardinian phonology and morphology.
*Lingua nostra.* Florence, 1939—.
Migliorini, Bruno. *Tra il latino e l'italiano: Primordi della lingua italiana (476-960).* Florence, 1953.
Monaci, E. *Crestomazia italiana dei primi secoli,* ed. F. Arese. Rome, 1955.
Olivieri, D. *Dizionario etimologico italiano.* Milan, 1953.
Pei, Mario. *The Italian Language.* New York, 1941.
Prati, A. *Vocabolario etimologico italiano.* Rome, 1951.
Rohlfs, Gerhard. *Historische Grammatik der italienischen Sprache und ihrer Mundarten.* 3 vols. Berne, 1949-54.
Wagner, Max Leopold. *La lingua sarda.* Berne, 1951.

# 7. Balkan Romance

Bartoli, M. *Das Dalmatische.* 2 vols. Vienna, 1906.

Cioranescu, Alexandre. *Diccionario etimológico rumano. Fascículos 1-4 (A-POAL).* Canary Islands: Universidad de la Laguna, 1958-60.

*Limba romîna.* Bucharest, 1952—.

Nandris, G. *Colloquial Rumanian.* London, 1945.

Pop, Sever. *Grammaire roumaine. Berne,* 1947.

Puşcariu, S. *Etymologisches Wörterbuch der rumänischen Sprache.* Heidelberg, 1905.

————. *Limba română.* Bucharest, 1940.

Rosetti, A. *Istoria limbii române.* 6 vols. Bucharest, 1938.—

————. *Istoria limbii, române: Noţiuni generale.* Bucharest, 1942.

Rothe, W. *Einführung in die historische Laut- und Formenlehre des Rumänischen.* Halle, 1957.

Tiktin, H. *Rumänisches Elementarbuch.* Heidelberg, 1905.

# INDEX

adjectives   Ct., 100b; Fr., 99a; It., 102a; Pt., 100c; Pr., 99b; Rm., 103; Sd., 102b; Sp., 100a; SS, 101; VL, 98

adverbs   Rom., 105; VL, 104

articles   Ct., 94b; Fr., 93a; It., 96a; Pg., 94c; Pr., 93b; Rm., 97; Sd., 96b; Sp., 94a; SS, 95; VL, 92

Balkan Romance   5; see *Rumanian*

*barbarus*   vs. *romanicus*, 1

Castilian   see *Spanish*

Catalan   and Ibero-Romance, 5; *morphology*: adjectives, 100b; adverbs, 105; articles, 94b; nouns, 96; numerals, 108b; pronouns (adverbial, 105; demonstrative, 88h; indefinite, 88n; interrogative, 88k; personal, 88b; possessive, 88e; relative, 88k); verbs (conditional, 82r; conjugations, 82b; future indicative, 82r; gerunds, 82b; imperatives, 82gg; imperfect indicative, 82h; imperfect subjunctive, 82aa; infinitives, 82b; passive voice, 82ff; past participles, 82b; perfect indicative, 82u; perfect subjunctive, 82ee; present indicative, 82e; present participles, 82b; present subjunctive, 82x; preterites (periphrastic, 82n; strong, 82m; weak, 82*l*); *phonology*: consonants (final, 70b; initial, 49b; initial groups, 54; intervocalic, 59b; medial groups, 65b; VL -*cc*-, 63b, -*ll*-, 63c, -*nn*-, 63d, -*rr*-, 63e); diphthong [au̯], 45; vowels (final, 41b; initial, 31b; posttonic, 36b; pretonic, 36b; stressed [a], 13, [ẹ], [ę], 18b, [i], 27, [ọ], [ǫ], 23b, [u], 27)

consonants   double (VL -*cc*-, 63b, -*ll*-, 62c, -*nn*-, 63d; -*rr*-, 63e, others, 63a), final (Ct., 70b; Fr., 69a; It., 72a; Pg., 70c; Pr., 69b; Rm., 73; Sd., 72b; Sp., 70a; Sd., 71), initial (Ct., 49b; Fr., 48; It., 51a; Pg., 49c; Pr., 48; Rm., 52; Sd., 51b; Sp., 49a; SS., 50), initial groups (Ct., 54; Fr., 53; It., 56a; Pg., 54; Pr., 53; Rm., 57; Sd., 56b; Sp., 54; SS, 55), intervocalic (Ct., 59b; Fr., 58a; It., 61a; Pg., 59c; Pr., 58b; Rm., 62; Sd., 61b; Sp., 59a; SS, 60)

Dalmatian   and Balkan Romance, 5

diphthong   [au̯] in Romance, 45

French   and Gallo-Romance, 5; *morphology*: adjectives, 99a; adverbs, 105; articles, 93a; nouns, 75; numerals, 107a; pronouns (adverbial, 87k; demonstrative, 87e; indefinite, 87i; interrogative, 87g; personal, 87a; possessive, 87c; relative, 87g; verbs (conditional, 81*l*; conjugations, 81a; future indicative, 81*l*; gerunds, 81a; imperatives, 81t; imperfect indicative, 81e; imperfect subjunctive, 81p; infinitives, 81a; passive voice, 81s; past participles, 81a; perfect

voice, 82ff; past participles, 82c; perfect indicative, 82v; perfect subjunctive, 82ee; present indicative, 82f; present participles, 82c; present subjunctive, 82y; preterites (strong, 82p; weak, 82o); *phonology*: consonants (final, 70c; initial, 49c; initial groups, 54; intervocalic, 59c; medial groups, 65c; VL -*cc*-, 63b; -*ll*-, 63c, -*nn*-, 63d, -*rr*-, 63e); diphthong [aṷ], 45; vowels (final, 41c; initial, 31c; post-tonic, 36c; pretonic, 36c; stressed [a], 13, [ẹ], [ę], 18a, [i], 27, [ọ], [ǫ], 23c, [u], 27)

pronouns  adverbial (Ct., 88p; Fr., 87k; It., 90k; Pg., 88p; Pr., 87k; Sd., 90k; Sp., 88p; VL, 86f); demonstrative (Ct., 88h; Fr., 87e; It., 90e; Pg., 88i; Pr., 87f; Rm., 81c; Sd., 90f; Sp., 88g; SS, 89c; VL, 86c); indefinite (Ct., 88n; Fr., 87i; It., 90i; Pg., 88o; Pr., 87j; Rm., 91e, Sd., 90j; Sp., 88m; SS, 89e, VL, 86e); interrogative and relative (Ct., 88k; Fr., 87g; It., 90g; Pg., 88l; Pr., 87h; Rm., 91d; Sd., 90h; Sp., 88j; SS, 89d; VL, 86d); personal (Ct., 88b; Fr., 87a; It., 90a; Pg., 88c; Pr., 87b; Rm., 91a; Sd., 90b; Sp., 88a; SS, 89a; VL, 86a); possessive (Ct., 88e; Fr., 87c; It., 90c; Pg., 88f; Pr., 87d; Rm., 91b; Sd., 90d; Sp., 88d; SS, 89b; VL, 86b); relative (see *interrogative*)

Provençal  and Gallo-Romance, 5; *morphology*: adjectives, 99b; adverbs, 105; articles, 93b; nouns, 75; numerals, 107b; pronouns (adverbial, 87k; demonstrative, 87f; indefinite, 87j; interrogative, 87h; personal, 87b; possessive, 87d; relative, 87h); verbs (conditional, 81l; conjugations, 81b; future indicative, 81l; gerunds, 81b; imperatives, 81u; imperfect indicative, 81f; imperfect subjunctive, 81q; infinitives, 81b; passive voice, 81s; past participles, 81b; perfect indicative, 81d; present participles, 81b; present subjunctive, 81o; preterites (periphrastic, 81k; strong, 81j; weak, 81h); *phonology*: consonants (final, 69b; initial, 48; initial groups, 53; intervocalic, 58b; medial groups, 64b; VL, -*cc*-, 63b, -*ll*-, 63c, -*nn*-, 63d, -*rr*-, 63e); diphthong [aṷ], 45; vowels (final, 40; initial, 30; post-tonic, 35b; pretonic, 35a; stressed [a], 12b, [ẹ], [ę], 17, [i], 27, [ọ], [ǫ], 22, [u], 27)

Rheto-Romance  5; see *Surselvan*

Romance  Balkan, 5; Eastern, 5, 6; Gallo-, 5; Ibero-, 5; Italo-, 5; Rheto-, 5; Western, 5, 6

Romania  vs. Rome, 1

*romanicus*  vs. *romanus*, 1

Romansch-  and Rheto-Romance, 5; see *Surselvan*

*romanus*  vs. *romanicus*, 1

Rumanian  and Balkan Romance, 5; *morphology*: adjectives, 103; adverbs, 105; articles, 97; nouns, 79; numerals, 111; pronouns (demonstrative, 91c; indefinite, 91e; interrogative, 91d; personal, 91a; possessive, 91b; relative, 91d); verbs (conditional, 85g; conjugations, 85a; future indicative, 85f; gerunds, 85a; imperatives, 85l; imperfect indicative, 85c; infinitives, 85a; passive voice, 85k;

intervocalic, 60; medial groups, 66; VL -cc-, 63b, -ll-, 63c, -nn-, 63d, -rr-, 63e); diphthong [aṷ], 45; vowels (final, 42; initial, 32; post-tonic, 37; pretonic, 37; stressed [a], 14, [ẹ], [ę], 19, [i], 27, [ǫ], [ọ], 24, [u], 27)

verbs   Latin (Vulgar), 80; *Romance*: conditional (see *future indicative*); conjugations and gerunds, infinitives, past participles, present participles (Ct., 82b; Fr., 81a; It., 84a; Pg., 82c; Pr., 81b; Rm., 85a; Sd., 84b; Sp., 82a; SS, 83a); future indicative and conditional (Ct., 82r; Fr., 81*l*; Rm., 85f; Sd., 84*l*; Sp., 82q; SS, 83e,f; gerunds (see *conjugations*); imperatives (Ct., 82gg Fr., 81t; It., 84v; Pg., 82gg; Pr. 81u; Rm., 85*l*; Sd., 84w; Sp., 82gg; SS, 83*l*); imperfect indicative (Ct., 82h; Fr., 81e; It., 84e; Pg., 82i; Pr., 81f; Rm., 85c; Sd., 84f; Sp., 82g; SS, 83c); imperfect subjunctive (Ct., 82aa; Fr., 81p; It., 84q; Pg., 82bb; Pr., 81q; Sd., 84r; Sp., 82z; SS, 83i); infinitives (see *conjugations*); passive voice (Ct., 82ff; Fr., 81s; It., 84u; Pg., 82ff; Pr., 81s; Rm., 85d; Sd., 84u; Sp., 82ff; SS, 83k); past participles (see *conjugations*); perfect indicative (Ct., 82u; Fr., 81m; It., 84m; Pg., 82v; Pr., 81m; Rm., 85h; Sd., 84u; Sp., 82t; SS, 83d,g); perfect subjunctive (Ct., 82ee; Fr., 81r; It., 84s; Pg., 82ee; Pr., 81r; Rm., 85j; Sd., 84t; Sp., 82ee; SS, 83j); present indicative (Ct., 82e; Fr., 81c; It., 84c; Pg., 82f; Pr,. 81d; Rm., 85b; Sd., 84d; Sp., 82d; SS, 83b); present subjunctive (Ct., 82x; Fr., 81n; It., 84o; Pg., 82y; Pr., 81o; Rm., 85i; Sd., 84p; Sp., 82w; SS, 83h); present participles (see *conjugations*); preterites: periphrastic (Ct., 82n; Pr., 81k); strong (Ct., 82m; Fr., 81i; It., 84i; Pg., 82p; Pr., 81j; Rm., 85e; Sd., 84j; Sp., 82k); weak (Ct., 82*l*; Fr., 81g; It., 84g; Pg., 82o; Pr., 81h; Rm., 85d; Sd., 84h; Sp., 82j)

vowels   Latin (Vulgar), 8, 10, 11, 28, 29; *Romance*: final (Ct., 31b; Fr., 30; It., 33; Pg., 31c; Pr., 30; Rm., 34; Sd., 33; Sp., 31a; SS, 32); initial (Ct., 31b; Fr., 30; It., 33; Pg., 31c; Pr., 30; Rm., 34; Sd., 33; Sp., 31a; SS, 32); post-tonic (Ct., and pretonic, 36b; Fr., 35b; It., and pretonic, 38; Pg., and pretonic, 36c; Pr., 35b; Rm., and pretonic, 39; Sd., and pretonic, 38; Sp., and pretonic, 36a; SS, and pretonic, 37); pretonic (Ct., and post-tonic, 36b; Fr., 35a; It., and post-tonic, 38; Pg., and post-tonic, 36c; Pr., 35a; Rm., and post-tonic, 39; Sd., and post-tonic, 38; Sp., and post-tonic, 36a; SS, and post-tonic, 37); stressed [a] (Ct., 13; Fr., 12a; It., 15; Pg., 13; Pr., 12b; Rm., 16; Sd., 15; Sp., 13; SS, 14), [ɛ], [ę] (Ct., 18b; Fr., 17; It., 20; Pg., 18a; Pr., 17; Rm., 21; Sd. [e], 20; Sp., 18a; SS, 19), [ǫ], [ọ] (Ct., 23b; Fr., 22; It., 25; Pg., 23c; Pr., 22; Rm. [o], 26; Sd., [o], 25; Sp., 232; SS, 24); [i], [u], 27